CW01667787

GCSE Edexcel

Spanish

Say '*Buenos días*' to this brilliant GCSE Spanish Revision Guide.

It covers the full Edexcel course, with lots of examples, practice questions and all the vocab and grammar you'll need for the exams.

It also has lots of online revision in the CGP RevisionHub — there are quick quizzes, summary tests, audio, Q&A videos and more, all matched to your book! Mmm, sounds even better than a plate of *paella*.

Unlock **CGP RevisionHub**

Just scan a QR code in the book to access the CGP RevisionHub. Or go to **cgpbooks.co.uk/revise** and enter this code!

1236 1798 3589 6244

Revision Hub

By the way, this code only works for one person. If somebody else has used this book before you, they might have already claimed the code.

Revision Guide

with new **CGP RevisionHub**

Published by CGP

Editors:
Siân Butler
Daniel Chapero-Hall
Becca Clifford
Heather Cowley
Elliott Garraway
Brooke McCreight
Hannah Roscoe
Matt Topping

With thanks to Rebecca Greaves for the proofreading.
With thanks to Alice Dent for the copyright research.

Acknowledgements:

Audio produced by Voice Talent Online.

Questions throughout are based on Pearson Edexcel type questions.

ISBN: 978 1 83774 130 4
Printed by Elanders Ltd, Newcastle upon Tyne.
Clipart from Corel®

Based on the classic CGP style created by Richard Parsons.

Contents

Contents

Contents

How to Use this Book

This isn't a book. Or rather, this isn't *just* a book. It's full of online resources designed to help you get top marks. To learn how it all works, read these pages or scan the QR code for a walkthrough.

Video

This book follows the Edexcel specification

1) The content for Edexcel GCSE Spanish is divided into six themes.

My personal world	Lifestyle and wellbeing	My neighbourhood
Media and technology	Studying and my future	Travel and tourism

2) In this book, these six themes have been split into ten sections to make things more manageable.
3) There are also three grammar sections that cover the grammar you need to know.
4) The resources on the CGP RevisionHub are split up in the same way as the book.

There's also a 'General Stuff' topic in the book and online with content that's useful across the course.

The CGP RevisionHub is full of resources

- You can use the online resources on the CGP RevisionHub alongside this book as you're revising.
- There's audio, quick quizzes and summary tests, as well as printable vocab lists and transcripts.

There are resources for Foundation tier and Higher tier on the CGP RevisionHub. The Hub is automatically set to Higher, but you can switch to Foundation to only see Foundation content.

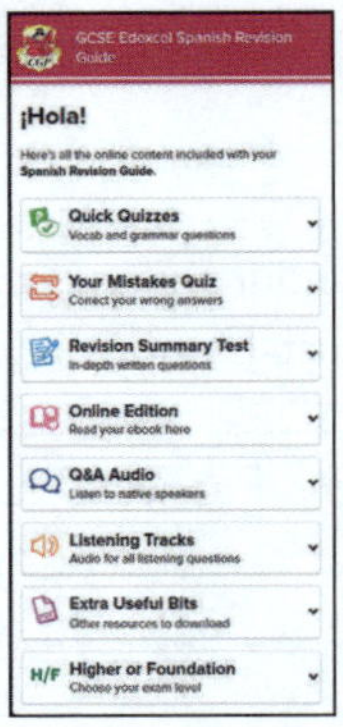

Revision Hub

Scan this QR code to access the CGP RevisionHub, or if you're on a computer, go to www.cgpbooks.co.uk/Gracias.

Get ready for the exams

1) In your exams, you can sit Foundation-tier or Higher-tier papers.
2) In each tier, there are four papers: Listening, Speaking, Reading and Writing. You have to choose the same tier for all four papers.

For more about the exams, see p.148-151.

- In Foundation tier, there's less vocabulary and less grammar to learn and the questions are slightly easier. In this tier, you can earn up to Grade 5.
- In Higher tier, you can achieve Grades 4-9, but you'll need to learn more vocab and more complex grammar.

3) Throughout this book, there's practice for all the key skills you'll need in the exams.
4) Most of this book is helpful for both tiers, but some vocab and questions have been marked with a bracket if they only apply to one tier.
5) If you aren't sure which tier to take, trying out the questions should help you and your teacher make a decision.

Higher

hacia	*toward, towards*
lejano/a	*distant*
situarse	*to be located*

H

el hogar	*home*
la planta	*floor*

Learn the set vocabulary

- The Edexcel specification contains a list of words you could be tested on in your Listening and Reading papers, depending on your tier.
- This vocab will also help you in your Speaking and Writing papers. In these two papers, you can use non-specification vocab, too.
- The key vocab is on the main pages of each section. At the end of each section, there's a list of all the vocab relevant to the topic. Every word on the specification is on at least one of these lists.
- There are printable versions of these lists on the CGP RevisionHub.

Practise your listening skills

1) In this book, you'll find questions and example answers:

Q&A Audio	Question	Simple Answer	Extended Answer
	¿Qué tipo de habitación le gustaría a usted?	Me gustaría una habitación con vistas al mar.	Somos una familia de tres, así que necesitamos dos habitaciones — una individual y una doble.
	What type of room would you like?	*I would like a room with sea views.*	*We are a family of three, so we need two rooms — a single and a double.*

Scan the QR code to hear the sentences out loud and to practise your pronunciation.

2) There are also QR codes that take you to Listening Tracks. Each track comes with questions that test you on what you've heard.

Test your knowledge

Quick Quizzes

- The QR codes at the top of the page take you to a quick quiz.
- These quizzes test you on the vocab (or the grammar in Sections 11-13) on that page.
- They're a great way to keep your knowledge fresh.
- You can easily revisit questions that you answer incorrectly by doing the 'Your Mistakes' quiz.

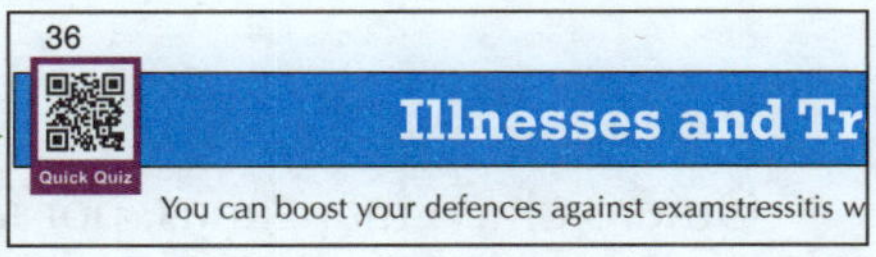

Revision Summary Tests

- For more of a challenge, try a revision summary test. These are found at the end of each section.
- These tests cover the most important information in a topic and are a good way to see how much you can remember.
- You can do these tests on paper or you can complete them online. Online, you can find sample answers, assess your progress, and look at previous topics to see the areas you need to work on.

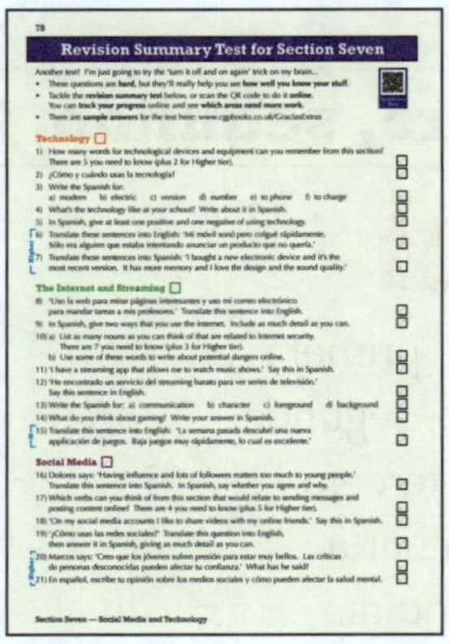

Fun fact — rearrange the letters of 'RevisionHub' and you get...

...'SnoivierUbh', which makes no sense. But do you know what *does* make sense? Using the RevisionHub alongside this book — it'll help you to get the most out of your revision and impress all those examiners.

Numbers and Times

Quick Quiz

Your GCSE Spanish Revision is ready to launch in 3...2...1...

Remember there's also lots of online content here: www.cgpbooks.co.uk/Gracias

Uno, dos, tres — *One, two, three*

Vocabulary

cero	*0*	veinte, veinti-	*20*
uno	*1*	veintiuno	*21*
dos	*2*	veintidós	*22*
tres	*3*	veintitrés	*23*
cuatro	*4*	treinta	*30*
cinco	*5*	treinta y uno	*31*
seis	*6*	cuarenta	*40*
siete	*7*	cincuenta	*50*
ocho	*8*	sesenta	*60*
nueve	*9*	setenta	*70*
diez	*10*	ochenta	*80*
once	*11*	noventa	*90*
doce	*12*	cien(to)	*100*
trece	*13*	ciento uno	*101*
catorce	*14*	doscientos	*200*
quince	*15*	quinientos	*500*
dieciséis	*16*	setecientos	*700*
diecisiete	*17*	novecientos	*900*
dieciocho	*18*	mil	*1000*
diecinueve	*19*	un millón	*1 000 000*

All twenty-something numbers are rolled into one — like 'veintiuno' (twenty-one). After 30, numbers are joined by 'y' (and), but written separately — like 'treinta y uno' (thirty-one).

Grammar — using 'one' with masculine nouns

When you put 'one' in front of a masculine word, uno becomes 'un'.

veintiún alumnos — ***21 pupils***
treinta y un alumnos — ***31 pupils***

Before a feminine word, the 'o' changes to 'a':

veintiuna naranjas — ***21 oranges***

See p.101 for more on masculine and feminine nouns.

'Cien' becomes 'ciento' when used in front of another number (except 'mil').

mil ochocientos veintiséis	*1826*
mil novecientos ochenta y cuatro	*1984*
dos mil once	*2011*

Quiero cinco manzanas, por favor. — *I want five apples, please.*

Tenemos treinta y tres bolígrafos. — *We have 33 pens.*

Hay ciento veintiún alumnos. — *There are 121 students.*

Nací en dos mil diez. — *I was born in 2010.*

Each of our 33 pens can hold up to 6 students.

Primero, segundo, tercero — *First, second, third*

Vocabulary

primero, primera	*1st*
segundo, segunda	*2nd*
tercero, tercera	*3rd*
cuarto, cuarta	*4th*
quinto, quinta	*5th*

Grammar — 'primero', 'tercero' + masculine nouns

You can drop the 'o' at the end of 'primero' or 'tercero' when they appear in front of a masculine word.

el primer baile — ***the first dance***
el tercer cantante — ***the third singer***

Vivo en la primera planta del edificio. — *I live on the first floor of the building.*

Mi hermano terminó en el tercer lugar. — *My brother finished in third place.*

¿Qué hora es? — *What time is it?*

Vocabulary

Es la...	*It's...*
Son las...	*It's...*
y cuarto	*quarter past*
y media	*half past*
el segundo	*second (time measurement)*
el minuto	*minute*
la hora	*hour, time (specific)*

Grammar — at / it's X o'clock

To say '<u>at X o'clock</u>', you need '<u>a</u>':

a <u>la una</u> — ***at <u>one o'clock</u>***
a <u>las ocho</u> — ***at <u>eight o'clock</u>***

'La' changes to 'las' for anything other than 'one o'clock'.

To say '<u>it's X o'clock</u>', use '<u>es</u>' or '<u>son</u>':

<u>es</u> la una — ***<u>it's</u> one o'clock***
<u>son</u> las ocho — ***<u>it's</u> eight o'clock***

'Es' changes to 'son' for anything other than 'one o'clock'.

Es la una y media.	*It's half past one.*
Es la una menos veinte.	*It's twenty to one.*
Son las ocho y cinco.	*It's five past eight.*
Son las cinco y cuarto.	*It's quarter past five.*

five to — menos cinco

quarter to — menos cuarto

Instead of saying 'to' when telling the time in Spanish, you use 'menos' ('less' or 'minus'). So 'Son las cinco menos diez' literally means 'It's five o'clock minus ten'.

The 24-hour clock

The <u>24-hour clock</u> is also used in many Spanish-speaking countries, so make sure you can tell the time <u>both</u> ways.

(Son) <u>las veintiuna horas</u> treinta minutos. — ***(It's) <u>21</u>.30.***
(Son) <u>las tres horas</u> catorce minutos. — ***(It's) <u>03</u>.14.***
(Son) <u>las diecinueve horas</u> cincuenta y cinco minutos. — ***(It's) <u>19</u>.55.***

The only time Max cares about is nap time.

Practice Questions

Q1 *Read the text and answer the questions in English.*

READING

Laia tiene veintidós años. Su hermana solo tiene diecisiete años, pero su abuelo tiene ochenta y ocho años. Laia vive muy cerca — en la segunda calle a la derecha.

e.g. *How old is Laia?* She is 22.

a) How old is Laia's sister? *[1 mark]*

b) How old is Laia's grandad? *[1 mark]*

c) On which street does Laia live? *[1 mark]*

Higher

Q2 *Ignacio is talking about his routine. What does he say?*
Write A if only statement A is correct. Write B if only statement B is correct.
Write A + B if both statements A and B are correct.

LISTENING

Listening Track 01

a) Ignacio normally wakes up...
A. at half past seven. **B.** at nine o'clock. *[1 mark]*

b) At quarter to ten, Ignacio...
A. reads his book. **B.** gets out of bed. *[1 mark]*

c) Ignacio prefers to...
A. have a wash before breakfast. **B.** eat breakfast at half past ten. *[1 mark]*

1st the worst, 2nd the best, 3rd the one with the Spanish test...

They might feel like a basic topic, but numbers are quite important. You can do some pretty incredible things with them too: tell the time, give your birthday, ask for enormous quantities of cheese at the supermarket...

Quick Quiz

Times and Dates

I'm partial to prunes myself — dates get stuck in my teeth. Anyway, it's times and dates um... time.

Los momentos del día — *Times of the day*

Vocabulary

la mañana	*morning*	pasado/a	*last, past*
el mediodía	*noon, midday*	último/a	*last, latest*
la tarde	*afternoon, evening*	siguiente	*next, following*
la noche	*night, evening*	a veces	*sometimes*
hoy	*today*	de vez en cuando	*from time to time*
mañana	*tomorrow*	antes	*before, beforehand*
ayer	*yesterday*	después	*after, afterwards*
tarde	*late*		

You need to add 'de' after 'antes' or 'después' if you want to say before or after something. E.g. say 'después de la fiesta', not just 'después la fiesta'.

Iré a España mañana por la mañana. — *I will go to Spain tomorrow morning.*

Esta mañana fui al castillo. — *This morning I went to the castle.*

Perdió su cuaderno la semana pasada. — *He lost his notebook last week.*

Juego al fútbol por la mañana. — *I play football in the morning.*

tonight — esta noche

the following week — la semana siguiente

last night — anoche

Q&A Audio

Question

¿Qué haces el fin de semana?

What do you do at the weekend?

Simple Answer

Me gusta salir con mis amigos el fin de semana.

I like to go out with my friends at the weekend.

Extended Answer

A veces me gusta salir con mis amigos el fin de semana, pero prefiero descansar o leer si estoy cansada.

Sometimes I like to go out with my friends at the weekend, but I prefer to relax or read if I am tired.

Los días de la semana — *The days of the week*

Days of the week are always masculine and lower case.

Vocabulary

la fecha	*date*	lunes	*Monday*	viernes	*Friday*
el día	*day, daytime*	martes	*Tuesday*	sábado	*Saturday*
la semana	*week*	miércoles	*Wednesday*	domingo	*Sunday*
el fin de semana	*(at the) weekend*	jueves	*Thursday*		

Voy al centro comercial los sábados para ir de compras con mis amigos. — *I go to the shopping centre on Saturdays to go shopping with my friends.*

Intento salir todos los días. Paseo al perro después del colegio. — *I try to go out every day. I walk the dog after school.*

Fui a la biblioteca ayer porque tengo un examen de inglés el miércoles. — *I went to the library yesterday because I have an English exam on Wednesday.*

Suelo descansar los domingos. — *I tend to relax on Sundays.*

You don't translate 'at' here — you just say 'the weekend'.

at the weekend — el fin de semana

on Friday afternoons — los viernes por la tarde

Los meses del año — *The months of the year*

Just like the days of the week, the months of the year are all masculine and shouldn't have capital letters.

Vocabulary

enero	*January*	abril	*April*	julio	*July*	octubre	*October*
febrero	*February*	mayo	*May*	agosto	*August*	noviembre	*November*
marzo	*March*	junio	*June*	septiembre	*September*	diciembre	*December*

Voy a la playa todos los años en agosto.	*I go to the beach every year in August.*
En enero, iremos de vacaciones.	*In January, we will go on holiday.*
Mi hermano menor nació en abril.	*My younger brother was born in April.*

¿Qué fecha es? — *What's the date?*

In English, you say 'the third of May' or 'the twentieth of December'. In Spanish, you can say either 'el primero de' or 'el uno de' for the first of the month, but for all the other dates, you say 'the three of May' or 'the twenty of December'...

el tres de mayo	*(on) the third of May*
el veinte de diciembre	*(on) the twentieth of December*
Es el uno de / el primero de febrero.	*It's the first of February.*
Es el dos de octubre de dos mil veinticuatro.	*It's the second of October 2024.*

You don't translate 'on' at the start of dates in Spanish, so both 'the third of May' and 'on the third of May' are written 'el tres de mayo'.

Practice Questions

Q1 Read aloud the following text in Spanish. *[8 marks]*

SPEAKING

Mi cumpleaños es lunes el quince de agosto. Quiero tener una fiesta grande con mis amigos. Siempre me gusta pasar tiempo con ellos. Mañana a las seis, tengo que llamar a mi restaurante favorito. Quiero reservar una mesa que está al lado de la cocina.

Answer the following questions in Spanish.

a) ¿Cuándo es tu cumpleaños?
b) Describe tu fiesta perfecta.
c) ¿Qué te gusta hacer con tus amigos?
d) ¿Qué piensas de los restaurantes? *[4 marks]*

Top Tips for Higher Students
✓ Try to use complex structures like the subjunctive.
✓ Give at least two details in each answer.

Q2 Listen to what Carlos, Anabel and Julia have to say, and then answer the questions in English.

e.g. *How often does Carlos go to the sports centre?* *Every day.*
a) When was Anabel's birthday meal? *[1 mark]*
b) Where did Anabel go last week? *[1 mark]*
c) When is Julia going to the theatre? *[1 mark]*

Listening Track 02

LISTENING

Time to *fecha* your calendar and revise your days and months...

It might be tempting to put capital letters everywhere you'd expect to see them in English, but it's best avoided. Lots of Spanish words don't actually need them — even the word 'Spanish' (write 'español', not 'Español').

Quick Quiz

Questions

I'm afraid it's a bit late to question your GCSE options now... but if you wanted to do this *en español*, these pages will give you a few pointers. They're going to prove pretty handy in your speaking exam...

Question marks and tone of voice

To turn a statement into a question, put an upside down question mark at the beginning and a normal one at the end.

When speaking, raise your voice at the end of the sentence to show you're asking a question.

Literally: 'Your dress is blue?'

¿Tu vestido es azul? — *Is your dress blue?*

¿Tienes un coche? — *Do you have a car?*

Literally: 'You have a car?'

¿Qué... — *What...?*

If your question starts with 'What...', you normally need to start it with '¿Qué...' in Spanish.

¿Qué comes por la mañana? — *What do you eat in the morning?*

¿Qué quieres hacer el fin de semana? — *What do you want to do at the weekend?*

Go back to p.6-7 for more time phrases.

¿Cuál... — *Which one..? What...?*

1) '¿Cuál...' normally means 'Which...' or 'Which one...':

¿Cuál quieres? — *Which (one) do you want?*

2) However, sometimes you might need to use '¿Cuál...' even if you'd use 'What...' in English. This is usually when you use the verb 'ser' and you're asking for a piece of information, rather than a definition.

¿Cuál es tu problema? — *What is your problem?*

¿Cuál es tu dirección? — *What is your address?*

¿Cuándo? ¿Por qué? ¿Dónde? — *When? Why? Where?*

There are lots of other words you can use to begin a question — get them all learnt.

Vocabulary

¿Cuándo?	*When?*	¿Dónde?	*Where?*	¿Cuánto/a?	*How much?*	¿Quién(es)?	*Who?*
¿Por qué?	*Why?*	¿Cómo?	*How?*	¿Cuántos/as?	*How many?*	¿Cuál(es)?	*Which?*

Remember that question words need accents.

¿Cuántos/as tienes?	*How many do you have?*
¿Por qué haces eso?	*Why are you doing that?*
¿De dónde eres?	*Where are you from?*
¿Cuál prefieres?	*Which do you prefer?*

Noodles definitely has questions this time...

Question words like this are known as interrogatives. See p.107.

Tengo una pregunta — *I have a question*

Here are some of the most common ways you can use the question words.

¿Cuándo es tu cumpleaños?	*When is your birthday?*
¿Cuántos años tienes?	*How old are you?*
¿Cuánto cuesta(n)?	*How much does it (do they) cost?*

You shouldn't use '¿Cómo...?' to ask how old someone is in Spanish. You have to ask 'How many years do you have?' instead.

Q&A Audio

Question

¿Cuánto cuesta ir al cine?

How much does it cost to go to the cinema?

Simple Answer

Cuesta diecisiete euros.

It costs seventeen euros.

Extended Answer

Cuesta diecisiete euros, cincuenta céntimos. Es muy caro, y por lo tanto prefiero ver las películas en casa.

It costs seventeen euros, fifty cents. It's very expensive, and therefore I prefer to watch films at home.

Grammar (Higher only) — prepositions in questions

If you need to include a preposition (see p.108) in your question, it should come before the question word. Prepositions should never go at the end of a question in Spanish.

¿Con quién hablas?	***Who are you talking to? (literally 'With whom are you talking?')***
¿Para qué estudias?	***What are you studying for? (literally 'For what are you studying?')***

Practice Questions

Q1 *Read Carla and Olaya's role-play. Then, use the instructions on the role-play card to prepare your own role-play. You should address your friend as 'tú'. Aim to speak for about one and a half minutes.*

Top Tips for Higher Students
✓ Try to use multiple tenses in your role-play.
✓ Back up all of your opinions.

SPEAKING

Olaya: *¿Qué piensas de la televisión?*
Carla: *Me gusta la tele porque me ayuda a descansar.*
Olaya: *Y ¿qué tipos de libros te gustan?*
Carla: *Me gusta leer revistas. Me hacen feliz.*
Olaya: *¿Hay alguna actividad que te gustaría hacer?*
Carla: *Me gustaría aprender a tocar el piano.*
Olaya: *¿Cuántas veces haces deporte a la semana?*
Carla: *Juego al fútbol dos veces a la semana. ¿Qué deporte haces tú?*
Olaya: *Me gusta jugar al tenis y disfruto corriendo.*

You are talking to your friend.

1. *Say what you think about TV.*
2. *Say what sort of books you like.*
3. *Say an activity you would like to try in your free time.*
4. *Say how often you play sports.*
5. *Ask a question about sports.*

The last prompt is a question you need to ask.

[10 marks]

Higher

Q2 *Translate these sentences into Spanish.*

WRITING

a) *Which clock should I buy?*
b) *Who were you dancing with?*
c) *How many dishes are there?*
d) *What are you talking about?*

[8 marks]

Why does that hamster have a better film set-up than me?

Look at him — a sofa all to himself, free reign of the remote and even some popcorn. Who do I need to speak to about getting that? Whatever you want to question, make sure you know which words you need to use.

Quick Quiz

Being Polite

Can you learn all of the lovely vocab on these pages? Pretty please with a cherry on top?

Tú y usted — *Informal and formal 'you'*

In Spanish, there are four different ways of saying 'you' depending on how formal you want to be.

Grammar — 'tú' and 'usted'

Tú	Vosotros/as	Usted	Ustedes
Informal singular 'you'. For one person who's your friend, a family member or of a similar age.	Informal plural 'you'. For a group of two or more people that you know. Only use 'vosotras' if everyone you're talking to is female.	Formal singular 'you'. For one person that is older than you or someone you don't know.	Formal plural 'you'. For a group of two or more people that you don't know.

Ewe better learn these...

So, there are four different ways to ask a question like 'Where are you from?':

Tú	Vosotros/as	Usted	Ustedes
¿De dónde eres?	¿De dónde sois?	¿De dónde es?	¿De dónde son?

You need to use the 'he/she/it' part of the verb for 'usted' (see p.125-145). For 'ustedes', use the 'they' part of the verb.

Hola y adiós — *Hello and goodbye*

You can also say '¿Cómo estás?' (informal) or '¿Cómo está?' (formal) to ask how someone is.

Vocabulary

hola	*hello, hi*	¿Qué tal?	*How are you?*	mal	*badly*
¡Buenos días!	*Good morning!*	bien	*well*	adiós	*goodbye*

Q&A Audio

Question	Simple Answer	Extended Answer
¿Qué tal? *How are you?*	Bien, gracias. *Well, thanks.*	Me siento enfermo. Tengo dolor de cabeza. *I feel sick. I've got a headache.*

See p.36 for more illnesses.

Las presentaciones — *Introductions*

1) To introduce someone in Spanish, you can say 'Este / Esta es...' ('This is...').

Shula:	Hola Señora Valls. ¿Cómo está?	*Hello Señora Valls. How are you?*
Señora Valls:	Muy bien, gracias.	*Very well, thank you.*
Shula:	Este es Arturo, mi novio.	*This is Arturo, my boyfriend.*
Señora Valls:	Encantada.	*Pleased to meet you.*
Arturo:	Encantado.	*Pleased to meet you.*
Señora Valls:	Lo siento, tengo que irme. ¡Hasta luego!	*I'm sorry, I have to go. See you soon!*
Shula & Arturo:	¡Adiós!	*Goodbye!*

Shula is using the 'usted' form because Señora Valls is older than her.

Señora Valls says 'Encantada' because she is female.

Arturo says 'Encantado' because he is male.

See you on Monday! — ¡Hasta el lunes!
See you tomorrow! — ¡Hasta mañana!

H 2) You can also introduce someone using the verb 'presentar' and an indirect object pronoun — usually 'te' (informal) or 'le' (formal). For example, 'Le presento a Arturo.' ('May I introduce Arturo?')

Por favor y gracias — *Please and thank you*

Vocabulary

por favor	*please*	claro	*of course*
gracias	*thank you, thanks*	lo siento	*I'm sorry, I apologise*
vale	*OK?*	perdón	*(I am) sorry*

'Perdone' is the formal version of 'perdón' — it's used to get someone's attention, e.g. when asking someone the way. 'Con permiso' is used if you want to get past someone.

¿Me puedes ayudar, por favor?	*Can you help me, please?*
Sí, claro.	*Yes, of course.*
¡Perfecto! ¡Muchas gracias!	*Perfect! Thank you very much!*
¡No te preocupes!	*No worries!*

You're welcome! — ¡De nada!

Quisiera... — *I would like...*

1) Don't just say 'I want to...' — make sure you ask what you would like to do politely using 'quisiera' and an infinitive.
2) You can also ask for a specific object if you put a noun after 'quisiera'.
3) Or you can phrase what you would like to do as a question using 'puedo' and an infinitive.

Quisiera hablar.	*I would like to talk.*
Quisiera un café.	*I would like a coffee.*
¿Puedo sentarme?	*May I sit down?*

go to the toilet — ir al baño

eat here — comer aquí

Practice Question

Q1 Andrés is introducing his two friends Mateo and Sakura to each other. WRITING

Andrés: *¡Buenos días, Mateo! ¿Qué tal?*
Mateo: *Muy bien, gracias, ¿y tú?*
Andrés: *Sí, bien. Esta es mi amiga, Sakura.*
Mateo: *¡Hola Sakura! Encantado.*
Sakura: *Encantada.*
Mateo: *¿Cómo estás, Sakura?*
Sakura: *No muy bien. Estoy enferma.*
Mateo: *Ay, ¡qué lástima!**
Sakura: *Sí, es una pena.*
Andrés: *Pues, hasta luego, Mateo.*
Mateo: *¡Adiós!*

**Ay, ¡qué lástima!* — Oh, what a shame!

Top Tips for Higher Students
✓ Ask additional questions to develop your conversation.
✓ Use varied adjectives to talk about how you feel.

Now have a go yourself:

Write a conversation between you and your friend Diego. Write approximately 50 words in Spanish.

You should:

- *say how you both feel.*
- *introduce another friend to Diego.*
- *say what you and Diego will do tomorrow.*

[14 marks]

Mind your manners — and yours and yours and yours...

If you're unsure which 'you' to use, it's better to start with 'usted(es)' as it's politer. If whoever you're speaking to thinks 'usted' is too formal, they might say that you can 'tutear', which just means you can use the 'tú' form.

Quick Quiz

Opinions

Having opinions is great, but spicing them up with exotic adjectives makes them even better.

Las opiniones — *Opinions*

Vocabulary

gustar	*to like, be pleasing to*	la razón	*reason*	Higher	parecer	*to seem*
encantar	*to love*	odiar	*to hate*		imaginar(se)	*to imagine*
encontrar	*to find*	creer	*to think, believe*		proponer	*to suggest*
interesar	*to interest, be of interest*	pensar (de)	*to think (of / about)*		mencionar	*to mention*
de acuerdo	*in agreement*	significar	*to mean*		considerar	*to consider*

Grammar — 'gustar' and 'encantar'

Use 'me gusta' and 'me encanta' when you want to say you like or love a singular thing.
If you want to say you like or love a plural thing, add an 'n' to the end.

Me gustan los churros. ***I like churros.*** **Me encantan las películas.** ***I love films.***

To say you like doing an activity, use an infinitive (see p.125) after the correct form of 'gustar' or 'encantar'.

Me gusta escribir. ***I like writing.*** **Me encanta dormir.** ***I love sleeping.***

(No) me gustan las verduras.	*I (don't) like vegetables.*
Los idiomas (no) me interesan.	*Languages (don't) interest me.*
Encuentro la paella deliciosa.	*I find paella delicious.*
Me encantan los perros.	*I love dogs.*
¿Qué piensas de mi amigo? Pienso que es muy simpático.	*What do you think of my friend? I think he's very friendly.*
Estoy de acuerdo contigo. Me parece un chico amable.	*I am in agreement with you. He seems to me like a kind boy.*

You need an indirect object pronoun with verbs like 'gustar' because you're literally saying 'it pleases me'. See p.105 for more information.

What's your opinion of...? — ¿Cuál es tu opinión de...?

I am not in agreement — No estoy de acuerdo

shy — tímido

Prefiero... — *I prefer...*

If you dislike something, try to say what you prefer:

Me gusta el té, pero prefiero el café.	*I like tea, but I prefer coffee.*
No me gusta pintar — prefiero correr.	*I don't like painting — I prefer running.*

Grammar — 'preferir' is a stem-changing verb

'Preferir' (*to prefer*) is a stem-changing verb (see p.126). The second 'e' changes to 'ie' in the present tense:

prefiero	***I prefer***
prefieres	***you prefer***
prefiere	***he/she/it prefers***
prefieren	***they prefer***

The stem doesn't change for the 'we' form ('preferimos'), nor does it change for the 'you inf., pl.' form ('preferís').

Porque — *Because*

To start justifying your opinion, you need 'porque' (because).

Look out, though — 'porque' and '¿por qué?' sound very similar, but they're written differently and mean different things.

¿Por qué te gusta cocinar?	*Why do you like cooking?*
Me gusta cocinar porque...	*I like cooking because...*

(No) me gusta porque es... — *I (don't) like it because it's...*

Vocabulary

bueno/a	*good*	agradable	*nice, pleasant*	divertido/a	*funny, amusing*
excelente	*excellent*	increíble	*incredible, unbelievable*	aburrido/a	*boring*
guay	*cool*			malo/a	*bad*
emocionante	*exciting, touching, moving*	bonito/a	*beautiful, nice*	terrible	*terrible*
		maravilloso/a	*marvellous, wonderful*	precioso/a (Higher)	*beautiful*
				irritante (Higher)	*annoying*
perfecto/a	*perfect*	interesante	*interesting*	decepcionante (Higher)	*disappointing*

Grammar — nouns and adjectives agree

The ending of the adjective must agree with the noun (p.115).

El libro es bueno. ***The book is good.*** 'el libro' is masculine so 'bueno' must end in 'o'.

La película es buena. ***The film is good.*** 'la película' is feminine so the adjective ends in 'a'.

Q&A Audio

Question

¿Cuál es tu opinión de esta revista?

What is your opinion of this magazine?

Simple Answer

Me gusta mucho esta revista.

I really like this magazine.

Extended Answer

Me gusta mucho esta revista porque es muy interesante.

I really like this magazine because it's very interesting.

If an adjective doesn't end in an 'o', it usually stays the same for both masculine and feminine nouns.

Practice Questions

Q1 Dike and Elena are discussing the cinema. Read the dialogue and answer the questions in English.

READING

Dike: *¿Te gusta ir al cine, Elena?*

Elena: *Sí, ir al cine es emocionante. Me gustan las películas de acción. ¿Y tú qué piensas?*

Dike: *No me gusta ir al cine. Prefiero ver las películas en casa. Me encantan las películas de terror pero odio las de ciencia ficción porque son aburridas. ¿Qué piensas, Elena?*

Elena: *No estoy de acuerdo. Creo que pueden ser muy divertidas.*

e.g. *Why does Elena like going to the cinema?* *Because it's exciting.*

a) Does Dike prefer going to the cinema or watching films at home? *[1 mark]*

b) What is Dike's opinion of science fiction films? *[1 mark]*

c) What does Elena think of science fiction films? *[1 mark]*

Higher

Q2 Carolina and Antonio are talking about what they do at the weekend. What are their opinions? Write P for a positive one, N for a negative one, or P+N for a positive and negative one.

LISTENING — Listening Track 03

e.g. *Carolina — dancing* P

a) i) Carolina — reading *[1 mark]*

ii) Carolina — listening to music *[1 mark]*

b) i) Antonio — cooking *[1 mark]*

ii) Antonio — going out with friends *[1 mark]*

I think sharing your opinions is positively splendiferous...

It is a real word — I checked. Though I wonder how you say it in Spanish... Anyway, whenever you do share your opinion, you should try to explain why you like or dislike something — you'll pick up more marks for it.

General Stuff — Vocabulary

Phew that was a lot, but don't worry — I've popped all the words you need across the next four pages. How kind of me...

Numbers

el número	*number*
cero	*zero*
uno	*one*
dos	*two*
tres	*three*
cuatro	*four*
cinco	*five*
seis	*six*
siete	*seven*
ocho	*eight*
nueve	*nine*
diez	*ten*
once	*eleven*
doce	*twelve*
trece	*thirteen*
catorce	*fourteen*
quince	*fifteen*
dieciséis	*sixteen*
diecisiete	*seventeen*
dieciocho	*eighteen*
diecinueve	*nineteen*
veinte, veinti-	*twenty*
veintiuno	*twenty-one*
veintidós	*twenty-two*
veintitrés	*twenty-three*

treinta	*thirty*
treinta y uno	*thirty-one*
cuarenta	*forty*
cincuenta	*fifty*
sesenta	*sixty*
setenta	*seventy*
ochenta	*eighty*
noventa	*ninety*
cien(to)	*one hundred (and...)*
ciento uno	*one hundred and one*
doscientos	*two hundred (and...)*
quinientos	*five hundred (and...)*
setecientos	*seven hundred (and...)*
novecientos	*nine hundred (and...)*
mil	*one thousand*
un millón	*one million*
dos millones	*two million*
primer	*first (pre-noun, m only)*
primero/a	*first*
segundo/a	*second*
tercer	*third (pre-noun, m only)*
tercero/a	*third*
cuarto/a	*fourth*
quinto/a	*fifth*
varios/as	*several*

la mayoría	*majority*	
la mitad	*half*	
el cuarto	*quarter*	
doble	*double*	
máximo/a	*maximum*	
mínimo/a	*minimum*	
juntos/as	*together*	
entero/a	*entire, whole, complete*	Higher
superior	*superior, higher, upper*	Higher
numeroso/a	*numerous*	Higher
la minoría	*minority*	Higher
el par	*pair, couple*	Higher

Time

el tiempo	*time*
Es la...	*It's...*
Son las...	*It's...*
y cuarto	*quarter past*
y media	*half past*
el segundo	*second (time measurement)*
el minuto	*minute*
la hora	*hour, time (specific)*
ahora	*now*
en este momento	*at the moment*
el presente	*present (time)*
luego	*later, afterwards*
el comienzo	*start, beginning*
el final	*end, ending*
el momento	*moment*
el pasado	*past*
la vez	*time (once, twice...)*
la mañana	*morning*
el mediodía	*noon, midday*
la tarde	*afternoon, evening*
la noche	*night, evening*

hoy	*today*
mañana	*tomorrow*
ayer	*yesterday*
reciente	*recent*
tarde	*late*
pasado/a	*last, past*
último/a	*last, latest*
siguiente	*next, following*
constante	*constant*
a veces	*sometimes*
de vez en cuando	*from time to time*
antes	*before, beforehand*
después	*after, afterwards*
finalmente	*finally, at last*
H el principio	*start, beginning*
H breve	*brief, short*
H la frecuencia	*frequency*

'Antes' and 'después' can be followed by 'de' + noun (Foundation) or 'de' + infinitive (Higher). See p.109 for more.

For more information about words related to telling the time, head to p.5. For other time words, see p.6.

Dates

la fecha	*date*
el día	*day, daytime*
la semana	*week*
el fin de semana	*(at the) weekend*
lunes	*Monday*
martes	*Tuesday*
miércoles	*Wednesday*
jueves	*Thursday*
viernes	*Friday*
sábado	*Saturday*
domingo	*Sunday*
el mes	*month*
el año	*year*
la estación	*season*
la primavera	*spring*
el verano	*summer*
el otoño	*autumn*
el invierno	*winter*

enero	*January*
febrero	*February*
marzo	*March*
abril	*April*
mayo	*May*
junio	*June*
julio	*July*
agosto	*August*
septiembre	*September*
octubre	*October*
noviembre	*November*
diciembre	*December*
H hace X años	*X years ago*
H anterior	*previous, preceding*
H la década	*decade*

If you want to say 'on Mondays', you shouldn't use 'en'. Instead, just add 'los' before 'lunes' or any other day of the week. E.g. 'I dance on Mondays' would be 'Bailo los lunes'.

Questions

¿Qué?	*What?*
¿Cuál(es)?	*Which?, What?*
¿Cuándo?	*When?*
¿Por qué?	*Why?*
¿Dónde?	*Where?*
¿Cómo?	*How?*
¿Cuánto/a?	*How much?*
¿Cuántos/as?	*How many?*
¿Quién(es)?	*Who?*
sí	*yes*
no	*no*
la pregunta	*question*
responder	*to answer*

When writing questions in Spanish, don't forget to add an upside down question mark at the start of your question. If you're asking a question out loud, remember to raise your voice at the end of the sentence.

For more on interrogative pronouns, see p.107.

Quick, they're looking! Let's pretend I've said something really witty and inspiring.

Being Polite

hola	*hello, hi*
¡Buenos días!	*Good morning!*
¡Buenas tardes / noches!	*Good afternoon, evening / night!*
el saludo	*greeting, regards*
¿Qué tal (estás / está)?	*How are you?*
¿Qué (te) pasa?	*What's wrong?, What's happened?, What's up?*
bien	*well*
mal	*badly*
adiós	*goodbye*
¡Hasta luego / pronto!	*See you later / soon!*
la presentación	*introduction*
por favor	*please*

el favor	*favour*
gracias	*thank you, thanks*
de nada	*you are welcome, not at all*
vale	*OK (I agree), OK?*
claro	*of course*
me da igual	*I don't mind*
lo siento	*I'm sorry, I apologise*
perdón	*(I am) sorry*
quisiera	*(I) would like (formal)*
el señor	*Mr., sir*
la señora	*Mrs., lady, madam*
H presentar	*to present, introduce (someone)*
H presentarse	*to introduce (oneself)*
H por supuesto	*indeed, of course*

General Stuff — Vocabulary

Opinions

la opinión	*opinion*
gustar	*to like, be pleasing to*
me/te/le gustaría	*(I, you, he, she, it, you (sing. form)) would like (informal)*
encantar	*to love*
encontrar	*to find*
encontrarse	*to feel*
interesar	*to interest, be of interest*
de acuerdo	*in agreement*
la razón	*reason*
tener razón	*to be right, correct*
la decisión	*decision*
la idea	*idea*
el ejemplo	*example*
el punto	*point, full stop, dot*
el detalle	*detail*
odiar	*to hate*
creer	*to think, believe*
pensar (de)	*to think (of / about)*
la verdad	*truth*
la posibilidad	*possibility*
significar	*to mean*
preferir	*to prefer*
bueno/a	*good*
excelente	*excellent*
guay	*cool*
emocionante	*exciting, touching, moving*
perfecto/a	*perfect*
agradable	*nice, pleasant*
increíble	*incredible, unbelievable*
bonito/a	*beautiful, nice*
maravilloso/a	*marvellous, wonderful*
extraordinario/a	*extraordinary*
interesante	*interesting*
divertido/a	*funny, amusing*
exacto/a	*exact*
verdadero/a	*real, true*
aburrido/a	*bored, boring*
malo/a	*bad*
terrible	*terrible*
falso/a	*false*
general	*general*
personal	*personal*
típico/a	*typical*
común	*common*
original	*original*
diferente	*different*
distinto/a	*different*
imposible	*impossible*
posible	*possible*
simple	*simple, straightforward*

Higher

parecer	*to seem*
imaginar(se)	*to imagine*
desear	*to desire*
sentir	*to regret, sense*
proponer	*to suggest, propose*
considerar	*to consider*
mencionar	*to mention*
ignorar	*to ignore, not know*
la encuesta	*survey*
la conclusión	*conclusion*
la duda	*doubt*
vale la pena	*it's worth it*
precioso/a	*beautiful*
irritante	*annoying*
decepcionante	*disappointing*
universal	*universal*
similar	*similar*
contrario/a	*contrary, opposite*
complejo/a	*complex, complicated*
evidente	*obvious*
evidentemente	*evidently, obviously*

Useful Nouns

la manera	*way*
la forma	*way, form, shape*
la parte	*part*
el tipo	*type, kind, sort*
la caja	*box*
el miedo	*fear*
la pena	*shame, sadness*
el recuerdo	*memory*
la calidad	*quality*
la condición	*condition*
el plan	*plan*
la letra	*letter*
la cosa	*thing*
la asociación	*association*
la situación	*situation*

H

la impresión	*impression*
la expresión	*expression*

Higher

el concepto	*concept*
el sentido	*sense, direction*
el fondo	*background, bottom*
el signo	*sign*
la fila	*line, row*
el objeto	*object*
la colección	*collection*
la variedad	*variety*
la capacidad	*capacity*
el acceso	*access*
un montón (de)	*a lot (of), pile*
la característica	*characteristic, quality*
el orgullo	*pride*
el deseo	*desire, wish*
la intención	*intention*
la ocasión	*occasion*
la sesión	*session*

When you learn a new noun, make sure you learn its article too. That way, you'll know how to make any adjectives agree with it.

Useful Adjectives & Adverbs

Remember — Spanish adjectives need to agree in gender and number with the noun they describe. However, adverbs don't need to agree.

corto/a	*brief*
lento/a	*slow*
libre	*free, vacant*
vacío/a	*empty*
ligero/a	*light*
completo/a	*complete, full*
medio/a	*half*
real	*real*
seguro/a	*sure*
incluido/a	*included, inclusive of*
diverso/a	*diverse*
inútil	*useless*
esencial	*essential*
normal	*normal, usual, regular*
como	*like*
encima (de)	*above*
rápidamente	*quickly*
completamente	*completely*
realmente	*really*
seguramente	*surely, certainly*
totalmente	*totally, completely*

Higher:

pesado/a	*heavy, boring, annoying*
inmenso/a	*immense, huge, great*
amplio/a	*large, wide, loose*
lleno/a	*full, filled*
suave	*soft, gentle, mild*
auténtico/a	*authentic*
adecuado/a	*appropriate, adequate*
listo/a	*ready (after estar)*
de hecho	*actually, in fact*

Colours

el color	*colour*
amarillo/a	*yellow*
azul	*blue*
blanco/a	*white*
gris	*grey*
marrón	*brown*
naranja	*orange*
negro/a	*black*
rojo/a	*red*
rosa	*pink*
verde	*green*
claro/a (H)	*clear, light (in colour)*
oscuro/a (H)	*dark*

Mercè believed in a 'more is more' approach.

Useful Verbs

abrir	*to open*
afectar	*to affect*
bajar	*to lower, reduce*
cambiar	*to change, exchange*
decidir	*to decide*
dejar	*to leave, allow*
depender (de)	*to depend (on)*
encontrarse	*to run into*
entrar	*to enter, go in*
escoger	*to choose*
esperar	*to hope, wait, expect*
hablar	*to speak*
intentar	*to try*
mirar	*to look, watch*
mostrar	*to show*
mover(se)	*to move*
necesitar	*to need*
oír	*to hear*
ponerse	*to get, become (+ adjective)*
pronunciar	*to pronounce*
quedar	*to meet up*
recordar	*to remember, remind*
repetir	*to repeat*
romper	*to break (object)*
tener ganas de	*to look forward to, be keen to*
tirar	*to pull*

Higher:

acabar	*to finish*
acompañar	*to go with, accompany*
acordarse (de)	*to remember*
agradecer	*to thank*
alcanzar	*to reach*
apreciar	*to appreciate*
arreglar	*to repair, resolve*
asegurarse de	*to ensure*
atreverse	*to dare*
bañar	*to bathe*
comprobar	*to check*
consistir (en)	*to consist (of)*
contar	*to count, tell*
conversar	*to chat, talk*
crear	*to create*
esconder(se)	*to hide*
experimentar	*to experience*
faltar	*to be missing, lack*
formar	*to form*
inventar	*to invent*
irse (de)	*to leave*
limitar	*to limit*
llenar	*to fill, fulfil*
marcharse	*to leave, go away*
me apetece + infinitive / noun	*I feel like + ing / noun*
meter (en)	*to put (into)*
notar	*to notice*
poseer	*to possess*
recuperar	*to get (something) back*
relacionar	*to relate*
saltar	*to jump*
separar	*to separate, sort*
sustituir	*to replace, substitute*
traducir	*to translate*
tratar de + infinitive	*to try to + verb*

Revision Summary Test for Section One

That's the first section (nearly) done and dusted. Time to test yourself on what you can remember.

- These questions are **hard**, but they'll really help you see **how well you know your stuff**.
- Tackle the **revision summary test** below, or scan the QR code to do it **online**. You can **track your progress** online and see **which areas need more work**.
- There are **sample answers** for the test here: www.cgpbooks.co.uk/GraciasExtras

Summary Test

Numbers and Times

1) Count out loud from 0 to 20 in Spanish.
2) How do you say these numbers in Spanish? a) 25 b) 37 c) 60 d) 104 e) 2003
3) 'Hay mil setecientas cuarenta y nueve razones.' What does this mean in English?
4) Say the following phrases in Spanish: a) the first example b) the second day c) the third detail
5) Describe your daily routine using at least three different times.

H 6) 'The maximum number of points you can reach is five hundred.' Translate this into Spanish.

Times and Dates

7) Say all 7 days of the week and all 12 months of the year in Spanish.
8) ¿Cuándo es tu cumpleaños?
9) Say these words and phrases in English:
a) ahora b) luego c) el mediodía d) la tarde e) la noche f) hoy g) ayer
10) Your Chilean friend says: 'Decidiré mañana por la mañana.' What does this mean in English?
11) Describe what you like to do at the weekend.

H 12) Paloma says: 'Esta década será el principio de unas posibilidades extraordinarias. Es un deseo mío crear millones de recuerdos bonitos llenos de felicidad.' What is she saying?

Questions

13) What is the difference between '¿Qué...?' and '¿Cuál...?'?
14) '¿Cuánto cuestan los calcetines naranja? El precio no está en la caja.' What is this person asking?
15) Write a question for each of the following question words:
a) ¿Quién...? b) ¿Cuántos/as...? c) ¿Dónde...? d) ¿Cómo...? e) ¿Por qué...?

Being Polite

16) What are the differences between 'tú', 'vosotros/as', 'usted' and 'ustedes'?
17) How do you say these in English?
a) hola b) ¿Qué tal? c) bien d) mal e) adiós f) por favor g) gracias h) lo siento
18) Imagine you're introducing a friend to your headteacher. Write out 2 sentences for each person.
19) How would you ask someone politely to repeat their idea in Spanish?

Opinions

20) In Spanish, say that you always look forward to watching different kinds of original series.
21) Pepe says: 'Me gusta jugar al baloncesto porque es emocionante.' What's he saying?
22) 'I find this situation terrible and completely unbelievable.' How would you say this in Spanish?
23) Gonzalo asks: '¿Estás de acuerdo con mi opinión?' What does he want to know?
24) a) Explain why you dislike your least favourite school subject in Spanish.
b) Say a subject that you like using the word 'prefiero'. Give a reason why you like it.

H 25) How would you say that you love to invent objects that don't seem real in Spanish?
26) Give a review of a book that you have recently read or a film that you have recently watched.

About Yourself

Quick Quiz

I know you're probably not supposed to admit this, but I do love talking about myself. And why wouldn't I when I can limbo skate better than the pros...

Head to the CGP RevisionHub for all your online content: www.cgpbooks.co.uk/Gracias

Me llamo... — *I'm called...*

Vocabulary

el nombre	*name*	europeo/a	*European*	la religión	*religion*
llamarse	*to be called*	transgénero	*transgender*	religioso/a	*religious*
la edad	*age*	bisexual	*bisexual*	la discapacidad	*disability*
el año	*year*	gay	*gay*	la silla de ruedas	*wheelchair*
inglés(a)	*English*	lesbiana	*lesbian*	H nacer	*to be born*
español(a)	*Spanish*	heterosexual	*straight*	H crecer	*to grow up*

¡Hola! Me llamo Riku y tengo quince años.	*Hello! I'm called Riku and I'm 15 years old.*
Mi cumpleaños es el dos de abril. Nací en dos mil doce.	*My birthday is the 2nd of April. I was born in 2012.*
Vivo en España, pero soy francesa.	*I live in Spain, but I am French.*
Mi familia es religiosa.	*My family is religious.*
Varios aspectos forman mi identidad, como la edad y el género.	*Various aspects form my identity, like age and gender.*

I'm... — Soy...
My name is... — Mi nombre es...

Check p.7 for a reminder of how to say dates.

Scottish — escocés / escocesa
Irish — irlandés / irlandesa
Welsh — galés / galesa

See p.28 for more nationalities.

Grammar — saying your age

In Spanish, you 'have' an age, so you need 'tener' to say how old you are. 'Tener' is a stem-changing verb — see p.126.

Tengo 16 años. ***I'm 16 years old.***

Grammar — nationalities

Nationalities are adjectives. Some have an accent in the masculine singular form, but drop the accent and add 'a' in the feminine form.

inglés (m., sing.) — **inglesa** (f., sing.)
ingleses (m., pl.) — **inglesas** (f., pl.)

The accent is dropped in the plural forms too.

Practice Question

Q1 Read the following text out loud.

SPEAKING

¡Hola! Me llamo Estefanía y soy de Venezuela. Vivo en el norte del país, cerca de la ciudad de Caracas. Tengo dieciséis años y mi cumpleaños es el veinticuatro de julio.

[8 marks]

Now answer the questions about yourself below in Spanish.

a) *¿Cómo te llamas?*
b) *¿Dónde vives?*
c) *¿Cuántos años tienes?*
d) *¿Cuándo es tu cumpleaños?* *[4 marks]*

Top Tip for Higher Students
✓ Try to give more than one detail for your answers, e.g. say the year you were born in.

The only llamas I'm interested in have four legs and a fluffy tail...

When you're introducing yourself to someone new in Spanish, you could say the same stuff as you would in English, like your name, age, and where you're from. Or you could make up a cool alter ego instead...

Quick Quiz

My Family and Friends

OK, it's not *all* about you — you'll have to be able to talk about your family and friends too. Examiners are a nosy bunch, so prepare yourself for a friendly interrogation...

Mi familia — *My family*

Vocabulary

los padres	*parents*	los hijos	*children*	la prima	*cousin (f)*
el padre	*father*	el hijo	*son, child (m)*	el perro	*dog*
el papá	*dad*	la hija	*daughter, child (f)*	el gato	*cat*
la madre	*mother*	el hermano	*brother, sibling (m)*	el conejo	*rabbit*
la mamá	*mum*	el hermanastro	*stepbrother*	el caballo	*horse*
el padrastro	*stepfather*	la hermana	*sister, sibling (f)*	el/la menor (Higher)	*the youngest*
la madrastra	*stepmother*	la hermanastra	*stepsister*	el/la mayor (Higher)	*the oldest*
los abuelos	*grandparents*	el tío	*uncle*	gemelo/a (adj.) (Higher)	*twin*
el abuelo	*grandfather*	la tía	*aunt*	el pájaro (Higher)	*bird*
la abuela	*grandmother*	el primo	*cousin (m)*	el pez (Higher)	*fish*

Háblame de tu familia — *Tell me about your family*

Grammar — saying 'my' and 'your'

Possessive adjectives like 'my' and 'your' have to agree with the noun they come before (see p.117). Remember — 'su(s)' could also mean 'your' if you're being formal.

mi padre	*my father*	tu hermana	*your sister*	su tía	*his / her / their aunt*
mis padres	*my parents*	tus hermanas	*your sisters*	sus tías	*his / her / their aunts*

I wonder who the favourite is...

Tengo una hermana mayor. Se llama Ramona.
I have an older sister. She is called Ramona.

> *a younger sister* — una hermana menor
> *a bird* — un pájaro

Hay cinco personas en mi familia: mi madre, mi padrastro, mis dos hermanos menores y yo. Mis hermanos se llaman Waisea y Gabriel.
There are five people in my family: my mother, my stepfather, my two younger brothers and me. My brothers are called Waisea and Gabriel.

> *older brothers* — hermanos mayores

Soy hijo único, pero me gustaría tener hermanos.
I'm an only child (m), but I'd like to have siblings.

> *an only child (f)* — hija única
> *the oldest* — el/la mayor
> *the youngest* — el/la menor

> *I like not having siblings* — me gusta no tener hermanos

Para mí, mi perro Joey es parte de la familia también.
For me, my dog Joey is part of the family too.

Q&A Audio

Question

¿Cómo es tu familia?
What's your family like?

Simple Answer

Soy hijo único, pero tengo muchos primos.
I'm an only child, but I have a lot of cousins.

Extended Answer

Soy hijo único, pero mi padre tiene cinco hermanos y cada uno tiene hijos. Entonces, en realidad mi familia es muy grande. Mis primos viven cerca de aquí y siempre lo pasamos bien juntos.
I'm an only child, but my father has five siblings and each one has children. So, in reality my family is very big. My cousins live near here and we always have a good time together.

Mis amigos — *My friends*

Vocabulary

el amigo	*friend (m)*	conocer	*to know (person, place), meet (for the first time)*
la amiga	*friend (f)*	pasar	*to spend (time)*
cercano/a	*close*	H la amistad	*friendship*
viejo/a	*long-standing (pre-noun)*		

Grammar — prenominal adjectives

'Bueno' becomes 'buen' before masculine singular nouns. 'Buen' is a prenominal adjective (see p.116).

Eres un buen amigo.
You're a good friend.

The other forms don't need to change.

Sois buenos amigos.
You're good friends.

Para mí, es bastante fácil hacer amigos. Pero a veces puede ser difícil. — *For me, it's quite easy to make friends. But sometimes it can be difficult.*

Tengo muchas amigas pero no tengo una amiga muy cercana. — *I have lots of friends but I don't have a very close friend.*

Mis amigos y yo somos muy similares. — *My friends and I are very similar.*

La amistad es muy importante. Soy feliz porque tengo buenos amigos. — *Friendship is very important. I am happy because I have good friends.*

Mi buen amigo Benicio es argentino. Me gusta cuando pasamos tiempo juntos porque le conozco muy bien. — *My good friend Benicio is Argentinian. I like it when we spend time together because I know him really well.*

to meet new people — conocer a nueva gente

a best friend — un/a mejor amigo/a

Mexican — mexicano
Chilean — chileno
Colombian — colombiano

'Conozco' (I know) is the only irregular bit of the verb 'conocer' in the present tense.

Practice Questions

Q1 *Write a description of your family and friends.*
You should write about 40-50 words in Spanish. Mention:

WRITING

- *who's in your family*
- *your opinion of family events*
- *an activity that you will do with your friends in the future.* *[14 marks]*

Top Tip for Higher Students
✓ Use possessive pronouns to talk about your family, e.g. 'Tu amigo es mayor que el mío.'

Higher

Q2 *Qori has written about her family.*
Read her comments and then answer the questions below in English.

READING

> *Vivo con mi mamá y mis tres hermanas. Paso mucho tiempo con la mayor de mis hermanas porque disfrutamos de las mismas actividades y compartimos varios intereses comunes. Los fines de semana, visito a mi padre, su mujer italiana y mi hermanastro, que se llama Marco. Tenemos la misma edad y el mismo cumpleaños. Sí, ¡nació el mismo día que yo! Me gustaría pasar más tiempo allí con ellos porque nos llevamos muy bien.*

a) Which of her sisters does Qori spend lots of time with? *[1 mark]*

b) Why does Qori spend lots of time with her? (1 detail) *[1 mark]*

c) Who does Qori visit on the weekend? *[1 mark]*

d) What coincidence does Qori mention? *[1 mark]*

Pineapple on pizza — that's what true friendship looks like...

You can tut all you like, but it won't change my mind. No matter who makes up your family or friendship groups, you need to be able to talk about them in your exams. You'd better give these pages another read...

Quick Quiz

Describing People

Adjectives are a key ingredient of Spanish success, so it's always worth having some to hand...

¿Cómo eres? — *What are you like?*

You'll need the verbs 'tener' (to have) and 'ser' (to be) for this page. They're irregular, so check p.127-128 to see how they work.

Vocabulary

bello/a	*beautiful*	verde	*green*	el/la adulto/a	*adult*
alto/a	*tall*	azul	*blue*	el/la anciano/a	*old person*
bajo/a	*short*	gris	*grey*	la gente	*people*
pequeño/a	*small, little, young*	el pelo	*hair*	el estilo	*style, elegance*
joven	*young*	corto/a	*short (hair)*	parecerse a (Higher)	*to look like*
viejo/a	*old, aged (post-noun)*	largo/a	*long*	la belleza (Higher)	*beauty*
describir	*to describe*	rubio/a	*blonde, light (skin)*	precioso/a (Higher)	*beautiful*
la cara	*face*	castaño/a	*chestnut brown*	oscuro/a (Higher)	*dark*
las gafas	*glasses*	negro/a	*black*	moreno/a (Higher)	*dark (hair), tanned (skin)*
los ojos	*eyes*	pelirrojo/a	*red-haired, ginger*	la altura (Higher)	*height*
marrón	*brown*	la persona	*person*		

'Marrón' loses its accent in the plural form.

Tengo... — *I have...*

Q&A Audio

Question

¿Cómo eres?

What are you like?

Simple Answer

Soy alta. Tengo los ojos azules y tengo el pelo castaño.

I'm tall. I have blue eyes and I have chestnut brown hair.

Extended Answer

Soy de altura media — no soy ni alta ni baja. Tengo los ojos azules y llevo gafas. Tengo una cara pequeña y tengo el pelo corto.

I am average height — I'm neither tall nor short. I have blue eyes and I wear glasses. I have a small face and I have short hair.

Soy muy bajo como mis padres. Sin embargo, mi hermano es mucho más alto que yo. Tengo el pelo rubio y tengo los ojos verdes.

I'm very short like my parents. However, my brother is much taller than me. I have blonde hair and I have green eyes.

Grammar — adjectives agree

Adjectives must agree with the noun they describe.
'Los ojos' are masculine plural, so adjectives like 'blue' must be in the masculine plural form — 'azules'.
'El pelo' is masculine singular, so adjectives like 'short' need to be in the masculine singular form — 'corto' — even if you're a girl.

No soy ni gorda ni delgada. Tengo los ojos marrones y el pelo negro.
I'm neither fat nor slim. I have brown eyes and black hair.

tanned skin — la piel morena
dark hair — el pelo oscuro

Creo que te pareces a tu padre, pero él es más bajo y tiene el pelo gris.
I think that you look like your father, but he is shorter and has grey hair.

Mis abuelos son viejos pero mi abuelo todavía se considera joven.
My grandparents are old but my grandfather still considers himself young.

he's red-haired — es pelirrojo

Tiene el pelo rubio y largo. Es altísima. Lleva gafas y tiene los ojos azules.
She has long, blonde hair. She's really tall. She wears glasses and she has blue eyes.

really short — bajísima

Es un chico bellísimo con los ojos verdes. Tiene una sonrisa preciosa.
He's a very beautiful boy with green eyes. He has a beautiful smile.

face — cara

Mi personalidad — *My personality*

Vocabulary

simpático/a	*nice, kind, friendly*	serio/a	*serious*	fiel	*loyal, faithful*
alegre	*lively, cheerful, happy*	estricto/a	*strict*	orgulloso/a	*proud*
contento/a	*happy, content*	independiente	*independent*	nervioso/a	*nervous, anxious*
feliz	*happy*	tranquilo/a	*calm, relaxed*	(ser) listo/a	*(to be) clever*
trabajador(a)	*hardworking*	triste	*sad, unhappy*	optimista	*optimistic*
		enfadado/a	*angry*	artístico/a	*artistic*

(Higher: fiel, orgulloso/a, nervioso/a, (ser) listo/a, optimista, artístico/a)

Grammar — making adjectives agree

Adjectives must agree with the nouns they describe — see p.115.

Some adjectives don't follow the normal rules:

1) '-or' endings, e.g. '**trabajador**' — add an 'a' on the end for the feminine form and then 'es' and 'as' for the masculine and feminine plurals.
2) '-ísta/-ista' endings, e.g. '**optimista**' — stay the same in the singular and add an 's' for both the masculine and feminine plurals.

Grammar — 'ser' vs 'estar'

Both 'ser' and 'estar' mean 'to be'.

To describe someone's personality use 'ser', but to describe how they feel at a given moment, use 'estar' — see p.128.

Está tranquilo. ***He is feeling calm.***

Es tranquilo. ***He is calm. (a calm person)***

Mi mejor amigo es muy fiel. Es optimista también. Sin embargo, hoy está triste. — *My best friend is very loyal. He's optimistic too. However, today he is feeling sad.*

He has a good sense of humour — Tiene un buen sentido del humor

Mis padres son estrictos pero divertidos al mismo tiempo. Mi madre es muy deportiva pero mi padre es más artístico. — *My parents are strict but fun at the same time. My mother is very sporty but my father is more artistic.*

Mis profesoras son listas y simpáticas. — *My teachers are clever and friendly.*

understanding — comprensivas

Practice Questions

Q1 *Ana and Pablo are describing these four people. Write the correct order in which they are mentioned.*

LISTENING — Listening Track 04

A 
B 
C 
D 

[4 marks]

Q2 *Write a blog post about you and a close friend. Write about 80-90 words in Spanish. You must include the following points:*

- *your friend's appearance and personality*
- *your opinion of your friend's style*
- *how you met your friend*
- *where you would like to go with them this weekend.*

WRITING

Top Tip for Higher Students
✓ Use a wide range of adjectives, e.g. superlatives, to talk about your friend's best qualities.

[18 marks]

I reckon I'm funny, intelligent and humble...

Oh, this space isn't for me to keep describing myself? Shame. Remember — if you want to say your sister is serious, you'll need the feminine form of the adjective. Also, try to avoid describing everyone in the same way.

Quick Quiz

Relationships and Partnerships

Here's your chance to say who you get on best with — or vent about someone who winds you up...

Las relaciones — *Relationships*

Vocabulary

llevarse (con)	*to get on (with)*
discutir	*to argue, discuss*
escuchar	*to listen*
respetar	*to respect*
comprender	*to understand*
reír(se)	*to laugh*
ayudar	*to help*

Higher

entender	*to understand*
confiar en	*to rely on*
contar con	*to count on*
animar	*to encourage, cheer up*
molestar	*to annoy*
pelearse	*to fight, argue*
apoyar	*to support*

Willow could always lean on her friends for support.

Grammar — reflexive verbs

'Llevarse', 'reírse', 'pelearse' and 'enamorarse' are reflexive verbs. Take off the 'se' and add the correct ending to the stem like a normal verb (see p.125). Then choose the right pronoun (see p.135) and put it in front of the verb.

Me llevo bien con mi hermana.	***I get on well with my sister.***
¿Te ríes con ella?	***Do you laugh with her?***
Nos peleamos mucho.	***We fight a lot.***

Grammar (Higher only) — 'confiar'

'Confiar' is an irregular verb. In the present tense, the 'i' has an accent on it in every form except the 'we' and 'you inf., plural' forms.

Confío en él. ***I rely on him.***

¿Te llevas bien con ellos? — *Do you get on well with them?*

Mis padres tienen una buena relación pero yo no me llevo bien con ellos.

My parents have a good relationship but I don't get on with them.

I find it difficult to interact with them — me resulta difícil relacionarme con ellos

Me llevo mejor con mi hermana porque me ayuda mucho. La encuentro muy graciosa.

I get on better with my sister because she helps me a lot. I find her very funny.

I don't like to argue with my sister — No me gusta discutir con mi hermana

Mi hermano y yo nos peleamos mucho porque me molesta.

My brother and I fight a lot because he annoys me.

I can't stand my brother — No aguanto a mi hermano

Un buen amigo siempre te escucha y te apoya.

A good friend always listens to you and supports you.

helps you and cheers you up — te ayuda y te anima

El amor — *Love*

Vocabulary

amar	*to love*
el cariño	*affection, love*
el beso	*kiss*
la cita	*date*
el novio	*boyfriend*
la novia	*girlfriend*
el marido	*husband*
la mujer	*wife*
la unión	*union (marriage)*
casarse	*to get married*

Higher

la pareja	*partner, couple*
el/la compañero/a	*companion*
el sentimiento	*feeling*
enamorarse	*to fall in love*
separarse	*to split up*

En el futuro... — *In the future...*

Q&A Audio

Question

¿Te gustaría casarte y tener hijos en el futuro?

Would you like to get married and have children in the future?

Simple Answer

No sé si quiero casarme, pero me gustaría tener hijos.

I don't know if I want to get married, but I'd like to have children.

Extended Answer

Quiero casarme porque me importa mucho. Me gustaría tener hijos cuando tenga treinta años, pero no sé cuántos hijos quiero tener.

I want to get married because it matters a lot to me. I'd like to have children when I'm 30, but I don't know how many children I want to have.

Grammar (Higher only) — When I'm X years old...

To say 'when I'm 30' (or to say 'when' with a future event), use the subjunctive. See p.140.

Cuando tenga 60 años...
When I'm 60 years old...

¿Te gustaría casarte? — *Would you like to get married?*

Me gustaría enamorarme y casarme porque parece emocionante.

I would like to fall in love and get married because it seems exciting.

Debo decir que preferiría no casarme, porque una boda puede costar mucho dinero.

I must say that I would prefer not to get married, because a wedding can cost a lot of money.

En mi opinión, no es necesario casarse antes de tener hijos, pero todavía me gustaría hacerlo.

In my opinion, it's not necessary to get married before having children, but I'd still like to do it.

I never want to get married — no quiero casarme nunca

I'd prefer to buy myself a house — preferiría comprarme una casa

marriage can give you security — el matrimonio te puede dar seguridad

Practice Questions

Q1 Read Chea's message about her boyfriend and choose the correct options below. READING

> *Conocí a mi novio en una fiesta de cumpleaños cuando tenía quince años. Me llevo muy bien con él porque lo encuentro muy divertido y me hace reír. Discutimos muy poco, pero no quiero casarme con él ahora porque somos muy jóvenes. Todo podría cambiar en unos años ¡si todavía estamos juntos!*

a) *Where did Chea meet her boyfriend?*

A. A party **C.** At school
B. A cafe **D.** Online *[1 mark]*

b) *When does she want to get married?*

A. In 15 years **C.** Never
B. She's not sure **D.** Now *[1 mark]*

Higher

Q2 Miguel is talking about his relationships. Choose the correct statement from each list below to complete the sentences in English. LISTENING

Listening Track 05

a) Miguel used to fight with...

A. his mum.
B. his dad.
C. his brother. *[1 mark]*

b) Miguel's boyfriend says that Miguel...

A. is happy.
B. is proud.
C. isn't always friendly. *[1 mark]*

Luckily, I get on really well with Spanish revision...

I know it feels a bit weird to talk to a stranger about your relationships, but have a think about who you do or don't get on with (and why) so you'll be ready for whatever the examiner might throw your way.

Quick Quiz

Role Models

Time to talk about who inspires you and why — it's a great opportunity to use plenty of adjectives...

Tu modelo de conducta — *Your role model*

Vocabulary

positivo/a	*positive*	el grupo	*group, band*	reconocer	*to recognise, admit*
negativo/a	*negative*	seguir	*follow*	la estrella (Higher)	*star*
famoso/a	*well-known, famous*	el/la seguidor(a)	*follower*	la entrevista (Higher)	*interview*
la actriz	*actress, actor (f)*	el/la aficionado/a	*fan*	el público (Higher)	*public, audience*
el actor	*actor (m)*	el papel	*role*	la juventud (Higher)	*youth*
el/la artista	*artist*	la influencia	*influence*	la oportunidad (Higher)	*opportunity, chance*
el/la modelo	*model*	la atención	*attention*	criticar (Higher)	*to criticise*
el/la jugador(a)	*player*	merecer	*to deserve*		
		el respeto	*respect*		

Me gusta esta persona porque... — *I like this person because...*

Mi modelo de conducta es un cocinero famoso. Parece una persona muy simpática y me gustaría trabajar en su restaurante algún día.

My role model is a famous chef. He seems like a really nice person and I would like to work in his restaurant some day.

role model — ídolo

Una persona que me inspira es científica. Ganó un Premio Nobel por sus contribuciones a la medicina.

One person who inspires me is a scientist. She won a Nobel Prize for her contributions to medicine.

Soy fan de un director que ha grabado muchos documentales sobre la naturaleza. Me ha inspirado a trabajar con los animales en el futuro.

I'm a fan of a director who has recorded a lot of nature documentaries. He has inspired me to work with animals in the future.

shares their short films on social media — comparte sus cortometrajes en las redes sociales

Hay una artista que me hace ser más consciente de los problemas sociales. Los critica a través de su arte.

There's an artist who makes me more aware of social problems. She criticises them through her art.

I'm a huge fan of — Soy un gran aficionado/a a

Practice Question

Q1 *Read the following text out loud, then answer the questions below in Spanish.*

SPEAKING

> *Los modelos de conducta son importantes para los jóvenes porque pueden tener una influencia muy positiva en sus vidas. A menudo llaman la atención sobre causas importantes.*

Top Tip For Higher Students
✓ Use 'desde hace' to talk about how long someone has been your role model.

a) *¿Quién es tu modelo de conducta y por qué?*
b) *¿Qué piensas de la idea de ser famoso/a?* *[12 marks]*

My local bakery is full of roll models...

Their bread is star quality. If you can't think of a role model, you can always make one up. For example, you could describe the mysterious figure who writes your revision jokes and list your favourite things about them...

Quick Quiz

Celebrations

I hope you like surprises because I've secretly been making this page on celebrations for you. I even went to the trouble of giftwrapping it, so do give it a read through.

¿Qué celebras? — *What are you celebrating?*

Vocabulary

celebrar	*to celebrate*	el regalo	*present, gift*
reunirse	*to gather, meet*	la tarjeta	*card*
el cumpleaños	*birthday*	el pastel	*cake*
Nochevieja	*New Year's Eve*	juntarse (Higher)	*to meet, get together*
el evento	*event*	sorprender (Higher)	*to surprise*
la fiesta	*party*	regalar (Higher)	*to give (as a present)*
la sorpresa	*surprise*	ofrecer (Higher)	*to offer*
invitar	*to invite*	la alegría (Higher)	*joy, happiness*
recibir	*to receive, welcome*	el ambiente (Higher)	*atmosphere*

Jorge decided the best way to celebrate his birthday was a good old-fashioned siesta.

Me encanta reunirme con mis amigos. — *I love meeting up with my friends.*

Celebré mi cumpleaños en familia. Organizaron una fiesta para mí. Fue una sorpresa. Recibí regalos y unas tarjetas. — *I celebrated my birthday with family. They organised a party for me. It was a surprise. I received presents and some cards.*

Mi prima me invitó a su fiesta de Nochevieja. El ambiente era muy feliz. Le regalé un cuadro. — *My cousin invited me to her New Year's Eve party. The atmosphere was very happy. I gave her a painting as a gift.*

with my best friends — con mis mejores amigos

on holiday — de vacaciones

wedding — boda

was full of joy — estaba lleno de alegría

Q&A Audio

Question

¿Celebraste algo recientemente?

Did you celebrate something recently?

Simple Answer

El mes pasado fui a una fiesta en la playa.

Last month I went to a party on the beach.

Extended Answer

El mes pasado fui a una fiesta en la playa. Desafortunadamente, el ambiente no era ideal porque ¡todos teníamos demasiado calor!

Last month I went to a party on the beach. Unfortunately, the atmosphere wasn't ideal because we were all too hot!

Practice Question

Q1 Write a blog post about celebrations.
You should write about 80-90 words in Spanish. Write about:

- *your favourite event to celebrate*
- *your opinion of surprise parties*
- *how you celebrated your birthday last year*
- *a celebration you'll be part of in the future.* [18 marks]

WRITING

Top Tip for Higher Students
✓ Use relevant Higher-tier verbs, e.g. 'juntarse', 'sorprender', and 'regalar'.

I went to a party on the moon — there was no atmosphere...

Celebrations is a really helpful topic for practising your tenses — try writing some sentences about what you did for your last birthday or what you'll do next year. I'm thinking something with a live kazoo band...

Identity and Relationships — Vocabulary

Use the next three pages to strike up a friendship with all the vocab from this section.

About Yourself

el nombre	*name*
llamar	*to call*
llamarse	*to be called*
la edad	*age*
el año	*year*
tener ... años	*to be ... years old*
la identidad	*identity*
británico/a	*British*
inglés(a)	*English*
español(a)	*Spanish*
europeo/a	*European*
latino/a	*Latin*
mexicano/a, mejicano/a	*Mexican*
cubano/a	*Cuban*
chileno/a	*Chilean*
colombiano/a	*Colombian*
argentino/a	*Argentinian*
peruano/a	*Peruvian*
el género	*gender*
transgénero	*transgender*
no binario	*non-binary*
bisexual	*bisexual*
gay	*gay*
lesbiana	*lesbian*
heterosexual	*straight*
la religión	*religion*
religioso/a	*religious*
la discapacidad	*disability*
con discapacidad	*disabled*
la silla de ruedas	*wheelchair*

Higher

presentar	*to present, introduce (someone)*
nacer	*to be born*
el nacimiento	*birth*
crecer	*to grow up*
la fe	*faith*

My Family and Friends

la familia	*family*
el miembro	*member*
los padres	*parents*
el padre	*father*
el papá	*dad*
la madre	*mother*
la mamá	*mum*
el padrastro	*stepfather*
la madrastra	*stepmother*
los abuelos	*grandparents*
el abuelo	*grandfather*
la abuela	*grandmother*
los hijos	*children*
el hijo	*son, child (m)*
la hija	*daughter, child (f)*
el hermano	*brother, sibling (m)*
el hermanastro	*stepbrother*
la hermana	*sister, sibling (f)*
la hermanastra	*stepsister*
menor	*younger, youngest*
mayor	*elder, eldest*
el tío	*uncle*
la tía	*aunt*
el primo	*cousin (m)*
la prima	*cousin (f)*
el niño	*child (m), (young) boy*
la niña	*child (f), (young) girl*
el bebé	*baby*
el animal	*animal*
el perro	*dog*
el gato	*cat*
el conejo	*rabbit*
el caballo	*horse*
familiar	*familiar, of the family, family-sized*
el amigo	*friend (m)*
la amiga	*friend (f)*
cercano/a	*close, closely-related*
viejo/a	*old, long-standing (pre-noun)*
conocer	*to know (person, place), meet (for the first time), experience*
pasar	*to spend (time)*

Higher

el/la menor	*the youngest*
el/la mayor	*the oldest*
gemelo/a (adj.)	*twin*
la generación	*generation*
el pájaro	*bird*
el pez	*fish*
la amistad	*friendship*

Describing People — Appearances

bello/a	*beautiful*
alto/a	*tall*
bajo/a	*short (height)*
pequeño/a	*small, little, young*
joven	*young*
viejo/a	*old, aged (post-noun)*
describir	*to describe*
la cara	*face*
sonreír	*to smile*
llevar	*to wear*
las gafas	*glasses*
los ojos	*eyes*
marrón	*brown*
verde	*green*
azul	*blue*
gris	*grey*
rojo/a	*red*
el pelo	*hair*
corto/a	*short (hair)*
largo/a	*long*
rubio/a	*blonde, light (skin)*
castaño/a	*chestnut brown*
negro/a	*black*
pelirrojo/a	*red-haired, ginger*

la persona	*person*
el chico	*boy*
la chica	*girl*
la mujer	*woman*
el hombre	*man*
el/la adulto/a	*adult*
el/la anciano/a	*old person*
la gente	*people*
el estilo	*style, elegance, manner*

To describe someone who is non-binary, you could use 'la persona' instead of 'el chico' / 'la chica'.

Higher

el aspecto	*appearance*
parecerse a	*to look like*
la belleza	*beauty*
precioso/a	*beautiful*
lindo/a	*beautiful*
oscuro/a	*dark*
moreno/a	*dark (hair), tanned (skin)*
el cabello	*hair*
la sonrisa	*smile*
la altura	*height*
el pañuelo	*headscarf*

Describing People — Personalities and Emotions

la personalidad	*personality*
simpático/a	*nice, kind, friendly*
alegre	*lively, cheerful, happy*
contento/a	*happy, content*
feliz	*happy*
trabajador(a)	*hardworking*
serio/a	*serious*
estricto/a	*strict*
independiente	*independent*
individual	*individual*
tranquilo/a	*calm, relaxed*
triste	*sad, unhappy*
enfadado/a	*angry*

'listo/a' changes its meaning depending on whether you use it with 'ser' or 'estar'. Use 'ser' if you want to say that someone is clever, e.g. 'Es un hombre listo.' Use 'estar' if you want to say that someone is ready, e.g. 'La mujer está lista.'

Higher

fiel	*loyal, faithful*
orgulloso/a	*proud*
nervioso/a	*nervous, anxious*
(ser) listo/a	*(to be) clever*
optimista	*optimistic*
artístico/a	*artistic*
el humor	*humour*

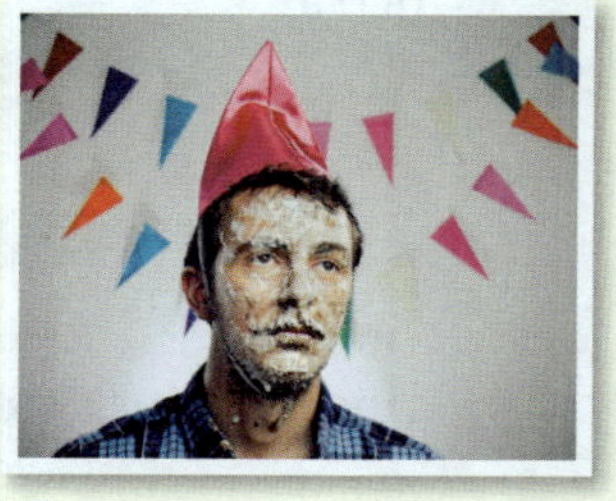

Eneko didn't appreciate his brother's sense of humour.

Identity and Relationships — Vocabulary

Relationships and Partnerships

la relación	*relationship, relation*
llevarse (con)	*to get on (with)*
discutir	*to argue, discuss*
escuchar	*to listen*
respetar	*to respect*
comprender	*to understand*
reír(se)	*to laugh*
llorar	*to cry*
ayudar	*to help*
amar	*to love*
el amor	*love*
el cariño	*affection, love*
el beso	*kiss*
la cita	*date*
el novio	*boyfriend*
la novia	*girlfriend*
el marido	*husband*
la mujer	*wife*
la unión	*union (marriage)*
casarse	*to get married*
adoptar	*to adopt*
la independencia	*independence*
solo/a	*alone*

Higher

pertenecer	*to belong*
relacionarse (con)	*to relate to, interact (with)*
entender	*to understand*
confiar en	*to rely on*
contar con	*to count on*
animar	*to encourage, cheer up*
molestar	*to annoy*
pelearse	*to fight, argue*
apoyar	*to support*
prometer	*to promise*
abrazar	*to hug*
cuidar (de)	*to look after*
la pareja	*partner, couple*
el/la compañero/a	*companion*
el sentimiento	*feeling*
enamorarse	*to fall in love*
separarse	*to split up*
civil	*civil*

Role Models

el modelo de conducta	*role model*
positivo/a	*positive*
negativo/a	*negative*
famoso/a	*well-known, famous*
la actriz	*actress, actor (f)*
el actor	*actor (m)*
actuar	*to act, perform*
el/la artista	*artist*
el/la modelo	*model*
el/la jugador(a)	*player*
el grupo	*group, band*
seguir	*to follow*
el/la seguidor(a)	*follower*
el/la aficionado/a	*fan*
el papel	*role, part (movie, play)*
la influencia	*influence*
la atención	*attention*
merecer	*to deserve*
el respeto	*respect*
la imagen	*image, picture*
la revista	*magazine*
el periódico	*newspaper*
el dinero	*money*
rico/a	*rich*
reconocer	*to recognise, admit*

Higher

la estrella	*star*
la figura	*figure*
la entrevista	*interview*
el público	*public, audience*
la juventud	*youth*
mantener	*to maintain, keep*
la oportunidad	*opportunity, chance*
criticar	*to criticise*
juzgar	*to judge*
identificarse (con)	*to identify (with)*

Celebrations

celebrar	*to celebrate*
reunirse	*to gather, meet*
el cumpleaños	*birthday*
Nochevieja	*New Year's Eve*
el evento	*event*
la fiesta	*party*
la sorpresa	*surprise*
invitar	*to invite*
recibir	*to receive, welcome*
el regalo	*present, gift*
la tarjeta	*card*
el pastel	*cake*

Higher

juntarse	*to meet, get together*
sorprender	*to surprise*
regalar	*to give (as a present)*
ofrecer	*to offer*
la alegría	*joy, happiness*
el ambiente	*atmosphere*

Revision Summary Test for Section Two

Improve your relationship with family and friendship vocab by giving this test a go.

- These questions are **really tricky**, but they'll help you see **how well you know your stuff**.
- Tackle the **revision summary test** below, or scan the QR code to do it **online**. You can **keep track of your progress** online and see **which areas need more work**.
- There are **sample answers** here: www.cgpbooks.co.uk/GraciasExtras

Summary Test

About Yourself

1) Da tu nombre, edad y cumpleaños en español.
2) How many words related to gender, sexuality and religion can you list in Spanish? There are 9 in this section (plus 1 for Higher tier).
3) How would you say these words in Spanish? a) identity b) disability c) disabled d) wheelchair
4) List the 11 Spanish words from this section that describe where you're from.
5) H Pablo says: 'Te presento a mi amigo cercano. Se llama Carlos y su lugar de nacimiento es Barcelona. Yo nací en Madrid, pero ambos crecimos en el mismo pueblo.' Translate his sentences into English.

My Family and Friends

6) How many words related to family members can you name in Spanish? There are at least 23 you need to know (plus 1 for Higher tier).
7) In Spanish, write about why you like your friends. Give at least two details.
8) Would you like to have any pets? Why (or why not)? Answer in Spanish.
9) H 'De los niños en mi familia, Anwar es el menor y Leya es la mayor. Esa niña es de una generación completamente diferente a la mía.' Translate these sentences into English.

Describing People

10) How would you say the following words in Spanish? a) beautiful b) tall c) short (height) d) small e) young f) old g) ginger h) people
11) 'Tiene el pelo largo y rubio, los ojos azules y lleva gafas rojas.' Translate this description into English.
12) ¿Cómo te describirías físicamente y cómo describirías tu personalidad?
13) How many adjectives can you think of to describe someone's personality or emotions in Spanish? There are 11 you need to know in this section (plus 6 for Higher tier).
14) H 'La anciana tenía una cara feliz y una sonrisa linda. También llevaba un pañuelo de un estilo tradicional.' Translate these sentences into English.

Relationships and Partnerships

15) What is your relationship like with your family and friends? Answer in Spanish.
16) How would you say the following words in Spanish? a) boyfriend b) girlfriend c) husband d) wife e) to get married f) to adopt g) alone
17) H 'My parents don't understand my feelings. It annoys me a lot.' Translate this into Spanish.
18) H In Spanish, write about the qualities you think are most important in a relationship.

Role Models

19) In Spanish, describe your role model and give at least one reason why you like them.
20) What's the Spanish for: a) actress b) model c) player d) band e) respect f) rich
21) ¿Crees que las personas famosas merecen la atención que reciben? ¿Por qué?

Celebrations

22) ¿Qué haces para celebrar tu cumpleaños? Answer in Spanish, including as much detail as possible.
23) H Describe una fiesta a la que asististe recientemente.

Quick Quiz

Food

It's time to devour some tasty food vocab. My stomach's already rumbling...

Don't forget you can access your online content here: www.cgpbooks.co.uk/Gracias

Voy a comer... — *I'm going to eat...*

Vocabulary

la comida	*food, meal*	el pescado	*fish*	el té	*tea*
la comida rápida	*fast food*	el queso	*cheese*	el azúcar	*sugar*
la fruta	*fruit*	el huevo	*egg*	tomar	*to have (drink, food)*
la verdura	*vegetable*	la bebida	*drink*	beber	*to drink*
el pan	*bread*	caliente	*hot*	el alimento (Higher)	*food*
la pasta	*pasta*	el agua (f)	*water*	la copa (Higher)	*cup*
el arroz	*rice*	la leche	*milk*	el vaso (Higher)	*glass*
la carne	*meat*	el café	*coffee*		

En mi familia comemos mucha comida rápida, ya que mis padres trabajan mucho.
In my family we eat a lot of fast food, since my parents work a lot.

Ayer traje conmigo una naranja al colegio y comí verduras con la cena.
Yesterday I brought an orange with me to school and I ate vegetables with dinner.

Siempre he puesto azúcar en mi té. Sé que no es muy bueno para la salud, pero está rico.
I have always put sugar in my tea. I know it isn't very good for your health, but it's tasty.

Por la tarde normalmente tomo una bebida caliente. Sin embargo, prefiero tomar una bebida fría cuando tengo sed.
I normally have a hot drink in the evening. However, I prefer to have a cold drink when I'm thirsty.

I love a glass of cold water — me encanta un vaso de agua fría

Las horas de comer — *Meal times*

Vocabulary

el desayuno	*breakfast*	la merienda	*afternoon snack*	el entrante	*starter*
el almuerzo	*lunch*	la cena	*dinner*	el postre	*dessert*

Suelo comer una ensalada de frutas para el desayuno.
I usually eat a fruit salad for breakfast.

'Soler' (*to usually do something*) is a stem-changing verb ('o' to 'ue'). See p.126.

Para el almuerzo, me gustaría comer un bocadillo de huevo.
For lunch, I would like to eat an egg sandwich.

Odio el té. Prefiero tomar un café con el desayuno.
I hate tea. I prefer to have a coffee with breakfast.

Este domingo voy a cenar en mi restaurante favorito. Creo que tomaré pescado asado como entrante.
This Sunday I'm going to have dinner at my favourite restaurant. I think I will have grilled fish as a starter.

Cada día tomo la merienda después del colegio.
Every day I have an afternoon snack after school.

Grammar — meal times

These are the nouns for Spanish meals:

el desayuno	***breakfast***
el almuerzo	***lunch***
la cena	***dinner***

These nouns can be made into verbs:

desayunar	***to have breakfast***
almorzar	***to have lunch***
cenar	***to have dinner, tea***

¿Qué te gusta comer? — *What do you like to eat?*

Vocabulary

la tortilla	*omelette, corn pancake (in Latin America)*	vegetariano/a	*vegetarian*
la paella	*paella (dish usually of rice and seafood)*	vegano/a	*vegan*
el bocadillo	*sandwich*	el hambre (f)	*hunger*
las patatas fritas	*chips*	la sed	*thirst*
la hamburguesa	*burger, hamburger*	el gusto	*taste, pleasure*
el chocolate	*chocolate*	rico/a	*tasty, rich*
el pastel	*cake*	la comida basura (Higher)	*junk food*
los churros	*churros*	probar (Higher)	*to try, taste*
el helado	*ice cream*	dulce (Higher)	*sweet*
		agrio/a (Higher)	*sour*
		fresco/a (Higher)	*fresh*

I said paella — not pie, Ella...

Mi padre es vegano, entonces nunca prepara comida con productos animales.

My dad is vegan, so he never prepares food with animal products.

Los churros son un postre típico de España. Se comen a menudo en la calle.

Churros are a typical dessert from Spain. They are often eaten in the street.

No me gusta comer pasteles. Son demasiado dulces y ricos para mí.

I don't like eating cakes. They're too sweet and rich for me.

Me encanta comer hamburguesas. Sin embargo, no como una todos los días porque sería bastante malsano.

I love eating hamburgers. However, I don't eat one every day because it would be quite unhealthy.

butter — mantequilla
cream — nata

Corn pancakes are of Mexican origin — Las tortillas son de origen mexicano

junk food — la comida basura

I only have them on special occasions — sólo las tomo en ocasiones especiales

Q&A Audio

Question

¿Cuál es tu comida favorita?

What is your favourite food?

Simple Answer

El helado es mi comida favorita. Me encantan los postres.

Ice cream is my favourite food. I love desserts.

Extended Answer

Cuando era pequeña, me encantaban las hamburguesas. Sin embargo, ahora soy vegetariana entonces ya no como carne. La tortilla es mi plato favorito en este momento.

When I was little, I loved hamburgers. However, now I'm vegetarian so I no longer eat meat. Omelette is my favourite dish at the moment.

Practice Question

Q1 Joaquín, Alejandra and Raquel are talking about food. Answer the questions in English.

LISTENING — Listening Track 06

e.g. What did Joaquín eat a lot of when he was younger? chocolate

a) What food does Joaquín say he avoids? *[1 mark]*

b) What does Alejandra say she needs to eat more of? *[1 mark]*

c) What does Raquel find difficult as a vegetarian? *[1 mark]*

Why did the tomato blush? Because it saw the salad dressing...

It doesn't get much better than food, so savour every morsel of this page. If you're struggling to remember how to say certain foods, give them a label in the kitchen and repeat the Spanish word every time you see it.

Quick Quiz

Physical and Mental Wellbeing

It's time for two whole pages all about wellbeing. The important thing to remember is that it's all about balance. It's why I always eat biscuits in pairs — one for each hand.

Una vida sana — *A healthy life*

Vocabulary

la vida	*life*	el ejercicio	*exercise*		la costumbre	*habit*
la salud	*health*	en forma	*fit, in shape*		diario/a	*daily*
la discapacidad	*disability*	la dieta	*diet (general)*		mantener	*to maintain, keep*
con discapacidad	*disabled*	descansar	*to rest*	Higher	mantenerse	*to keep, stay*
la silla de ruedas	*wheelchair*	el descanso	*break, rest*	Higher	equilibrado/a	*balanced*
sano/a	*healthy*	la cantidad	*quantity, amount*	Higher	suficiente	*enough*
malsano/a	*unhealthy*	el riesgo	*risk*	Higher	evitar	*to avoid*
llevar	*to lead*	la droga	*drug*	Higher	el humo	*smoke*
activo/a	*active*	fumar	*to smoke*	Higher	probar	*to try*
físico/a	*physical*					

Q&A Audio

Question	Simple Answer	Extended Answer
¿Crees que es importante estar en forma? *Do you believe it's important to be fit?*	Sí, pienso que es importante hacer ejercicio y comer bien. *Yes, I think it's important to exercise and to eat well.*	Diría que es importante mantenerse en forma, pero no tengo tiempo para hacer ejercicio todos los días. Voy al gimnasio dos veces a la semana y siempre elijo comida sana. *I would say that it's important to keep fit, but I don't have time to exercise every day. I go to the gym twice a week and I always choose healthy food.*

La salud física — *Physical health*

Es importante intentar comer una dieta sana todos los días.	*It's important to try to eat a healthy diet every day.*
Hago ejercicio los fines de semana porque no tengo mucho tiempo libre durante la semana.	*I do exercise at weekends because I don't have much free time during the week.*
Vale la pena tener buenas costumbres como beber dos litros de agua todos los días.	*It's worth having good habits like drinking two litres of water every day.*
Mi hermano juega al rugby en silla de ruedas y practica tres veces por semana. Es mucho más activo que yo.	*My brother plays wheelchair rugby and he practises three times a week. He's much more active than me.*
Fumar afecta la salud y puede causar enfermedades graves. Si fumas, deberías dejar de hacerlo.	*Smoking affects your health and can cause serious illnesses. If you smoke, you should stop doing it.*
No quiero probar las drogas porque son peligrosas.	*I don't want to try drugs because they are dangerous.*

to have a balanced diet — tener una dieta equilibrada

I prefer to rest after school — prefiero descansar después del colegio

eating at least five portions of fruit and vegetables — comer al menos cinco porciones de frutas y verduras

Grammar — to stop ...ing

To say '<u>to stop ...ing</u>', use '<u>dejar de</u>' followed by the <u>infinitive</u>.

Quiero <u>dejar de fumar</u>.
I want <u>to stop smoking</u>.

La salud mental — *Mental health*

Vocabulary

mental	*mental*	la mente	*mind*
cansado/a	*tired*	sentirse	*to feel (+ adjective)*
dormir	*to sleep*	acostarse (Higher)	*to go to bed*
dormirse	*to fall asleep*	relajarse (Higher)	*to relax*
el sueño	*sleep*	apoyar (Higher)	*to support*
la siesta	*afternoon nap, siesta*	preocupar (Higher)	*to worry*
relajante	*relaxing*	preocuparse (de / por) (Higher)	*to worry (about)*

Grammar — reflexive verbs

'dormirse' is a reflexive verb (see p.135).

Me duermo.
I fall asleep.

Leer un libro por la tarde es relajante y me ayuda a dormirme. — *Reading a book in the evening is relaxing and it helps me to fall asleep.*

Mucha gente se preocupa por su apariencia y por lo que piensan otras personas de ellos. — *Lots of people worry about their appearance and about what other people think of them.*

Dormir lo suficiente es muy importante para cuidar la salud mental. — *Getting enough sleep is very important for looking after your mental health.*

En mi opinión, la mente y el cuerpo son igualmente importantes. Por lo tanto, siempre reservo tiempo para hacer actividades que me relajan. — *In my opinion, the mind and the body are equally important. Therefore, I always make time to do activities that relax me.*

daily life causes a lot of stress — la vida diaria causa mucho estrés

Practice Questions

Q1 Write an article for a magazine about healthy living. You should write about 80-90 words in Spanish. Mention:

WRITING

- *whether you exercise or not*
- *if you have a healthy diet*
- *how much sleep you get*
- *two things you could do to lead a healthier life.* *[18 marks]*

Top Tips for Higher Students
✓ Give plenty of details about what makes your diet healthy.
✓ Use impersonal phrases like 'vale la pena' to say what is worth doing.

Higher

Q2 Read Karima's thoughts on alcohol and drugs. Answer the questions in English.

READING

Para mí, beber alcohol es tan peligroso como tomar drogas. Los jóvenes piensan que no importa si toman unas copas con los amigos, pero no consideran las consecuencias. A veces, no saben ni dónde están ni cuánto han bebido. El año pasado, mi amigo bebió demasiado y tuvo que ir al hospital. Era muy irresponsable.

a) What is Karima's opinion on drinking alcohol? *[1 mark]*
b) What two consequences of drinking alcohol does Karima mention? *[2 marks]*
c) What happened to Karima's friend? *[1 mark]*

Balance is key — you won't get very far if you keep falling over...

I must be a magician because all the biscuits have disappeared... This topic isn't just about physical health, so practise talking about mental health as well. And make sure you cover both healthy and unhealthy living.

Quick Quiz

Illnesses and Treatments

You can boost your defences against examstressitis with a daily dose of vocab practice.

Las partes del cuerpo — *Body parts*

The verb 'romper' means 'to break', but you need the reflexive verb (see p.135) 'romperse' to talk about broken bones.

Vocabulary

la cabeza	*head*	el brazo	*arm*	romper(se)	*to break (bones)*
los ojos	*eyes*	el hombro	*shoulder*	roto/a	*broken*
la nariz	*nose*	la pierna	*leg*	enfermo/a	*ill, sick*
la boca	*mouth*	el pie	*foot*	alérgico/a	*allergic*
la lengua	*tongue*	la espalda	*back*	la piel (Higher)	*skin*
el diente	*tooth*	el corazón	*heart*	la herida (Higher)	*injury, wound*
la garganta	*throat*	el estómago	*stomach*	sufrir (Higher)	*to suffer, be in pain*
la mano	*hand*	doler	*to hurt*	el dolor (Higher)	*pain, ache*
el dedo	*finger*	el virus	*virus*	la fiebre (Higher)	*fever*

Me rompí... — *I broke my...*

Ayer me caí mientras corría y me rompí el brazo. — *Yesterday I fell over while I was running and I broke my arm.*

I broke my wrist — me rompí la muñeca
I twisted my ankle — me torcí el tobillo

El año pasado, un familiar mío sufrió una fiebre muy alta. Me preocupé mucho por él. — *Last year, a relative of mine suffered from a very high fever. I worried a lot about him.*

In Spanish, you need to use the definite article ('the') instead of 'my' when you talk about body parts that you've hurt.

Me duele muchísimo la garganta y apenas puedo hablar. He tenido que beber muchos líquidos durante unos días. — *My throat hurts a lot and I can hardly speak. I have had to drink a lot of liquids for a few days.*

Siempre me siento enferma. Es muy duro porque me impide hacer actividades físicas. — *I always feel ill. It's very hard because it stops me doing physical activities.*

I get tired quickly — me canso rápidamente

Mientras estaba de vacaciones, contraje un virus. No era muy serio, pero me ha afectado el oído un poco. — *While I was on holiday, I caught a virus. It wasn't very serious, but it has affected my hearing a little.*

Q&A Audio

Question

¿Cuál es el problema?
What's the problem?

Simple Answer

Me duele la mano.
My hand hurts.

Extended Answer

Me duelen el pie y la pierna.
Tengo dolor de cabeza también.
My foot and leg hurt.
I have a headache too.

Grammar — 'doler' — to hurt

'Doler' works in a similar way to 'gustar' — to say what's hurting you, you need to use an indirect object pronoun (see p.105) before the verb. You also need to add an 'n' in the plural.

Me duele la rodilla. — ***My knee hurts.***
Me duelen los pies. — ***My feet hurt.***
Le duele el brazo. — ***His / her arm hurts.***

Literally, 'the knee hurts me'.

You also need to remember that 'doler' is a stem-changing verb. See p.126.

Necesito ir al doctor — *I need to go to the doctor*

Vocabulary

el hospital	*hospital*	la medicina	*medicine*	tratar (Higher)	*to treat*
el/la doctor(a)	*doctor*	la tableta	*tablet (medicine)*	ocuparse (de) (Higher)	*to look after, take care of*
la cita	*appointment*	la emergencia (H)	*emergency*	recuperarse (Higher)	*to recover, get better*
la farmacia	*pharmacy, chemist's*	el/la médico/a (H)	*doctor*		

Tengo una cita con la doctora porque me duele una herida en la mano. — *I have an appointment with the doctor because a wound on my hand hurts.*

Cuando era niño, tenía que tomar medicina para poder respirar mejor. — *When I was a child, I had to take medicine to be able to breathe better.*

Vivir con una enfermedad mental puede ser muy difícil. Es importante hablar con alguien si tienes problemas. — *Living with a mental illness can be very difficult. It's important to speak to someone if you have problems.*

Los médicos pueden ofrecer a los pacientes tanto apoyo como sea posible. — *Doctors can offer patients as much support as possible.*

Descubrí que soy alérgico al pescado hace dos años — tuve que ir al hospital después de comer paella. Ahora tengo medicina para eso. — *I discovered that I'm allergic to fish two years ago — I had to go to the hospital after eating paella. Now I have medicine for that.*

I have a pain in my back — tengo un dolor en la espalda

appropriate treatments — tratamientos apropiados

lots of useful advice — muchos consejos útiles

Practice Questions

Q1 *Read the following text out loud, then answer the questions below in Spanish.*

> *Mi hermano tuvo un accidente.*
> *Se cayó del equipo de patio.*
> *Ahora le duele mucho la cabeza.*
> *Mi madre quiere llevarle al hospital.*
> *Él no quiere hablar a los doctores porque tiene miedo.*

Top Tip for Higher Students
✓ Use relative pronouns to add more detailed clauses to your sentences, e.g. 'El médico siempre me da consejos excelentes, lo que me ayuda mucho.'

a) *¿Qué piensas de ir al doctor?*
b) *¿Cuándo estuviste enfermo/a el año pasado? ¿Qué hiciste?* *[12 marks]*

Higher

Q2 *Listen to the conversation between Aitor and the doctor, then answer the questions below.*

Listening Track 07

a) What caused Aitor to start feeling unwell? *[1 mark]*
b) What does the doctor ask Aitor? *[1 mark]*
c) Why is Aitor having trouble falling asleep? *[1 mark]*
d) Write down two pieces of advice that the doctor gives Aitor. *[2 marks]*

My friend gets heartburn when they eat birthday cake...

I told them to try taking the candles off first. Revision is the best medicine for GCSE Spanish woes, so don't skip over the vocab for this topic. Doing all the right prep will help you feel fighting fit for your exams.

Healthy Living — Vocabulary

It's time for a recap of all the vocab from this section before you hop, skip and jump to the next topic.

Food

la comida	*food, meal*
la comida rápida	*fast food*
la fruta	*fruit*
la verdura	*vegetable*
el pan	*bread*
la pasta	*pasta*
el arroz	*rice*
la carne	*meat*
el pescado	*fish*
el queso	*cheese*
el huevo	*egg*
la bebida	*drink, beverage*
caliente	*hot (temperature)*
la botella	*bottle*
el agua (f)	*water*
la leche	*milk*
el café	*coffee*
el té	*tea*
el azúcar	*sugar*
preparar	*to prepare*
cocinar	*to cook*
tomar	*to have (drink, food)*
comer	*to eat*
beber	*to drink*
el desayuno	*breakfast*
el almuerzo	*lunch*
la merienda	*afternoon snack*
la cena	*dinner*
el entrante	*starter*

el postre	*dessert*
la tortilla	*omelette, corn pancake (in Latin America)*
la paella	*paella (dish usually of rice and seafood)*
el bocadillo	*sandwich*
las patatas fritas	*chips*
la hamburguesa	*burger, hamburger*
el chocolate	*chocolate*
el pastel	*cake*
los churros	*churros*
el helado	*ice cream*
vegetariano/a	*vegetarian*
vegano/a	*vegan*
el hambre (f)	*hunger*
la sed	*thirst*
el gusto	*taste, pleasure*
rico/a	*tasty, rich*
gustar	*to like, be pleasing to*
odiar	*to hate*

Higher

el alimento	*food, nourishment*
la copa	*cup*
el vaso	*glass*
la comida basura	*junk food*
probar	*to try, taste*
dulce	*sweet*
agrio/a	*sour*
fresco/a	*fresh*

Physical Wellbeing

la vida	*life*
la salud	*health*
la discapacidad	*disability*
con discapacidad	*disabled*
la silla de ruedas	*wheelchair*
sano/a	*healthy, wholesome*
malsano/a	*unhealthy*
la importancia	*importance, significance*
se necesita	*you need (to) (general), one needs (to)*
llevar	*to lead*
activo/a	*active*
físico/a	*physical*
el ejercicio	*exercise*
pasear	*to go for a walk, ride*
en forma	*fit, in shape*
la dieta	*diet (general)*
descansar	*to rest*
el descanso	*break, interval, rest*

demasiado(s)/a(s)	*too much, too many*
la cantidad	*quantity, amount*
perder	*to lose*
el riesgo	*risk*
la droga	*drug*
fumar	*to smoke*
dejar de (+ infinitive)	*to stop + verb (-ing)*

Higher

la costumbre	*habit*
diario/a	*daily*
mantenerse	*to keep, stay*
mantener	*to maintain, keep*
equilibrado/a	*balanced*
suficiente	*enough*
evitar	*to avoid*
el humo	*smoke*
la consecuencia	*consequence*
probar	*to try*

Mental Wellbeing

mental	*mental*
cansado/a	*tired, tiring*
dormir	*to sleep*
dormirse	*to fall asleep*
el sueño	*sleep*
la siesta	*afternoon nap, siesta*
relajante	*relaxing*
H la mente	*mind*
H sentirse	*to feel (+ adjective)*
H sentir	*to sense*

Higher

acostarse	*to go to bed*
relajarse	*to relax*
apoyar	*to support*
preocupar	*to worry*
preocuparse (de / por)	*to worry (about)*

Use 'preocuparse' with 'de' or 'por' to say you are worried about something or someone, e.g. 'Me preocupo por mi amiga.'

Use 'sentirse' when you want to talk about how you feel physically or mentally, e.g. 'Me siento mal'. Use 'sentir' when you want to talk about general feelings, emotions or sensations, e.g. 'Siento frío'.

Illnesses and Treatments — Body Parts

el cuerpo	*body*
la cabeza	*head*
los ojos	*eyes*
el oído	*ear*
la nariz	*nose*
la boca	*mouth*
la lengua	*tongue*
el diente	*tooth*
la garganta	*throat*
la mano	*hand*
el dedo	*finger*
el brazo	*arm*
el hombro	*shoulder*
la pierna	*leg*
la rodilla	*knee*
el pie	*foot*
la espalda	*back*
el corazón	*heart*
el estómago	*stomach*
H la piel	*skin*

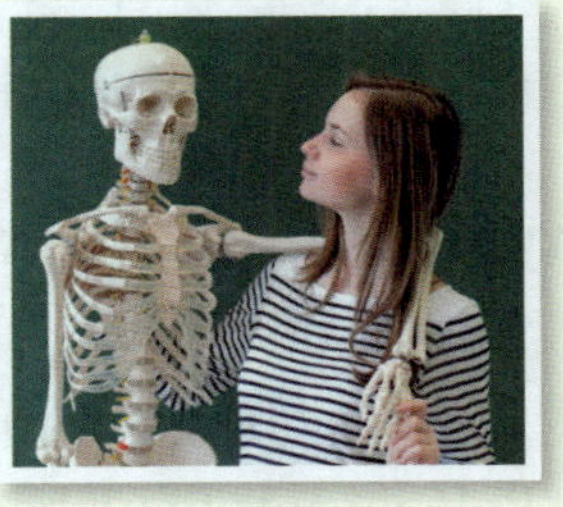

Señor Esqueleto wished Sophie would stop trying to steal his left hand...

Illnesses and Treatments — Medicine

romper(se)	*to break (bones)*
roto/a	*broken*
doler	*to hurt*
el virus	*virus*
el oído	*hearing*
enfermo/a	*ill, sick*
muerto/a	*dead*
alérgico/a	*allergic*
el accidente	*accident*
caer(se)	*to fall*
cortar(se)	*to cut (oneself)*
quemar(se)	*to burn (oneself)*
el hospital	*hospital*
el/la doctor(a)	*doctor*
la cita	*appointment*
el resultado	*result, outcome*
la farmacia	*pharmacy, chemist's*
la medicina	*medicine, medication*
la tableta	*tablet (medicine)*
tomar	*to take*
luchar	*to fight*
fuerte	*strong*
ayudar	*to help*

Higher

grave	*serious, grave*
humano/a	*human*
el dolor	*pain, ache*
la herida	*injury, wound*
sufrir	*to suffer, be in pain*
la fiebre	*fever*
la víctima	*victim, casualty*
la emergencia	*emergency*
el/la médico/a	*doctor*
tratar	*to treat*
ocuparse (de)	*to look after, take care of*
el cuidado	*care, carefulness*
recuperarse	*to recover, get better*

Revision Summary Test for Section Three

Give your mind a good workout by testing your knowledge on this section with these questions.

- Yep, these questions are **hard** — they'll really help you see **how well you know your stuff**.
- Tackle the **revision summary test** below, or scan the QR code to do it **online**. Use the CGP RevisionHub to **track your progress** and see **which areas need more work**.
- You can find **sample answers** here: www.cgpbooks.co.uk/GraciasExtras

Summary Test

Food

1) You're going shopping with your Argentinian friend. These foods are on their list: pan, arroz, pescado, queso, huevos, pastel y helado. What are these foods in English?
2) 'Tengo sed. Quisiera tomar una botella de agua con el almuerzo.' What does this mean in English?
3) In Spanish, give one food that you like and one food that you hate. Give a reason for each one.
4) What are these in English? a) un café fuerte b) un té con leche c) la merienda d) el postre
5) Iratxe says: 'I'm going to cook hamburgers and chips for dinner.' How would she say this in Spanish?
6) ¿Qué piensas de la comida vegana?
7) (H) 'Necesito evitar la comida basura y probar más frutas. Me gustan las que son muy dulces o agrias.' How would you say this in English?

Physical and Mental Wellbeing

8) 'Si quieres estar en forma, se necesita hacer ejercicio físico.' Translate this into English.
9) ¿Piensas que la mayoría de los jóvenes llevan una vida sana? ¿Por qué (no)?
10) Belén wants to be healthier. Which one of the following options would help her?
    a) comer más comida rápida b) dormir menos c) no tomar bebidas con mucho azúcar
11) What's the Spanish for...? a) disability b) afternoon nap c) to go for a walk d) to stop ... ing
12) 'It's unhealthy to smoke or take drugs. There are many risks for your health.' Say this in Spanish.
13) 'Participo en un club de voléibol sentado. Está bien para personas con discapacidad como yo, y me ayuda a estar en forma.' How would you say this in English?
14) What can someone do to look after their mental health? Answer this question in Spanish.
15) (H) Describe tus buenas costumbres.
16) (H) 'Me siento peor en mi vida diaria si no me relajo antes de acostarme.' What's this person saying?

Illnesses and Treatments

17) How many body parts can you name in Spanish? There are 18 in this section (plus 1 for Higher tier).
18) Nia says: 'Me duele todo el cuerpo y estoy cansadísima. Creo que tengo un virus. Compré unas tabletas en la farmacia para ayudarme.' What is Nia's health problem and how will she treat it?
19) Translate this into Spanish: 'I will study medicine because I would like to work in a hospital.'
20) 'La abuela de Juan tuvo un accidente y se cayó. En este momento tiene que usar una silla de ruedas.' Translate these sentences into English.
21) What's the English for...? a) romper(se) b) enfermo/a c) el/la doctor(a) d) la cita e) luchar
22) Imagine you've gone to see the doctor. Describe your health problem and what the doctor recommends in Spanish.
23) Translate these words into Spanish:
    a) broken b) dead c) result d) to cut (oneself) e) to burn (oneself)

Higher

24) Mahir tells you: 'Soy médico y ayer respondí a una emergencia. Había un fuego con mucho humo. Traté a dos víctimas inmediatamente.' What's he saying?
25) ¿Qué haces para recuperarte cuando estás enfermo/a?
26) 'I help my mum take care of my dad. He suffers from an old injury.' Translate this into Spanish.

Music

Quick Quiz

I love music, except when someone decides to share theirs with the rest of the bus. If I'd wanted alternative jazz, I'd have brought my saxophone.

Don't forget you can access your online content here: www.cgpbooks.co.uk/Gracias

La música — *Music*

When you're using the 'yo' form of 'tocar' in the preterite tense (see p.129), the 'c' changes to 'qu'.

Vocabulary

escuchar	*to listen*	el/la aficionado/a	*fan*
la canción	*song*	el grupo	*group, band*
la letra	*lyrics*	el/la cantante	*singer*
bajar	*to download*	tocar	*to play (an instrument)*
el rock	*rock (music)*	el instrumento	*instrument*
el pop	*pop (music)*	los auriculares (Higher)	*headphones, earbuds*
alto/a	*loud*	la orquesta (Higher)	*orchestra*
el concierto	*concert*	asistir (a) (Higher)	*to attend*

"Who wants to form a rock band?"

¿Te gusta la música? — *Do you like music?*

Es interesante encontrar nuevos grupos y nuevos tipos de música. Escucho de todo.	*It's interesting to find new groups and new types of music. I listen to everything.*
Toco el piano desde hace seis años. Espero ser músico cuando sea mayor.	*I have been playing the piano for six years. I hope to be a musician when I'm older.*
Me gusta usar mis auriculares para escuchar música porque me hace sentir tranquilo.	*I like to use my headphones to listen to music because it makes me feel calm.*
Me encanta ver una orquesta en vivo porque es una experiencia emocionante.	*I love seeing a live orchestra because it's an exciting experience.*
Asistí a un concierto el año pasado y no me divertí. La música estaba demasiado alta y no entendí lo que cantaban las cantantes.	*I went to a concert last year and I didn't enjoy myself. The music was too loud and I didn't understand what the singers were singing.*

the clarinet — el clarinete
the drums — la batería

the lyrics — la letra

Practice Question

LISTENING — Listening Track 08

Q1 *Marisol is a famous Spanish singer. Listen to the interview and then answer the questions in English.*

e.g. *Why did Marisol decide to be a singer?* thanks to her grandfather

a) Why does Marisol listen to music on the Internet? Give **one** detail. *[1 mark]*

b) What does Marisol always buy? *[1 mark]*

c) How many concert dates does Marisol have next year? *[1 mark]*

When I stick my headphones on, it's music to my ears...

And that's precisely what that person on the bus should have done. You know who you are. It doesn't matter what music you're into or what instrument you play — just make sure you can discuss it in Spanish.

Quick Quiz

Cinema and TV

Pop on your **3D glasses** because your cinematic revision is about to get real.

En el cine — *At the cinema*

Vocabulary

el cine	*cinema*	el personaje	*character*	recomendar	*to recommend*
la película	*film*	el papel	*role, part*	preferir	*to prefer*
el efecto especial	*special effect*	actuar	*to act, perform*	pensar	*to think*
la acción	*action*			la pantalla	*screen*
la ciencia ficción	*science fiction*	ver	*to see, watch*	la comedia (Higher)	*comedy*
el terror	*terror, horror*			basarse (en) (Higher)	*to be based (on)*

Me gusta mucho ir al cine porque siempre me divierto. — *I really like to go to the cinema because I always have a good time.*

I can eat lots of popcorn — puedo comer muchas palomitas

Pienso que vale la pena ver películas en la pantalla grande. — *I think it's worth seeing films on the big screen.*

Me encantan las películas que tienen personajes que me hacen reír. — *I love films that have characters who make me laugh.*

solve a mystery — resuelven un misterio

Prefiero las películas de aventura porque son emocionantes. — *I prefer adventure films because they are exciting.*

they scare me less than horror films — me dan menos miedo que las películas de terror

Para mí, los protagonistas deben contar una buena historia y el diálogo tiene que ser divertido. — *For me, the main characters must tell a good story and the dialogue has to be enjoyable.*

Cada escena debería tener sentido. Quiero creer lo que estoy viendo. — *Each scene should have meaning. I want to believe what I'm seeing.*

excellent special effects — efectos especiales excelentes

La última película que vi... — *The last film I saw...*

Q&A Audio

Question

Describe la última película que viste.

Describe the last film you saw.

Simple Answer

El sábado, vi una película de acción. Me gustó mucho.

On Saturday, I saw an action film. I really liked it.

Extended Answer

El fin de semana pasado, vi una película de acción. Se trataba de dos familias que luchaban durante cientos de años.

Last weekend, I saw an action film. It was about two families who were fighting for hundreds of years.

Grammar — I saw...

To say '<u>I saw...</u>' you need the <u>preterite</u> tense. Check how to form it on p.129.

El viernes, <u>vi</u> una película de terror.

On Friday, <u>I saw</u> a horror film.

<u>Unlike</u> most verbs when they're in the '<u>yo</u>' form of the <u>preterite</u> tense, '<u>vi</u>' <u>doesn't</u> have an <u>accent</u>.

Grammar (Higher only) — 'se trata de'

Use '<u>se trata de</u>' to say what a film is about:

<u>Se trata de</u> unos jóvenes muy ricos.

<u>It's about</u> some very rich young people.

And you can use it in the <u>imperfect</u> to say what a film <u>was</u> about:

<u>Se trataba del</u> amor. ***<u>It was about</u> love.***

Remember — 'de' + 'el' = 'del'.

¿Qué hay en la tele? — *What's on TV?*

Vocabulary

la tele(visión)	*TV*
el canal	*channel*
la serie	*series*
el programa	*show (TV, radio)*
las noticias	*news*
interesar	*to interest, be of interest*
encantar	*to love*

Higher

la cadena	*channel*
la temporada	*season (period of time, TV, series, food...)*
actual	*current*
el drama	*drama*
el documental	*documentary*
la entrevista	*interview*

¿Qué te gusta ver? — *What do you like watching?*

Suelo ver la televisión en Internet porque es más fácil encontrar los programas que prefiero. — *I usually watch TV on the internet because it's easier to find the programmes that I prefer.*

I prefer to watch series from other countries — prefiero ver las series de otros países

Me encantan los dramas porque hay amistades, discusiones, relaciones... ¡Nunca son aburridas! — *I love dramas because there are friendships, arguments, relationships... They're never boring!*

A mi abuela le gusta ver las noticias porque puede seguir eventos actuales. — *My grandma likes watching the news because she can follow current events.*

No me interesan la mayoría de los canales porque anuncian demasiado. — *The majority of channels don't interest me because they advertise too much.*

the shows aren't funny — los programas no son divertidos

Practice Questions

Q1 *Translate the following five sentences into Spanish.* WRITING

a) *She doesn't like the cinema at all.*
b) *I recommend films to my friends.*
c) *The characters did amusing things.*
d) *The special effects are extraordinary.*
e) *In the future, I would like to act in a horror film.*

[10 marks]

Higher

Q2 *Read Eli's email about TV and choose the correct options below.* READING

En la televisión británica, las entrevistas en las noticias duran demasiado. Sin embargo, no hay tantos descansos como en España. En mi familia, preferimos ver los documentales y los programas científicos porque nos interesa aprender nueva información sobre el mundo.

a) Eli believes...
A. news interviews are too long on British TV.
B. there are fewer breaks on Spanish TV.

b) Eli's family...
A. prefer to avoid documentaries
B. are interested in learning about the world.

[2 marks]

GCSE Spanish: The Movie. Now there's a thriller...

I know the TV is calling you, but first check you're confident with all the vocab for this topic. You need to be able to talk about what you watch (or don't watch) and be prepared to give an opinion or two on it.

Quick Quiz

Sport

It's time to get off the sofa and get moving with these pages on sport. On your marks, get set, go!

¿Practicas algún deporte? — *Do you practise any sports?*

Vocabulary

el deporte	*sport*	la natación	*swimming*	el vóleibol	*volleyball*
jugar (a)	*to play*	el ciclismo	*cycling*	el tenis	*tennis*
practicar	*to practise*	el fútbol	*football*	el/la jugador(a)	*player*
correr	*to run*	el baloncesto	*basketball*	H la práctica	*practice*
bailar	*to dance*	la silla de ruedas	*wheelchair*	H el atletismo	*athletics*

Grammar — 'jugar' + 'a' + sport

Use 'jugar a' to say what sports you play. In Spanish, you can't say 'Juego a el fútbol'. So if the sport is a masculine noun (like 'el fútbol'), the 'a' and the article 'el' combine to form 'al'.

Juegas al rugby. ***You play rugby.*** **Juego al netball.** ***I play netball.***

'Jugar' is a stem-changing verb — its stem changes from 'u' to 'ue' in the present tense. See p.126.

Monto a caballo varias veces a la semana. Me gusta porque puedo hacer deporte con mis amigos. — *I go horse riding a few times a week. I like it because I can do sport with my friends.*

Los fines de semana juego en un club de vóleibol. En el futuro, quiero ser jugador profesional de voleibol. — *At the weekends I play in a volleyball club. In the future, I want to be a professional volleyball player.*

I play tennis — juego al tenis

the sports centre is near my house — el polideportivo está cerca de mi casa

I am a volunteer at a sports club — soy voluntario en un club deportivo

¿Qué piensas del deporte? — *What do you think about sport?*

Q&A Audio

Question

¿Te gusta hacer deportes?

Do you like playing sports?

Simple Answer

Sí, me gusta jugar al baloncesto porque es emocionante.

Yes, I like playing basketball because it's exciting.

Extended Answer

Sí, me gusta jugar al baloncesto en silla de ruedas después del colegio. Siempre me divierto y me anima a ser parte de una comunidad unida a través del deporte.

Yes, I play wheelchair basketball after school. I always enjoy it and it encourages me to be part of a united community through sport.

Prefiero bailar porque es divertido incluir la música como parte de mi ejercicio. — *I prefer to dance because it's fun to include music as part of my exercise.*

Me gusta jugar a deportes de equipo. Es bueno para la salud y me ayuda a hacer amigos. — *I like to play team sports. It's good for my health and it helps me to make friends.*

El ciclismo es mi actividad favorita porque puedo viajar y mantenerme en forma a la vez. No me interesa hacer deportes y por lo tanto busco otras formas de ejercicio. — *Cycling is my favourite activity because I can travel and keep fit at the same time. Doing sports doesn't interest me and therefore I look for other forms of exercise.*

Las competiciones deportivas — *Sports competitions*

Vocabulary

participar	*to participate*
ganar	*to win*
la competición	*competition*
el partido	*match (sports)*
la final	*final (in competition)*
la carrera	*race*
deportivo/a	*sports*
el premio	*prize, reward*
H desde hace (+ present tense)	*to have been + -ing for + time*

Grammar (Higher only) — 'desde hace' + present tense

Use 'desde hace' with the present tense followed by a period of time to say how long you've been doing something for.

Juego al fútbol desde hace cinco años.

I have been playing football for five years.

Mis amigos y yo participamos en torneos de tenis desde hace dos años. Siempre nos divertimos mucho jugando juntos.

My friends and I have been participating in tennis tournaments for two years. We always have a lot of fun playing together.

A mí no me interesa la temporada de fútbol, pero veo la Copa Mundial porque mi país suele ganar sus partidos.

The football season doesn't interest me, but I watch the World Cup because my country usually wins its matches.

El mes pasado participé en una competición de baloncesto por una buena causa. Trabajé duro y muchas personas donaron dinero.

Last month I participated in a basketball competition for a good cause. I worked hard and many people donated money.

sharing a hobby — compartiendo un pasatiempo

athletics — el atletismo

the Olympic Games — los Juegos Olímpicos

lots of medals — muchas medallas

Practice Questions

Q1 *Write an article for a blog about sports. You should aim to write 80-90 words. Mention:* (WRITING)

- *what sports you do*
- *your opinion of sports competitions*
- *a sport you did last month*
- *a sport you'd like to try in the future.* *[18 marks]*

Top Tip for Higher Students
✓ Use 'desde hace' to talk about how long you've been doing a sport.

Higher

Q2 *Listen to Fátima and Emilio talking about sports they do. Choose the correct answer to complete each statement.* (LISTENING)

a) Fátima practises...	**A.** every day	**B.** almost every day	**C.** at weekends	*[1 mark]*
b) Fátima's team came...	**A.** first	**B.** second	**C.** third	*[1 mark]*
c) Emilio teaches...	**A.** football	**B.** volleyball	**C.** athletics	*[1 mark]*
d) Emilio broke his...	**A.** arm	**B.** foot	**C.** leg	*[1 mark]*

Listening Track 09

Racing a sibling to the kitchen for snacks is a sport, right?

Always try to give the reasons behind your opinions — those examiners are desperate to know why you do or don't like something. For example, I don't like tennis because my dog keeps stealing the ball...

Quick Quiz

Going Out and Other Hobbies

If music, cinema, TV or sport don't float your boat, you've come to the right place. I can't promise it'll be as exciting as extreme ironing, soap carving or duck herding, but it'll be pretty darn close...

Salir con los amigos — *Going out with friends*

Vocabulary

el tiempo libre	*free time*	vegetariano/a	*vegetarian*
salir	*to leave, go out*	vegano/a	*vegan*
el teatro	*theatre*	el entrante	*starter*
la entrada	*admission ticket*	el postre	*dessert*
gratuito/a	*free (of charge)*	las tapas	*small dishes of food*
el restaurante	*restaurant*	¡Buen provecho!	*Enjoy your meal!*
el bar	*bar*	la obra (Higher)	*play (theatre)*
la carta	*menu*	el escenario (Higher)	*stage (theatre)*
la cuenta	*bill*	elegir (Higher)	*to choose*
la opción	*option, choice*	el plato (Higher)	*plate, dish, course*

Q&A Audio

Question

¿Que le gustaría tomar?
What would you like?

Simple Answer

Quiero la sopa, por favor.
I want the soup, please.

Extended Answer

Para el entrante, quisiera la sopa y para el segundo plato, la paella.
For the starter, I'd like the soup and for main course, the paella.

Grammar — ordering politely

Use '<u>quisiera</u>' to order <u>what you'd like politely</u>. '<u>Quisiera</u>' comes from the verb '<u>querer</u>' (*to want*). See p.134.

<u>Quisiera</u> probar el filete.
<u>I'd like</u> to try the steak.

Me encanta ir a restaurantes, pero a veces es difícil elegir lo que quieres comer.

I love to go to restaurants, but sometimes it's hard to choose what you want to eat.

the dishes can be disappointing — los platos pueden ser decepcionantes

El fin de semana pasado, fui a un bar de tapas con mi hermano mayor. Las tapas costaron mucho dinero, pero nos divertimos muchísimo.

Last weekend, I went to a tapas bar with my older brother. The tapas cost a lot of money, but we had a great time.

there were a lot of options on the menu — había un montón de opciones en la carta

Mañana mis amigas y yo vamos al teatro a ver una obra sobre un evento histórico.

Tomorrow my friends and I are going to the theatre to see a play about a historical event.

a musical about the war — un musical sobre la guerra

Las actividades — *Activities*

Vocabulary

el pasatiempo	*hobby*	pintar	*to paint*	escribir	*to write*
cocinar	*to cook*	leer	*to read*	la historia	*story*
cantar	*to sing*	el género	*genre*	colgar (Higher)	*to hang up*
la videoconsola	*games console*	el periódico	*newspaper*	el artículo (Higher)	*article*
el arte	*art*	la revista	*magazine*	la novela (Higher)	*novel*
el dibujo	*drawing*	la ficción	*fiction*	soler (Higher)	*to usually do*

¿Qué haces en tu tiempo libre? — *What do you do in your free time?*

Hay muchas actividades que me interesan. Prefiero cocinar y hacer pasteles. — *There are lots of activities that interest me. I prefer to cook and make cakes.*

I have a lot of hobbies — Tengo muchos pasatiempos

Pinto cuando tengo tiempo libre porque el arte es mi pasatiempo favorito. — *I paint when I have free time because art is my favourite hobby.*

whenever I can — siempre que puedo

A mi hermana le encanta leer. Lee todos los géneros pero prefiere leer libros de ciencia ficción. — *My sister loves to read. She reads all genres but she prefers to read science fiction books.*

autobiographies — las autobiografías

detective stories — las novelas policíacas

¿Qué piensas? — *What do you think?*

Vocabulary

emocionante	*exciting, touching, moving*	guay	*cool*
excelente	*excellent*	divertido/a	*funny, amusing*
maravilloso/a	*marvellous, wonderful*	favorito/a	*favourite*
increíble	*incredible, unbelievable*	imposible	*impossible*
interesante	*interesting*	aburrido/a	*bored, boring*
		H decepcionante	*disappointing*

Mikolaj thinks your favourite film is really exciting. Absolutely incredible. Just marvellous. No, really.

Practice Questions

Q1 *Translate these sentences into English.*

READING

a) *La carta tiene mucha variedad.*
b) *Los entrantes son gratuitos para los niños.*
c) *Quiero probar un plato chino.*
d) *Pronto voy a pedir la cuenta.*

[8 marks]

Q2 *Choose one of the photos below. Talk in Spanish about what is in the photo. You should talk for about a minute and describe who is in the photo, where it takes place and what is happening.*

SPEAKING

[8 marks]

It's always good to leave a tip at the end of the ~~meal~~ page...

... but my boss didn't think that my dating advice was particularly appropriate. So I'll leave you with this instead — revision is best done in small, manageable chunks, so don't bite off more than you can chew.

Free-time Activities — Vocabulary

I've found a new hobby — reading all the words on these pages and seeing how many I can remember...

Music

escuchar	*to listen*
la música	*music*
la canción	*song*
la letra	*lyrics*
bajar	*to download*
musical (adj.)	*musical*
clásico/a	*classic, classical*
el rock	*rock (music)*
el pop	*pop*
la música pop	*pop (music)*
alto/a	*loud*
subir	*to turn up (music)*
el concierto	*concert*
el/la aficionado/a	*fan*
el grupo	*group, band*

There are two words for 'to play' in Spanish. Use 'jugar' to talk about playing sports (see p.44) and 'tocar' to talk about playing an instrument (see p.41).

la banda	*band*
el/la cantante	*singer*
la voz	*voice*
el ritmo	*rhythm*
tocar	*to play (an instrument), touch*
el instrumento	*instrument*

Higher

los auriculares	*headphones, earbuds*
el público	*public, audience*
la orquesta	*orchestra, dance band*
asistir (a)	*to attend*

Cinema

el cine	*cinema*
la película	*film*
el efecto especial	*special effect*
la acción	*action*
la aventura	*adventure*
la ciencia ficción	*science fiction*
el terror	*terror, horror*
el personaje	*character*
el papel	*role, part (movie, play)*
la actriz	*actress, actor (f)*
el actor	*actor (m)*
actuar	*to act, perform*
ver	*to see, watch*
seguir	*to continue*
recomendar	*to recommend*

preferir	*to prefer*
pensar (de)	*to think (of/about)*
divertirse	*to enjoy oneself*

Higher

la pantalla	*screen*
la comedia	*comedy*
representar	*to represent, play the role of*
tratarse (de/sobre)	*to be about*
basarse (en)	*to be based (on)*

The low special effects budget called for some improvisation...

TV

la tele(visión)	*TV*
el canal	*channel*
la serie	*series*
el programa	*show (TV, radio)*
la realidad	*reality*
las noticias	*news*
interesar	*to interest, be of interest*
encantar	*to love*

Higher

la cadena	*channel*
la temporada	*season (period of time, TV, series, food...)*
actual	*current*
el drama	*drama*
el documental	*documentary*
la entrevista	*interview*

Sport

el deporte	*sport*
jugar (a)	*to play*
hacer	*to do*
practicar	*to practise*
correr	*to run*
bailar	*to dance*
la natación	*swimming*
el ciclismo	*cycling*
el fútbol	*football*
el baloncesto	*basketball*
la silla de ruedas	*wheelchair*
el vóleibol	*volleyball*
la red	*net*
el tenis	*tennis*
el/la jugador(a)	*player*
el equipo	*team*
participar	*to participate*
ganar	*to win*
la competición	*competition*
el partido	*match (sports)*
la final	*final (in competition)*
la carrera	*race*
deportivo/a	*sports*

Higher

la práctica	*practice*
el atletismo	*athletics*
el premio	*prize, reward*
desde hace (+ present tense)	*to have been + -ing for + time*

Going Out

el tiempo libre	*free time*
salir	*to leave, go out*
el teatro	*theatre*
el espectáculo	*show (e.g. theatre)*
el programa	*programme (activity, plan)*
el descanso	*interval*
la entrada	*entrance, admission ticket*
gratuito/a	*free (of charge)*
el restaurante	*restaurant*
el bar	*bar*
la carta	*menu*
la cuenta	*bill*
la opción	*option, choice*
vegetariano/a	*vegetarian*
vegano/a	*vegan*
el entrante	*starter*
el postre	*dessert*
las tapas	*tapas (small dishes of food)*
¡Buen provecho!	*Enjoy your meal!*

Higher

la obra	*play (theatre)*
el musical	*musical*
el escenario	*stage (theatre)*
elegir	*to choose*
el plato	*plate, dish, course*
el tenedor	*fork*
el cuchillo	*knife*
la cuchara	*spoon*

Other Hobbies

el pasatiempo	*leisure activity, hobby*
la actividad	*activity*
la pasión	*passion*
el placer	*pleasure, amusement*
cocinar	*to cook*
cantar	*to sing*
la videoconsola	*games console*
el arte	*art*
el/la artista	*artist*
el dibujo	*drawing*
pintar	*to paint*
el cuadro	*painting*
leer	*to read*
la lectura	*reading*
el género	*genre*
el periódico	*newspaper*
la revista	*magazine*
la ficción	*fiction*
la publicación	*publication*
escribir	*to write*
la historia	*story*
la carta	*letter, (playing) card*
el contenido	*content*
emocionante	*exciting, touching, moving*
excelente	*excellent*
maravilloso/a	*marvellous, wonderful*
increíble	*incredible, unbelievable*
interesante	*interesting*
guay	*cool*
divertido/a	*funny, amusing*
favorito/a	*favourite*
imposible	*impossible*
aburrido/a	*bored, boring*

Higher

colgar	*to hang up*
el/la lector/a	*reader*
el artículo	*article*
la crítica	*review*
la novela	*novel*
soler	*to usually do*
decepcionante	*disappointing*

Revision Summary Test for Section Four

Before you whizz off to enjoy your spare time, give this summary test a whirl.

- These questions are **hard**, but they'll really help you see **how well you know your stuff**.
- Tackle the **revision summary test** below, or scan the QR code to do it **online**. You can **track your progress** online and see **which areas need more work**.
- There are **sample answers** for the test here: www.cgpbooks.co.uk/GraciasExtras

Summary Test

Music

1) Renata says: 'Soy cantante clásica. El mes que viene, voy a cantar una nueva canción en un concierto.' Translate what she says into English.
2) Aditi asks you about your music tastes. In Spanish, tell her what you like and don't like about music.
3) 'Soy gran aficionado a la música pop porque me encanta el ritmo que tiene.' What does this mean in English?
4) Say this in English: 'Cuando escucho el rock, siempre quiero subir la música y cantar en voz alta.'

Cinema and TV

5) 'No recomiendo películas de terror porque dan miedo.' What does this mean in English?
6) In Spanish, say that you prefer films that have exciting special effects and interesting characters.
7) Describe una película que has visto recientemente.
8) Say this in English: 'Ese actor actúa en muchas películas y me hacen reír. Escoge papeles divertidos.'
9) List the different types of TV programme in Spanish. There are 2 in this section (plus 3 for Higher tier).
10) 'No me interesan los canales de televisión. ¡Todos los programas recientes son aburridos!' How would you say this in English?
11) ¿Cuál es tu opinión sobre ver la televisión en Internet?
12) (H) Translate this into English: 'Mi serie favorita actual es una comedia que se basa en un libro que leí cuando era niño. La actriz que representa el personaje principal es excelente.'

Sport

13) Answer the following question in Spanish: ¿Practicas algún deporte?
14) 'Veo todas las competiciones de ciclismo que hay en la tele.' What is this person saying?
15) What's the Spanish for...? a) to dance b) wheelchair c) net d) player e) final
16) In Spanish, write about what you did in your last PE class.
17) Iván says: 'Participo en muchas actividades deportivas y gané mi última carrera.' What is he saying?
18) (H) 'The football season ends in May. When there are no matches to play, I attend practices each week.' Translate this sentence into Spanish.

Going Out and Other Hobbies

19) Say these English words in Spanish: a) interval b) menu c) bill d) starter e) dessert f) Enjoy your meal! g) letter
20) 'Los bares de tapas son mi opción favorita cuando salgo a comer.' What is this person saying?
21) There are 10 adjectives to describe hobbies (plus 1 for Higher tier). How many can you remember?
22) How would you tell your Cuban friend in Spanish that you think the theatre is a type of art?
23) In Spanish, describe your hobbies.

Higher

24) What's the Spanish for...? a) plate b) fork c) knife d) spoon
25) 'Mi tío escribe artículos de crítica para periódicos y revistas. Leo sus publicaciones en mi tiempo libre porque me encanta aprender sobre nuevas obras.' How would you say this in English?
26) Describe dos actividades que quieres probar en el futuro.

Where You Live

Quick Quiz

It doesn't matter if you live in the city, the countryside or under the sea — you'll need to know how to talk about where you live. Go to town on learning this page, then...

Don't forget you can access your online content here: www.cgpbooks.co.uk/Gracias

¿Dónde vives? — *Where do you live?*

Vocabulary

vivir	*to live*
la región	*region*
el campo	*countryside*
la ciudad	*city*
el pueblo	*village, town*
el centro	*centre, downtown*
el barrio	*neighbourhood, district*
la zona	*area, zone*
central	*central*
principal	*main*
la calle	*street, road*
urbano/a (Higher)	*urban*
el/la ciudadano/a (Higher)	*citizen*
las afueras (Higher)	*suburbs, outskirts*
el lugar (Higher)	*place*

Simón lives in 'the zone'.

Vivo en la zona industrial de una ciudad. No está en el centro, pero hay mucho ruido.
I live in the industrial area of a city. It isn't in the centre, but there is a lot of noise.

Mi pueblo está en el campo. Es muy bonito, pero no hay muchos sitios para visitar.
My village is in the countryside. It's very pretty, but there aren't many places to visit.

Me encanta vivir en la calle principal de mi barrio porque se encuentran aquí todos los mejores lugares para comer.
I love living on the main street of my neighbourhood because all the best places to eat are found here.

in the central district of my town — en el barrio central de mi pueblo

Q&A Audio

Question
¿Dónde vives?
Where do you live?

Simple Answer
Vivo en un pueblo en Cumbria.
I live in a village in Cumbria.

Extended Answer
Vivo en un pueblito en el campo. Preferiría vivir en una ciudad porque hay más que hacer. Aquí sólo hay bosques.
I live in a little town in the countryside. I would prefer to live in a city because there are more to do. Here there are only forests.

Grammar — adding 'ito'

In Spanish, you can add bits onto the ends of nouns and adjectives to change their meanings. Adding 'ito/a/os/as' makes the word smaller or cuter. Find out more on p.102.

Practice Question

Q1 *Translate the following sentences into Spanish.* WRITING

a) *I live in a pleasant neighbourhood.*
b) *I like living here because there is a lot to do.*
c) *This weekend, I am going to the town centre.*
d) *My friends and I are going to have lunch at a Spanish restaurant.*
e) *I went there last year and the food was incredible.*

[10 marks]

I used to live on a campsite, but the lifestyle was too in-tents...

You might love the area you live in, or maybe you wish you lived somewhere else entirely. Personally, I'd prefer to live in an area that's one giant obstacle course. I could use the monkey bars on my way to work...

Quick Quiz

At Home

Home is where the heart is — and where the marks are — so you need to be able to describe it.

¿Cómo es tu casa? — *What's your house like?*

Vocabulary

la casa	*house*	la cocina	*kitchen*
el piso	*flat, apartment*	el jardín	*garden*
el/la vecino/a	*neighbour*	el estudio	*study*
agradable	*nice, pleasant*	la puerta	*door*
cómodo/a	*comfortable*	la ventana	*window*
el cuarto	*room, bedroom*	la cama	*bed*
la habitación	*bedroom*	H el hogar	*home*
el baño	*bathroom, bath*	H la planta	*floor*

Grammar — there is / are

To say what there is in your house, use 'hay'. This word stays the same regardless of whether the thing you're talking about is singular or plural.

En mi, hay un estudio.
In my house, there is a study.

Hay seis cuartos.
There are six rooms.

Vivo en una casa muy agradable. Hay una cocina grande con muchas ventanas y tengo mi propia habitación también.

I live in a really nice house. There's a big kitchen with a lot of windows and I have my own bedroom too.

but I share my bedroom with my brother — pero comparto mi dormitorio con mi hermano

Vivimos en un piso pequeño con dos habitaciones. Está en la tercera planta y mi cuarto favorito es el salón.

We live in a small flat with two bedrooms. It's on the third floor and my favourite room is the living room.

I hate how many stairs there are — odio cuántas escaleras hay

Me gustaría vivir en una casa moderna.

I'd like to live in a modern house.

Q&A Audio

Question

¿Cómo sería tu casa perfecta?

What would your perfect house be like?

Simple Answer

Mi casa perfecta sería muy grande.

My perfect house would be very big.

Extended Answer

Mi casa perfecta tendría una piscina y un jardín enorme. Quisiera tener espacio para invitar a todos mis amigos.

My perfect house would have a swimming pool and a huge garden. I would like to have space to invite all of my friends over.

Un día típico — *A typical day*

Vocabulary

despertar(se)	*to wake up*
levantarse	*to get up*
lavarse	*to wash (oneself), have a wash*
vestirse	*to get dressed*
cambiarse	*to get changed*
dormirse	*to fall asleep*

Grammar — reflexive verbs

These verbs are reflexive — they say what you do to yourself. To use them, remove the reflexive pronoun (se), conjugate the verb as normal and put the reflexive pronoun back in front of the verb in its correct form (see p.135).

Me duermo a las diez de la noche. ***I fall asleep at 10 pm.***

Some of these verbs are stem-changing. See p.126.

Cada mañana, me despierto a las siete y luego me lavo.

Every morning, I wake up at seven o'clock and then I have a wash.

I always get dressed quickly — siempre me visto rápidamente

Después de volver del colegio me cambio y hago mis deberes.

After returning from school, I get changed and I do my homework.

I shower — me ducho

Las tareas — *Chores*

Vocabulary

habitual	*usual*	preparar	*to prepare*	lavar	*to wash*
hacer	*to do, make*	cocinar	*to cook*	H la tarea	*job, chore*
ayudar	*to help*	limpiar	*to clean*	H la basura	*rubbish, junk*

Cada mañana hago mi cama. También ayudo a preparar el desayuno. — *Every morning, I make my bed. I also help to prepare breakfast.*

I put the dishwasher on — pongo el lavavajillas

Después de la cena, tengo que lavar los platos y quitar la mesa. — *After dinner, I have to wash the dishes and clear the table.*

tidy my bedroom — arreglar mi dormitorio

Mis padres limpian la casa, y mis hermanos y yo no tenemos que hacer ninguna tarea. — *My parents clean the house, and my siblings and I don't have to do any chores.*

help them tidy up the living room — les ayudamos a arreglar el salón

Una tarea que no me gusta hacer es sacar la basura. — *One chore I don't like doing is taking out the rubbish.*

organising my clothes — ordenar mi ropa

Practice Questions

Q1 *Write a blog about your house.*
You should write about 80-90 words in Spanish. Mention:

WRITING

- *what the house you live in is like*
- *which chore you like/don't like doing and why*
- *what chores you did last week*
- *what your dream house would be like.* *[18 marks]*

Top Tip for Higher Students
✓ Use possessive adjectives to describe your house, e.g. 'en la casa nuestra' or 'en el cuarto mío'.

Q2 *Your pen-pal from Colombia sends you this email about their typical day at home.*
Read the passage and then write the correct letter for each question.

READING

Me encanta despertarme a las seis porque la casa está tranquila. Cuando me levanto, me visto y hago mi cama. Intento hacer mis deberes por la tarde, y a veces mis padres me ayudan. Cada noche, tengo que limpiar un cuarto de la casa. Ayer limpié el baño y ¡eso fue horrible!

a) They love...
A. falling asleep late. **B.** waking up early. **C.** waking up late. *[1 mark]*

b) In the afternoon, they...
A. do their homework. **B.** wash the dishes. **C.** get dressed. *[1 mark]*

c) Last night, they...
A. made their bed. **B.** cleaned the bathroom. **C.** helped their parents. *[1 mark]*

Ben treats revision like a chore — don't be like Ben...

To get to grips with this home vocab, you could try walking around your home and saying the room or part of the house in Spanish as you walk through it. Your family may think you're strange, but it might just help...

Quick Quiz

The Local Area

Ah, my local area. It's not much, but it's home. You'll need to say more than that to impress your examiner though, so crack on with pulling together some *100% truthful* details.

Háblame de tu región — *Talk to me about your region*

Vocabulary

describir	*to describe*	el teatro	*theatre*
se puede	*you can (general), one can*	la piscina	*swimming pool*
local	*local*	la farmacia	*pharmacy, chemist's*
bonito/a	*beautiful, nice*	el hospital	*hospital*
el edificio	*building*	la estación	*station (train, bus...)*
Correos	*post office*	el banco	*bank*
la oficina de correos	*post office*	el estadio	*stadium*
la biblioteca	*library*	el palacio	*palace*
el parque	*park*	la plaza	*square*
el café	*café*	el puente	*bridge*
el restaurante	*restaurant*	la comisaría (Higher)	*police station*
el bar	*bar*	el gimnasio (Higher)	*gym*
el cine	*cinema*	la fuente (Higher)	*fountain*

'Correos' is masculine, but it's not used with the article.

Q&A Audio

Question

¿Dónde te gusta ir en tu región?

Where do you like to go in your region?

Simple Answer

En mi región, hay un palacio bonito. Me gusta visitarlo con mi familia en verano.

In my region, there is a beautiful palace. I like to visit it with my family in the summer.

Extended Answer

Mi región es famosa por su arquitectura histórica. Me encanta ir a la plaza principal del barrio antiguo porque los edificios son bellísimos. La plaza se construyó hace cuatro siglos y vale la pena visitarla.

My region is well-known for its historic architecture. I love going to the main square of the old district because the buildings are extremely beautiful. The square was built four centuries ago and it's worth visiting it.

Grammar (Higher only) — 'vale la pena'

You can use 'vale la pena' to say something is worth doing. It's always followed by an infinitive.

Vale la pena ir.

It's worth going.

En mi barrio hay... — *In my neighbourhood, there is...*

Tenemos que viajar a un pueblo cercano para ir al hospital porque no hay ninguno aquí.

We have to travel to a nearby town to go to the hospital because there isn't one here.

to the city to go to the airport — a la ciudad para ir al aeropuerto

En mi barrio, hay un gran parque, un gimnasio y dos cafés.

In my neighbourhood, there's a big park, a gym and two cafés.

a famous restaurant — un restaurante famoso

Me gustaría ver una nueva piscina en mi pueblo.

I'd like to see a new swimming pool in my village.

more green spaces — más espacios verdes

Mi ciudad tiene varios edificios hermosos. Aquí se puede visitar una biblioteca muy antigua.

My city has various beautiful buildings. Here one can visit a really old library.

a historic mosque — una mezquita histórica

¿Qué haces en tu pueblo? — *What do you do in your town?*

Me gusta ir a la plaza principal para tomar un café. Es un lugar muy tranquilo con una fuente bella.	*I like going to the main square to have a coffee. It's a very tranquil place with a beautiful fountain.*
A menudo paseo por mi pueblo y lo admiro. Es muy agradable.	*I often go for a walk around my town and I admire it. It's very nice.*
Hay un cine enorme en mi pueblo. A mi familia le gusta ir allí dos veces al mes.	*There's an enormous cinema in my town. My family likes going there twice a month.*
Había un estadio famoso en mi pueblo, pero tuvo que cerrar. Ahora no hay un equipo de rugby local, lo que es decepcionante.	*There used to be a well-known stadium in my town, but it had to close. Now there isn't a local rugby team, which is disappointing.*
Cada día mis amigos y yo vamos al parque después de las clases. Se encuentra justo detrás del colegio.	*Every day my friends and I go to the park after our classes. It's located just behind the school.*

There are special events — Hay eventos especiales

ride our bikes through the forest — montamos en bicicleta por el bosque

Grammar — using prepositions for location

Some prepositions are used to describe the location of something or someone. See p.108 for more on prepositions.

El banco se encuentra entre dos puentes. ***The bank is located between two bridges.***

Practice Questions

Q1 Read aloud the following text. *[8 marks]*

> *Mi región es enorme. Vivo en un pueblo bastante grande. Creo que mi pueblo necesita más parques. Me gusta ir a la piscina. Mañana voy allí con mi hermana para hacer la natación.*

SPEAKING

Top Tip for Higher Students
✓ Use the subjunctive mood correctly, e.g. 'Es decepcionante que solo tenga un parque.'

Answer the questions below out loud in Spanish.

a) Describe tu pueblo.
b) ¿Qué no te gusta de tu pueblo?
c) ¿Qué se puede hacer en tu región?
d) ¿Qué harías para mejorar tu pueblo? *[4 marks]*

Higher

Q2 Ridwan is writing to you about what his region is like. Read the passage and then answer the questions below in English.

READING

> *La gente dice que no hay mucho que hacer en mi región. Claro, aquí no hay muchos cafés ni restaurantes y los que tenemos cobran mucho por su comida. No obstante, hay que reconocer los edificios maravillosos que tenemos aquí. Por ejemplo, yo podría pasar un día entero en el museo de arte porque me parece muy interesante.*

a) What is generally said about where Ridwan lives? *[1 mark]*
b) What does Ridwan say about the places to eat in his local area? (1 detail) *[1 mark]*
c) What does Ridwan say is positive about his local area? (1 detail) *[1 mark]*

My town has a square, but I'm more of a triangle person...

... But that's enough about my shape preferences. Remember to use 'ir' + the preposition 'a' + place when you're describing where you go in your local area. For example, 'voy al café para comer helado'... Mmm...

Quick Quiz

Shopping

Time to indulge in some retail therapy and pick up some marks along the way.

¡Vamos de compras! — *Let's go shopping!*

Vocabulary

el centro comercial	*shopping centre*
el supermercado	*supermarket*
la tienda	*shop*
abierto/a	*open*
cerrado/a	*closed*
la(s) compra(s)	*shopping, purchase*
ir de compras	*to go shopping*
el/la cliente	*customer*
la caja	*checkout, till*
la bolsa	*(shopping) bag*
la lista	*list*
la tarjeta	*credit card*
comprar	*to buy*
costar	*to cost*
vender	*to sell*
la venta	*sale (of a product)*
devolver	*to give back, return (an item)*

Higher

el negocio	*store, business*
la cadena	*chain (of store, necklace)*
la cola	*queue*
saltarse	*to jump (queue)*
valer	*to cost, be worth*
gastar	*to spend (money)*
el efectivo	*cash*
las rebajas	*sales (event)*
el producto	*product*

Los fines de semana me gusta ir de compras con mis amigos. Normalmente compramos caramelos y vemos una película en el cine.

On weekends, I like to go shopping with my friends. Normally we buy sweets and see a film at the cinema.

Cuando voy al supermercado, llevo mis bolsas reutilizables. Es mejor para el planeta que comprar bolsas nuevas cada vez.

When I go to the supermarket, I take my reusable shopping bags. It's better for the planet than buying new bags each time.

Las tiendas locales están cerrando porque mucha gente va a los centros comerciales más grandes. Creo que es triste para la comunidad.

The local shops are closing because many people are going to the bigger shopping centres. I think it's sad for the community.

Me gustaría... — *I would like...*

Vocabulary

la marca	*make, brand*
la talla	*size of clothing*
el tamaño	*size*
el número	*shoe size*
la ropa	*clothes*
la moda	*fashion*
a la moda, de moda	*fashionable*
la camisa	*shirt*
la camiseta	*T-shirt*
el jersey	*jumper*
la chaqueta	*jacket*
los pantalones	*trousers*
el vestido	*dress*
la falda	*skirt*
el calcetín	*sock*
el zapato	*shoe*
el sombrero	*hat*

Higher

el artículo	*article*
el material	*material*
la piel	*fur, leather*
mediano/a	*medium-sized*
probar	*to try on*
el conjunto	*outfit*

Me gustaría comprar un par de estos zapatos, pero no puedo encontrar el número correcto. ¿Tiene algunos otros?

I would like to buy a pair of these shoes, but I can't find the correct size. Do you have any others?

Me caso pronto y estoy buscando un vestido. Quiero que sea de moda pero no quiero gastar demasiado. ¿Me puede ayudar?

I'm getting married soon and I'm looking for a dress. I want it to be fashionable but I don't want to spend too much. Can you help me?

Las compras en línea — *Online shopping*

Prefiero ver la ropa en una tienda. Cuando hago las compras en línea, los artículos nunca son mi talla exacta y tengo que devolverlos.	*I prefer to see clothes in a shop. When I do online shopping, the items are never my exact size and I have to return them.*
Hago las compras en línea porque a menudo es más barato. Varios sitios tienen buenas rebajas.	*I do my shopping online because it's often cheaper. Several sites have good sales.*
Pienso que hacer las compras en línea es muy práctico porque no tienes que salir de casa.	*I think online shopping is very convenient because you don't have to leave the house.*

to try on clothes before buying them — probarme la ropa antes de comprarla

let you pay in instalments — te permiten pagar a plazos

SALE

Q&A Audio

Question

¿Te gusta hacer las compras en línea?

Do you like shopping online?

Simple Answer

Sí, me gusta mucho. Uso una aplicación para hacer las compras y es muy fácil.

Yes, I like it a lot. I use an app to do my shopping and it's very easy.

Extended Answer

Me encanta hacer compras en línea. Mi app favorita me ha permitido encontrar mucha ropa de segunda mano. Disfruto mucho mirando todos los artículos de ropa diferentes.

I love doing shopping online. My favourite app has let me find a lot of second-hand clothing. I really enjoy looking at all the different articles of clothing.

Practice Questions

Q1 *Choose one of the photos below. Talk in Spanish about what is in the photo. You should talk for about a minute and describe who is in the photo, where it takes place, and what is happening.*

SPEAKING

[8 marks]

Higher

Q2 *Karima is in a shop, asking about jackets. What does the employee say? Listen to the recording and answer the following questions in English.*

LISTENING

Listening Track 10

a) What type of jacket does the shop specialise in? *[1 mark]*

b) Where can Karima find the jackets? *[1 mark]*

c) What does Karima need to do once she has chosen an item? *[1 mark]*

d) What other information does the employee give Karima? *[1 mark]*

Why do trousers come in pairs? They're pantalonely...

'La ropa' is always a singular noun even when the English word is plural. So 'my clothes are sad' would be 'mi ropa está triste' rather than 'mis ropas están tristes'. Might want to give your poor clothing a pep talk...

Quick Quiz

Directions and Weather

The vocab on these pages will help you get by in Spain... and when you're in your exam.

¿Dónde está? — *Where is it?*

Vocabulary

aquí	*here*	fuera	*outside, away*		encontrar	*to find*
allí	*there, over there*	delante (de)	*(in) front (of)*		encontrarse	*to be located*
cercano/a	*close, nearby*	detrás (de)	*behind, at the back*	Higher	hacia	*toward, towards*
cerca (de)	*close, near*			Higher	lejano/a	*distant*
lejos (de)	*far (away, off)*	entre	*between, among*	Higher	situarse	*to be located*

La farmacia está entre la biblioteca y el banco. — *The pharmacy is between the library and the bank.*

Mi casa no está lejos del centro del pueblo. Está en la esquina de la calle. — *My house isn't far from the town centre. It's on the corner of the street.*

Hay un café delante del parque. Está fuera de la ciudad. — *There's a café in front of the park. It's outside of the city.*

quite close to here — bastante cerca de aquí

Grammar — 'estar' for locations

In Spanish, there are two verbs for 'to be' — 'ser' and 'estar'. To describe where things are, you need to use 'estar' — see p.128. You can also use 'encontrarse' or 'situarse' to say where something is located.

¿Cómo se llega a...? — *How do you get to...?*

Vocabulary

cruzar	*to cross*	la izquierda	*left*		el oeste	*west*
el kilómetro	*kilometre*	la derecha	*right, right hand*	Higher	andar	*to walk*
el metro	*metre*	el norte	*north*	Higher	atravesar	*to cross*
la ruta	*route*	el sur	*south*	Higher	girar	*to turn*
tomar	*to take*	el este	*east*	Higher	el camino	*path, way, route*

Toma la salida de la derecha y el parque temático no está muy lejos. — *Take the right exit and the theme park isn't too far.*

Follow the main road — Sigue la carretera

Si te pierdes, anda hacia el centro donde verás una iglesia alta. — *If you get lost, walk towards the centre where you'll see a tall church.*

El estadio está al oeste de la ciudad. Es muy fácil encontrarlo. — *The stadium is to the west of the city. It's very easy to find it.*

Ese camino te lleva en la dirección equivocada. Ve a la izquierda y el centro comercial está allí. — *That path leads you in the wrong direction. Go left and the shopping centre is there.*

Grammar — giving instructions

To give instructions, use the imperative. See how to form it on p.141.

Cruza la calle y luego sigue las señales.
Cross the street and then follow the signs.

Toma la segunda salida a la derecha.
Take the second exit on the right.

Ve en esta dirección — está cerca.
Go in this direction — it's nearby.

Hace buen / mal tiempo — *The weather is good / bad*

Vocabulary

el tiempo	*weather*	el calor	*heat, warmth, hot*	la temperatura	*temperature*
el clima	*climate*	el viento	*wind*	el grado	*degree*
hace (+ noun)	*it is (+ weather noun or adjective)*	llover	*to rain*	la lluvia (Higher)	*rain*
		nevar	*to snow*	húmedo/a (Higher)	*wet, humid*
el sol	*sun*	frío/a (adj.)	*cold*	fresco/a (Higher)	*cool, chilly*

Q&A Audio

Question

¿Qué tiempo hace donde vives?

What's the weather like where you live?

Simple Answer

De momento hace mucho frío.

It's very cold at the moment.

'frío' can be used as an adjective (e.g. 'No me gusta el tiempo frío.') or as a noun with the verb 'hacer' (e.g. 'Hace frío hoy.')

Extended Answer

Hoy hace mucho sol en el sur, pero mañana habrá nubes. Eso me parece perfecto, porque prefiero el tiempo cuando no hace demasiado calor.

Today it's very sunny in the south, but tomorrow there will be clouds. This seems perfect to me, because I prefer the weather when it's not too hot.

Esta semana lloverá en el este del país, pero hará sol aquí.	*This week it will rain in the east of the country, but it will be sunny here.*
Ayer hizo mal tiempo en mi región. Había un viento fresco.	*Yesterday the weather was bad in my region. There was a cool wind.*
Espero que haga sol esta primavera. No me gusta la lluvia.	*I hope that it's sunny this spring. I don't like the rain.*
El verano pasado pasé mal las vacaciones debido a las temperaturas altas.	*Last summer I didn't enjoy the holidays due to the high temperatures.*

Grammar — hace + noun

To describe the weather in English, you often use 'to be', e.g. 'it's sunny'. In Spanish, you have to use the verb 'hacer' instead:

Hace sol / viento / frío.
It's sunny / windy / cold.

Remember you can put the verbs into different tenses too.

Practice Questions

Q1 A tour guide is giving you directions to different places in a city you're visiting. Listen to the description of where each place is and choose the correct letter from the box for each question.

LISTENING — Listening Track 11

A. *Behind* **B.** *To the left of* **C.** *To the right of* **D.** *On the corner of*

a) The post office is ... the park.
b) The shopping centre is ... the cinema.
c) The clothes shop is ... this street.
d) The theatre is ... the swimming pool. *[4 marks]*

Higher

Q2 Translate the paragraph into Spanish.

WRITING

My region's climate is usually humid in autumn. However, last year it didn't rain a lot. It was very chilly and I had to wear a jumper every day. It seems that it will snow this winter, which is exciting. For me, cold temperatures are the best.

[10 marks]

Don't let revision rain on your parade...

I'd recommend writing out verb tables for both 'ser' and 'estar'. You'll end up using them a lot when you talk about directions and the weather. Of course, it'd be typical if you got nice weather during your exams.

Places in Town — Vocabulary

If you're looking for the vocabulary to describe where you live and what your region is like, look no further.

Where You Live

vivir	*to live*
la región	*region*
la provincia	*province*
la comunidad	*community*
el campo	*countryside, field*
la ciudad	*city*
el pueblo	*village, town*
el centro	*centre, downtown*
el barrio	*neighbourhood, district*
la zona	*area, zone*
central	*central*

principal	*main*
mayor	*larger, main*
la calle	*street, road*
la esquina	*corner*
la carretera	*main road*

Higher

urbano/a	*urban*
el/la ciudadano/a	*citizen*
el/la habitante	*inhabitant*
las afueras	*suburbs, outskirts*
el lugar	*place*

At Home

la casa	*house*
el piso	*flat, apartment, floor*
el/la vecino/a	*neighbour*
la visita	*guest at home*
agradable	*nice, pleasant*
cómodo/a	*comfortable*
el espacio	*space*
el cuarto	*room, bedroom*
la habitación	*bedroom*
el baño	*bathroom, bath*
la cocina	*kitchen*
el jardín	*garden*
el estudio	*study*
bajar	*to go down*
subir	*to go up*
la puerta	*door*
la ventana	*window*
la mesa	*table*
la cama	*bed*
despertar(se)	*to wake up*
levantarse	*to get up*

'Despertar' means 'to wake (someone else) up', whereas 'despertarse' means 'to wake up (yourself)'. 'Despertarse' is a reflexive verb — see p.135 for more on reflexive verbs.

lavarse	*to wash (oneself), have a wash*
vestir	*to wear, dress*
vestirse	*to get dressed*
cambiarse	*to get changed*
dormir	*to sleep*
dormirse	*to fall asleep*
habitual	*usual*
hacer	*to do, make*
ayudar	*to help*
preparar	*to prepare*
cocinar	*to cook*
limpiar	*to clean*
lavar	*to wash*

Higher

el hogar	*home*
la planta	*floor*
el/la dueño/a	*owner, landlord*
bañarse	*to have a bath*
acostarse	*to go to bed*
la tarea	*job, chore*
la basura	*rubbish, junk*
el vidrio	*glass, pane*

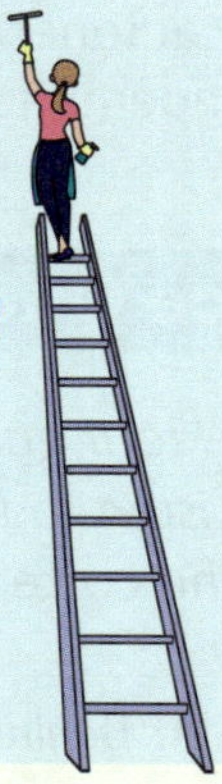

The Local Area

describir	*to describe*
se puede	*you can (general), one can*
local	*local*
bonito/a	*beautiful, nice*
el edificio	*building*
Correos	*post office*
la oficina de correos	*post office*
la biblioteca	*library*
el parque	*park*
el café	*café*
el restaurante	*restaurant*
el bar	*bar*
el cine	*cinema*

'Correos' is masculine, but it's not used with the article.

el teatro	*theatre*
la piscina	*swimming pool*
la farmacia	*pharmacy, chemist's*
el hospital	*hospital*
la estación	*station (train, bus...)*
el banco	*bank, bench*
el estadio	*stadium*
el palacio	*palace*
la plaza	*square*
el puente	*bridge*

H

la comisaría	*police station*
el gimnasio	*gym*
la fuente	*fountain*

Shopping

el centro comercial	*shopping centre*
el supermercado	*supermarket*
la tienda	*shop*
abierto/a	*open*
cerrado/a	*closed*
cerrar	*to close, shut*
la(s) compra(s)	*shopping, purchase*
ir de compras	*to go shopping*
el/la cliente	*customer*
el servicio	*service*
la caja	*checkout, till*
la bolsa	*(shopping) bag*
la lista	*list*
la tarjeta	*credit card*
comprar	*to buy*
costar	*to cost*
vender	*to sell*
la venta	*sale (of a product)*
devolver	*to give back, return (an item)*
la marca	*brand, mark*
la talla	*size of clothing*
el tamaño	*size, dimension*
el número	*shoe size*
la ropa	*clothes*
la moda	*fashion*
a la moda, de moda	*fashionable*
el estilo	*style*
la camisa	*shirt*
la camiseta	*T-shirt*
el jersey	*jumper*
la chaqueta	*jacket*
los pantalones	*trousers*
el bolsillo	*pocket*
el vestido	*dress*
la falda	*skirt*
el calcetín	*sock*
el zapato	*shoe*
las zapatillas de deporte	*trainers*
el sombrero	*hat*

Higher

el negocio	*store, business*
la cadena	*chain (of store, necklace)*
la cola	*queue*
saltarse	*to jump (queue)*
valer	*to cost, be worth*
gastar	*to spend (money)*
cobrar	*to charge (money)*
el efectivo	*cash*
el pago	*payment*
el plazo	*instalment (payment)*
las rebajas	*sales (event)*
el producto	*product*
el artículo	*article*
el material	*material*
la piel	*fur, leather*
mediano/a	*medium-sized*
ajustado/a	*tight*
probar	*to try on*
el conjunto	*outfit*
el reloj	*watch, clock*

Directions and Weather

la dirección	*address, direction*
aquí	*here*
allí	*there, over there*
cercano/a	*close, nearby*
cerca (de)	*close, near*
lejos (de)	*far (away, off)*
fuera	*out, outside, away*
delante (de)	*(in) front (of)*
detrás (de)	*behind, at the back*
entre	*between, among*
encontrar	*to find*
encontrarse	*to be located*
cruzar	*to cross*
el kilómetro	*kilometre*
el metro	*metre*
la ruta	*route*
perderse	*to get lost*
tomar	*to take*
la izquierda	*left*
la derecha	*right, right hand*
el norte	*north*
el sur	*south*
el este	*east*
el oeste	*west*
el tiempo	*weather*
el clima	*climate*
hace (+ noun)	*it is (+ weather noun or adjective)*
hacer sol	*to be sunny*
el sol	*sun*
el calor	*heat, warmth, hot*
hacer viento	*to be windy*
el viento	*wind*
la nube	*cloud*
gris	*grey, gloomy*
llover	*to rain*
nevar	*to snow*
la nieve	*snow*
frío/a (adj.)	*cold*
la temperatura	*temperature*
el grado	*degree*

la estación	*season (of the year)*
la primavera	*spring*
el verano	*summer*
el otoño	*autumn*
el invierno	*winter*

Higher

hacia	*toward, towards*
lejano/a	*distant*
situarse	*to be located*
andar	*to walk*
atravesar	*to cross*
girar	*to turn*
el camino	*path, way, route*
la lluvia	*rain*
húmedo/a	*wet, humid*
fresco/a	*cool, chilly*

Revision Summary Test for Section Five

I'm sure you're all fired up to go and get your chores done now, but have a go at this test first.

- These questions are **really tricky**, but they'll help you see **how well you know your stuff**.
- Tackle the **revision summary test** below, or scan the QR code to do it **online**. You can **keep track of your progress** online and see **which areas need more work**.
- There are **sample answers** here: www.cgpbooks.co.uk/GraciasExtras

Summary Test

Where You Live

1) 'Vivo en una calle muy amplia que está cerca del centro de la ciudad.' Translate this into English.
2) What's the Spanish for...? a) countryside b) village c) province d) corner e) main road
3) [H] You see this comment on an online forum: 'Prefiero vivir en las afueras de las zonas urbanas porque para mí hay demasiada gente en los lugares más centrales.' What's it saying?

At Home

4) How many nouns can you remember that relate to rooms and parts of a house? There are 9 in this section (plus 1 for Higher tier).
5) In Spanish, write about what you like and dislike about your house.
6) a) List the verbs from this section to do with a typical routine. There are 8 (plus 2 for Higher tier).
   b) Use some of these words to describe in Spanish what you typically do after school.
7) '¿Qué haces para ayudar en casa?' Translate this question into English, then answer it in Spanish.
8) [H] Translate this sentence into English: 'Nuestros vecinos nos han dicho que querían comprar una casa nueva, pero desafortunadamente el dueño de la casa se negó a venderla a ellos.'

The Local Area

9) En español, y con frases completas, describe tu barrio. ¿Qué hay? ¿Qué te gusta?
10) Translate this into English: 'En mi pueblo se puede encontrar un estadio famoso y un parque grande.'
11) Write the Spanish for: a) building b) café c) theatre d) pharmacy e) bench f) palace
12) [H] '¿Cómo mejorarías tu región?' Translate this question into English and answer it in Spanish.
13) [H] Tamya tells you: 'Tengo que pasar por la comisaría para llegar al gimnasio.' What's she saying?

Shopping

14) In Spanish, describe a time you went shopping, including as much relevant vocabulary as you can.
15) List the nouns from this section to do with clothing. There are 19 (plus 5 for Higher tier).
16) How do you say the following words in English?
    a) el supermercado b) abierto/a c) cerrado/a d) el servicio e) costar f) la lista
17) [Higher] Translate these sentences into Spanish: 'A new business is opening downtown and there will be some good sales. However, I will still spend a lot of money and the queues will be long.'
18) [Higher] What's the Spanish for...? a) to jump (queue) b) to be worth c) medium-sized d) tight

Directions and Weather

19) 'Para llegar al hospital, toma la calle a la izquierda.' Translate this sentence into English.
20) a) In Spanish, give all the directions on a compass.
    b) List the words in this section that describe an object's position. There are 9 (plus 2 for Higher tier).
21) How would you say in Spanish that the swimming pool is located to the right of a bar?
22) '¿Qué tiempo hace hoy?' Translate this question into English, then answer it in Spanish.
23) What's the English for...? a) la dirección b) el kilómetro c) el metro d) la ruta e) cruzar
24) 'Mañana nevará. Las temperaturas van a bajar a los 2 grados.' What's tomorrow's forecast?
25) In Spanish, write about your favourite season of the year. Include as much detail as you can.
26) [H] Pick two locations in your town, and in Spanish, say how to get from one to the other.

Environmental Problems

Quick Quiz

It's time to talk about the issues that affect the environment — serious stuff.

Remember there's also lots of online content here: www.cgpbooks.co.uk/Gracias

El medio ambiente — *The environment*

Vocabulary

el planeta	*planet*	perder	*to waste*	limpio/a	*clean*
causar	*to cause*	tirar	*to throw*	mundial (Higher)	*global, world*
la crisis	*crisis*	el plástico	*plastic*	aumentar (Higher)	*to increase*
el problema	*problem*	el uso	*use*	producir (Higher)	*to produce*
la polución	*pollution*	la energía	*energy*	la basura (Higher)	*rubbish, litter, junk*
cortar	*to cut*	los recursos	*resources*	destruir (Higher)	*to destroy*
el bosque	*forest, wood*	sucio/a	*dirty*	el árbol (Higher)	*tree*

El mundo ha perdido muchos de sus bosques. Se cortan árboles para producir más recursos.
The world has lost many of its forests. Trees are cut down to produce more resources.

El uso de algunos combustibles destruye el medio ambiente y producirlos no es sostenible.
The use of some fuels destroys the environment and producing them isn't sustainable.

En mi barrio... — *In my neighbourhood...*

Q&A Audio

Question

¿Qué problemas con el medio ambiente hay en tu barrio?
What environmental problems are there in your neighbourhood?

Simple Answer

En mi barrio las calles están muy sucias porque hay mucha polución.
In my neighbourhood the streets are very dirty because there is a lot of pollution.

Extended Answer

La polución acústica es un gran problema en el pueblo donde vivo. También hay demasiada basura en todos los parques. Debemos limpiarlos.
Noise pollution is a big problem in the town where I live. There is also too much litter in all the parks. We must clean them.

En mi región los ríos están sucios. La gente tira plástico y basura a ellos.
In my region the rivers are dirty. People throw plastic and rubbish in them.

smell awful — huelen fatal

Vivo en una zona con grandes fábricas. Usan mucha energía.
I live in an area with some big factories. They use a lot of energy.

They emit a lot of fumes — Emiten muchos humos

Practice Question

Q1 *Choose one of the photos below. Talk in Spanish about what is in the photo. You should talk for about a minute and describe who is in the photo, where it takes place, and what is happening.*

Top Tip for Higher Students
✓ Start a relative clause by using relative pronouns, e.g. 'lo cual' or 'donde', to add more detail to your sentences.

SPEAKING

[8 marks]

Pollution is rubbish...

You'll get fifteen minutes of prep time before the speaking exam to read the questions and jot down any notes. For the picture-based task, you'll only need to talk about one of the photos — just remember to say which one.

Quick Quiz

Effects on the Environment

Now you've seen some problems the environment faces, I've got a page for you about their effects.

Los efectos — *The effects*

Vocabulary

la naturaleza	*nature*	el nivel	*level*	debido a (Higher)	*due to*
natural	*natural*	el mar	*sea*	desaparecer (Higher)	*to disappear*
la tierra	*earth, land, ground*	el fuego	*fire*	el daño (Higher)	*damage, harm*
		climático/a (H)	*climate (adj.)*	la pérdida (Higher)	*loss, waste*
el cielo	*sky*	el cambio climático (H)	*climate change*	la especie (Higher)	*species, kind*

Los riesgos para la naturaleza — *The risks to nature*

Parece que no hay espacio suficiente para toda la basura que producimos. Sin embargo, si creamos más vertederos, podrían afectar a nuestros ríos.

It seems that there isn't enough space for all the rubbish that we produce. However, if we create more landfills, they could affect our rivers.

El cambio climático podría afectar negativamente los sistemas climáticos mundiales.

Climate change could negatively affect global weather systems.

Los científicos creen que si no actuamos ahora, el nivel del mar va a aumentar aún más.

Scientists believe that if we don't act now, the sea level will rise even more.

Algunas personas dicen que no habrá recursos suficientes para las generaciones del futuro si seguimos usándolos al ritmo actual.

Some people say that there won't be enough resources for future generations if we keep using them at the current rate.

Me preocupa que más especies desaparecerán si no dejamos de destruir los hábitats.

It worries me that more species will disappear if we don't stop destroying habitats.

Grammar — the inflectional/proper future

To talk about what things will happen in the future, you can use the inflectional future tense. See p.132.

La gente de mi pueblo reciclará más. ***The people from my town will recycle more.***

Practice Question

Q1 *Translate the following sentences into English.*

READING

a) *Nuestras acciones afectan el medio ambiente.*
b) *En este momento, no usamos bastante energía limpia.*
c) *Esto tiene efectos negativos en la naturaleza.*
d) *Hace cincuenta años, no había tantas opciones limpias.*
e) *En el futuro, se necesitará usar menos recursos naturales.*

[10 marks]

This page will have a positive effect on your Spanish...

The inflectional future tense is really handy for talking about your predictions for the future. It's worth making a verb table for all the future endings — then they'll all be in one place for when you need them.

Protecting the Environment

Quick Quiz

Time to round off these environment pages by looking at the ways we can protect it. Lovely stuff.

Proteger al medio ambiente — *Protecting the environment*

Vocabulary

proteger	*to protect*	reducir	*to reduce*	conservar	*to conserve*
salvar	*to save, rescue*	apagar	*to turn off, put out (e.g. a fire)*	resolver	*to solve, resolve*
ayudar	*to help*			recoger	*to pick up, tidy up*
el cambio	*change*	parar(se)	*to stop*	la campaña	*campaign*
reciclar	*to recycle*	parar de (+ infinitive)	*to stop + verb (-ing)*	la manifestación	*protest*
el reciclaje	*recycling*			consciente	*conscious, aware*

(Higher: conservar, resolver, recoger, la campaña, la manifestación, consciente)

¿Qué podemos hacer? — *What can we do?*

Q&A Audio

Question

¿Qué haces para proteger el medio ambiente?

What do you do to protect the environment?

Simple Answer

Nunca compro bolsas nuevas y reciclo mi papel.

I never buy new bags and I recycle my paper.

Extended Answer

Intento no utilizar bolsas nuevas sino reciclar las viejas. Mi padre y yo vamos al centro de reciclaje para reciclar el vidrio. Además, camino al colegio para conservar la energía y reducir el uso de combustible.

I try not to use new bags but rather recycle old ones. My dad and I go to the recycling centre to recycle glass. Also, I walk to school to conserve energy and to reduce fuel use.

Apoyo a organizaciones que quieren salvar nuestros bosques y reducir la deforestación.

I support organisations that want to save our forests and reduce deforestation.

Estoy participando en una campaña de ahorro de energía. Apagaré las luces de casa para reducir la cantidad de energía que uso. Si todos hacen este cambio pequeño, podría tener efectos muy positivos.

I'm participating in an energy-saving campaign. I'll switch off the lights at home to reduce the amount of energy I use. If everyone makes this small change, it could have very positive effects.

El mes pasado mi hermano mayor fue a una manifestación en contra de la moda rápida.

Last month my older brother went to a protest against fast fashion.

Practice Question

Q1 *Carmen is talking about what her town is doing to protect the environment. What does she say? Answer the following questions in English.*

LISTENING — Listening Track 12

a) i) What are the people of her town going to do in March? *[1 mark]*

ii) Why is Carmen in favour of this idea? *[1 mark]*

b) i) What have local teachers talked to young people about? *[1 mark]*

ii) What does Carmen suggest everyone does instead? *[1 mark]*

I once met a 'green' comedian — he only used recycled material...

You'll get more marks in the exams if you give reasons for your answers. Try adding 'porque' to your sentences to add extra detail, e.g. 'mi hermano no hizo sus deberes porque quería reducir su uso de papel'.

Quick Quiz

Equality and Social Issues

And the problems don't end there — you still have social issues to get through.

La igualdad social — *Social equality*

Vocabulary

justo/a	*fair, just*	la discriminación	*discrimination*
la sociedad	*society*	la representación	*representation*
la gente	*people*	la libertad	*freedom*
el racismo	*racism*	la justicia	*justice*
el sexismo	*sexism*	multicultural	*multicultural*

(Higher: la discriminación, la representación, la libertad, la justicia, multicultural)

Grammar — the verb 'should'

To say what someone should do, use '<u>deber</u>' in the conditional followed by the <u>infinitive</u>.

<u>Deberías</u> dar tu apoyo.
<u>You should</u> give your support.

La discriminación es un problema grave. Muchas personas son juzgadas por el color de su piel, su sexualidad o su género. Deberíamos trabajar juntos para crear un mundo igual.

Discrimination is a serious problem. Many people are judged for the colour of their skin, their sexuality or their gender. We should work together to create an equal world.

Los muy ricos tienen vidas de lujo en comparación con la gente más pobre. No parece justo.

The very rich have lives of luxury compared to poorer people. It doesn't seem fair.

Los problemas sociales — *Social problems*

Vocabulary

la dificultad	*difficulty, obstacle*	rico/a	*rich*	humano/a	*human*
el hambre	*hunger*	merecer	*to deserve*	proporcionar	*to provide, supply*
pobre	*poor*	el derecho	*right (legal)*	la falta (de)	*lack (of), shortage*

(Higher: humano/a, proporcionar, la falta (de))

Quiero que todo el mundo tenga acceso a la comida porque es un derecho básico. El hambre debería importarnos.

I want everyone to have access to food because it is a basic right. Hunger should matter to us.

we need it to survive — la necesitamos para sobrevivir

La falta de trabajos es una preocupación muy grave porque sin empleo es difícil vivir bien.

The job shortage is very a serious concern because without a job it's difficult to live well.

it can affect people's mental health — puede afectar la salud mental de la gente

El delito — *Crime*

Vocabulary

luchar	*to fight*	el delito	*crime, offence*	el conflicto	*conflict*
la violencia	*violence*	robar	*to steal, rob*	la ley	*law*

(H: el delito, robar; el conflicto, la ley)

El problema del delito es grave en mi barrio. Un grupo de ladrones robó a mi vecino el mes pasado pero por suerte la policía encontró a los culpables.

Crime is a serious problem in my neighbourhood. A group of thieves stole from my neighbour last month but luckily the police found the culprits.

Una manera en que podemos reducir la violencia es dar a la gente espacios seguros para expresar sus emociones y sentimientos.

One way that we can reduce violence is to give people safe spaces to express their emotions and feelings.

Ayudar a la sociedad — *Helping society*

Vocabulary

el partido	*(political) party*	dar	*to give*	la juventud (Higher)	*youth*
la actitud	*attitude*	importar	*to matter*	el desarrollo (Higher)	*development, progress*
la solución	*solution*	elegir (H)	*to choose*	el avance (Higher)	*advance, progress*
mejorar	*to improve*	votar (H)	*to vote*	el beneficio (Higher)	*benefit, profit*

Q&A Audio

Question

¿Qué haces para ayudar a tu comunidad?

What do you do to help your community?

Simple Answer

Los lunes ayudo en un club deportivo del colegio.

On Mondays I help out in a sports club at school.

Extended Answer

Llevo un año ayudando en un banco de alimentos. Estoy agradecido de poder apoyar a la gente porque siento que estoy ayudando a mejorar la situación.

I've been helping out in a food bank for a year. I'm grateful to be able to support people because I feel like I'm helping to improve their situation.

Dar apoyo a las organizaciones benéficas es una solución para mejorar la sociedad.

Giving support to charitable organisations is one solution to improve society.

Participo en un club juvenil cerca de mí. Es una idea genial porque ofrece muchos beneficios a los jóvenes.

I'm participating in a youth club near me. It's a great idea because it offers a lot of benefits to young people.

Los fines de semana ayudo a los ancianos de mi comunidad. Para mí es importante traerles felicidad especialmente cuando tanta gente sufre de soledad.

At the weekend I help the elderly in my community. It's important to me to bring them happiness, especially when so many people suffer from loneliness.

Practice Questions

Q1 *Write a letter to your friend about social problems in your town. You should write about 80-90 words in Spanish. Mention:*

WRITING

- *a social problem that affects people where you live*
- *your opinion of social equality with reasons*
- *what you've done in the past to make a difference in your area*
- *what you want to do in the future to help your local community.*

[18 marks]

Top Tip for Higher Students
✓ Use the plural form of the conditional, e.g. 'deberíamos...' (we should...).

Higher

Q2 *In an interview, Juan is talking about social problems in his area. Fill each gap in the sentences below with **one** word.*

LISTENING

Listening Track 13

a) Many people are affected by ______. *[1 mark]*

b) Others could help by supporting important ______. *[1 mark]*

c) In schools, ______ is an issue. *[1 mark]*

d) It is important that each student has equal ______. *[1 mark]*

I know — it's *justa* lot to take in sometimes...

Don't worry about all the tricky vocab here. You can always make it easier by sorting the vocab into smaller topics (e.g. jobs, food, crime, equality and helping people), then learning the words just one topic at a time.

Environmental and Social Issues — Vocabulary

This vocab list is made from 100% re-usable material. Give it a thorough read as you'll need to recycle it later...

Environmental Problems

el medio ambiente	*environment, natural world*
el planeta	*planet*
causar	*to cause*
la causa	*cause*
la crisis	*crisis*
el problema	*problem*
la polución	*pollution*
el ruido	*noise*
el aire	*air*
cortar	*to cut*
el bosque	*wood, forest*
perder	*to waste*
tirar	*to throw*
el plástico	*plastic*
usar	*to use*
el uso	*use*
la energía	*energy*
los recursos	*resources*
sucio/a	*dirty*
limpio/a	*clean*
puro/a	*pure, clean*

Higher

mundial	*global, world*
los alrededores	*surrounding area, vicinity*
alrededor (de)	*around, approximately*
existir	*to exist*
aumentar	*to increase*
construir	*to build*
utilizar	*to use*
producir	*to produce*
la basura	*rubbish, litter, junk*
el humo	*smoke*
el olor	*smell*
la industria	*industry, factory*
el vehículo	*vehicle*
amenazar	*to threaten*
la amenaza	*threat*
destruir	*to destroy*
el árbol	*tree*
grave	*serious, grave*
la luz	*light*
el vidrio	*glass*

Effects on the Environment

el clima	*climate*
el efecto	*effect*
la naturaleza	*nature*
natural	*natural*
la tierra	*earth, land, ground*
el cielo	*sky*
el nivel	*level*
el mar	*sea*
el fuego	*fire*

Higher

climático/a	*climate (adj.)*
el cambio climático	*climate change*
la consecuencia	*consequence*
debido a	*due to*
a causa de	*because of*
el/la científico/a	*scientist*

Higher

el río	*river*
la inundación	*flood*
desaparecer	*to disappear*
sufrir	*to suffer*
el daño	*damage, harm*
la pérdida	*loss, waste*
la especie	*species, kind*
la planta	*plant*
la hoja	*leaf*
seco/a	*dry*
quemar	*to burn*
sobrevivir	*to survive*
negar, negarse a	*to refuse*
preocupar	*to worry*
preocuparse (de/por)	*to worry (about)*

You use 'preocuparse' with the prepositions 'de' or 'por' when you want to say you are worried about something or someone, e.g. 'Me preocupo por mi amiga.'

Protecting the Environment

proteger	*to protect*
limpiar	*to clean*
salvar	*to save, rescue*
ayudar	*to help*
la ayuda	*help*
el cambio	*change*
reciclar	*to recycle*
el reciclaje	*recycling*
reducir	*to reduce*
apagar	*to turn off, put out (e.g. a fire)*
parar(se)	*to stop*
parar de (+ infinitive)	*to stop + verb (-ing)*
la acción	*action, act*
importante	*important*
responsable	*responsible*
la responsabilidad	*responsibility*
público/a (adj.)	*public*
los deberes	*duties*
(en) contra	*against*

Higher

conservar	*to preserve, conserve*
resolver	*to solve, resolve*
recoger	*to pick up, tidy up*
ahorrar	*to save (energy)*
sostenible	*sustainable*
renovable	*renewable*
la campaña	*campaign*
manifestarse	*to protest*
la manifestación	*protest*
la lucha	*fight*
defender	*to defend*
el debate	*debate*

Higher

por un lado	*on one hand*
por otro lado	*on the other hand*
la ventaja	*advantage, benefit*
la desventaja	*disadvantage*
informar	*to inform*
convencer	*to convince, persuade*
el público	*public*
consciente	*conscious, aware*
práctico/a	*practical, convenient*
fundamental	*essential*
profundo/a	*deep, profound*

Equality and Social Issues

la igualdad	*equality*
igual	*equal, same as*
justo/a	*fair, just*
la sociedad	*society*
la asociación	*association*
la gente	*people*
todo el mundo	*everyone*
los mayores	*adults, the elderly*
el racismo	*racism*
el sexismo	*sexism*
comparar	*to compare*
la diferencia	*difference*
enorme	*enormous, vast*
la dificultad	*difficulty, obstacle*
el hambre	*hunger, famine*
pobre	*poor*
rico/a	*rich*
el dinero	*money*
los medios	*means*
deber	*to have to, must*
merecer	*to deserve*
el derecho	*right (legal)*
luchar	*to fight*
la violencia	*violence*
el partido	*(political) party*
la actitud	*attitude*
la solución	*solution*
el acuerdo	*agreement*
mejorar	*to improve*
dar	*to give*
importar	*to matter*
el tema	*theme, topic*
H la discriminación	*discrimination*

Higher

la representación	*representation*
la libertad	*freedom*
la justicia	*justice*
integrar(se)	*to integrate*
la paz	*peace*
la felicidad	*happiness*
multicultural	*multicultural*
el ser	*being*
humano/a	*human*
proporcionar	*to provide, supply*
la falta (de)	*lack (of), shortage*
el delito	*crime, offence*
robar	*to steal, rob*
el conflicto	*conflict*
la ley	*law*
legal	*legal*
perseguir	*to pursue*
elegir	*to choose*
votar	*to vote*
el aspecto	*aspect*
la juventud	*youth*
el gobierno	*government*
el/la aliado/a	*ally*
el poder	*power*
el control	*control*
el estado	*state, condition*
desarrollar	*to develop*
el desarrollo	*development, progress*
el avance	*advance, progress*
el beneficio	*benefit, profit*
económico/a	*cheap, economic*
el comercio	*trade, business (shop)*

Revision Summary Test for Section Six

And as if by magic, it's another summary test. See, I told you you'd need to recycle that vocab...

- Yep, these questions are **hard** — they'll really help you see **how well you know your stuff**.
- Tackle the **revision summary test** below, or scan the QR code to do it **online**. Use the CGP RevisionHub to **track your progress** and see **which areas need more work**.
- You can find **sample answers** here: www.cgpbooks.co.uk/GraciasExtras

Summary Test

Environmental Problems

1) 'In my city there is too much pollution. The air isn't very clean, there are more clouds in the sky and there is always a lot of noise.' Translate this into Spanish.
2) Describe un problema con el medio ambiente en tu región.
3) In Spanish, write about one thing that people do that damages the environment. *(Higher)*
4) Translate these sentences into English: 'Hay varias industrias en los alrededores de mi barrio que producen mucho humo y olores terribles. Además, nunca se apagan las luces.' *(Higher)*

Effects on the Environment

5) ¿Qué efectos tiene en la naturaleza el uso de mucho plástico?
6) Write down the Spanish for... : a) sea level b) nature c) earth d) fire
7) Translate this sentence into Spanish: 'High energy use could lead to changes in the climate.'
8) In Spanish, describe the consequences of a global environmental problem that concerns you. *(Higher)*
9) Lin says: 'Si nos negamos a aceptar los efectos del cambio climático, podría ser grave. Aumentará el nivel del mar y una consecuencia es que mucha tierra desaparecerá.' Translate what he says. *(Higher)*
10) En tu opinión, ¿qué pasará con el medio ambiente en el futuro? *(Higher)*

Protecting the Environment

11) How do you say these words in Spanish?
    a) recycling b) to rescue c) help d) to reduce e) to stop f) duties g) against
12) What are two things you would like to do to help the environment? Write your answer in Spanish.
13) Now write in Spanish about something you've done in the past to protect the environment.
14) Translate this into English: 'Apoyo una campaña que defiende a los animales en peligro.' *(Higher)*
15) What's the Spanish for: a) to solve b) to pick up c) sustainable d) renewable e) to save (energy)? *(Higher)*
16) Translate this into English: 'Informar al público es fundamental para conservar el medio ambiente. Quiero que la gente sea consciente de su responsabilidad por el planeta de una manera positiva.' *(Higher)*

Equality and Social Issues

17) List the 6 nouns (plus 5 for Higher tier) for the social issues covered in this section.
18) In Spanish, describe a social problem in your area and how you think it could be improved.
19) Write down the English for the following words:
    a) los mayores b) pobre c) rico/a d) los medios e) la actitud f) la solución
20) In Spanish, write about something you've done recently to help your community.
21) Raúl says: 'La falta de trabajos es un problema serio. Tenemos que dar más dinero a varias industrias para crear más empleos.' Translate what he says into English. *(Higher)*
22) ¿Cuál es el problema social del mundo que más te importa? ¿Por qué? *(Higher)*
23) 'It isn't fair that many people have to fight to be equal. Equality and freedom of expression are rights that every human being deserves to have.' Translate these sentences into Spanish. *(Higher)*
24) 'It's important to vote for parties that will develop aspects of society that matter to you. For example, they could fight economic problems.' Translate these sentences into Spanish. *(Higher)*

Technology

Quick Quiz

You could sing technology's praises until the cows come home, but that won't be enough in the exams — you'll need to talk about its disadvantages as well.

Head to the CGP RevisionHub for all your online content: www.cgpbooks.co.uk/Gracias

La tecnología — *Technology*

CGP Moovies

Vocabulary

la versión	*version*	la tableta	*tablet*	positivo/a	*positive*
el ordenador (portátil)	*(laptop) computer*	el vídeo	*video*	negativo/a	*negative*
el móvil	*mobile phone*	funcionar	*to work*	el aparato (H)	*device*
el teléfono	*(tele)phone*	apagar	*to turn off*	la ventaja (H)	*advantage, pro*
		cargar	*to charge*	la desventaja (H)	*disadvantage, con*

Q&A Audio

Question

¿Cómo usas tu móvil?

How do you use your mobile phone?

Simple Answer

Uso mi móvil para mandar mensajes.

I use my mobile phone to send messages.

Grammar — the conditional

To imagine what you '<u>could do</u>' or '<u>couldn't do</u>', use the <u>conditional</u> of '<u>poder</u>' (see p.133) followed by the <u>infinitive</u>.

<u>No podría hacer</u> mis deberes sin un ordenador.

<u>I couldn't do</u> my homework without a computer.

Extended Answer

Tener un móvil es crucial para mí. Sin mi móvil, no podría ni mandar ni recibir mensajes.

Having a mobile phone is crucial to me. Without my mobile phone, I couldn't send or receive messages.

La tecnología es muy útil porque puedes encontrar información rápidamente.

Technology is really useful because you can find information quickly.

and it has improved our quality of life — y ha mejorado nuestra calidad de vida

Sin embargo, una desventaja es que siempre tienes que estar conectado.

However, one disadvantage is that you always have to be connected.

you have to charge your devices often — tienes que cargar tus aparatos a menudo

Uso mucho la tecnología en mi tiempo libre. Me gusta videollamar a mis amigos casi todas las noches en mi tableta.

I use technology a lot in my free time. I like to videocall my friends almost every night on my tablet.

Practice Question

Q1 *Indra and Lin are talking about how they use technology. What do they like and dislike doing? Choose the correct answer to complete each statement.*

LISTENING

Listening Track 14

a) i) Indra likes to...
- **A.** read the news.
- **B.** call her family.
- **C.** share news. *[1 mark]*

ii) She doesn't like to...
- **A.** download videos.
- **B.** charge her phone.
- **C.** upload images. *[1 mark]*

b) i) Lin likes to...
- **A.** play games.
- **B.** watch films.
- **C.** use a laptop. *[1 mark]*

ii) He doesn't like to...
- **A.** send messages.
- **B.** buy equipment.
- **C.** charge his tablet. *[1 mark]*

So many funny cat videos, so little time...

The thing is, I just find it so easy to get sucked into watching those adorable fluffy hooligans. I watch one video of them getting into mischief, then a recommended one — before I know it, three hours have gone by...

Quick Quiz

The Internet and Streaming

Ah, the Internet — handy for so many things, like that time I looked up how to make a flamingo out of bedsheets. It does have its problems though, so make sure you cover both sides...

¿Qué haces en Internet? — *What do you do on the Internet?*

Vocabulary

el Internet	*Internet*	bajar	*to download*
la web	*Internet, web*	el/la usuario/a (Higher)	*user*
en línea	*online*	conectarse (a Internet) (Higher)	*to connect (to the Internet)*
la comunicación	*communication*	la búsqueda (Higher)	*search*
la aplicación	*application, app*	comunicarse (Higher)	*to communicate*
la página	*page*	descubrir (Higher)	*to discover*
el correo electrónico	*email*		

Sofia had just discovered online makeup tutorials.

Me encanta usar Internet para descubrir nuevas canciones y bajarlas. — *I love using the Internet to discover new songs and download them.*

share images — compartir imágenes

Me gustan los sitios web que puedo usar para comunicarme con otra gente. — *I like websites that I can use to communicate with other people.*

Busco diferentes páginas de arte porque me encanta el dibujo. — *I search for different art pages because I love drawing.*

I receive emails about art classes — Recibo correos electrónicos sobre clases de arte

Es más práctico hacer las compras en línea. Sin embargo, me molesta cuando un producto no es lo mismo que la imagen en el sitio web. — *It's more convenient to do your shopping online. However, it annoys me when a product isn't the same as the image on the website.*

La seguridad en línea — *Online security*

Vocabulary

los datos	*data*	el virus	*virus*	la contraseña (Higher)	*password*
la información	*information*	el riesgo	*risk*	robar (Higher)	*to steal, rob*
proteger	*to protect*	peligroso/a	*dangerous*	desconocido/a (Higher)	*unknown*

Lo peor de Internet es que la gente puede usar tu contenido sin tu permiso. — *The worst thing about the Internet is that people can use your content without your permission.*

Es importante tener una contraseña segura para proteger tu identidad. Si alguien sabe tu contraseña, puede robar tus datos. — *It's important to have a secure password to protect your identity. If someone knows your password, they can steal your data.*

Siempre tengo cuidado en línea. Nunca abro correos electrónicos de direcciones desconocidas porque a veces pueden contener un virus. — *I am always careful online. I never open emails from unknown addresses because sometimes they can contain a virus.*

Me gusta tener acceso a recursos que mejoran mi seguridad en la web. — *I like having access to resources that improve my safety on the web.*

El streaming y los juegos — *Streaming and games*

Vocabulary

directo/a	*direct*	la videoconsola	*games console*	Higher	virtual	*virtual*
el contenido	*content*	el equipo	*equipment*		la pantalla	*screen, monitor*
la serie	*series*	el juego	*game*		el diseño	*design*
la realidad	*reality*	la atención	*attention*		la memoria	*memory*

Q&A Audio

Question

¿Qué piensas de los servicios de streaming?

What do you think of streaming services?

Simple Answer

Me gustan los servicios de streaming porque los puedo usar para ver muchas series.

I like streaming services because I can use them to watch lots of series.

Extended Answer

Creo que los servicios de streaming son una opción práctica para encontrar películas nuevas. Por otro lado, los precios de suscripción son bastante altos.

I think that streaming services are a convenient option for finding new films. On the other hand, subscription prices are quite high.

Los servicios de streaming son muy útiles para mí porque me dejan escuchar música y podcasts cuando viajo.	*Streaming services are very useful for me because they allow me to listen to songs and podcasts when I travel.*
Siempre es emocionante ver una nueva temporada de tu serie favorita.	*It's always exciting to watch a new season of your favourite series.*
El fin de semana pasado jugué con la videoconsola con mis hermanos. Probamos un juego de deportes muy popular. Pensé que todos los minijuegos eran divertidos.	*Last weekend I played on my games console with my siblings. We tried a really popular sports game. I thought all of the mini-games were fun.*
Cuando sea mayor me gustaría ganar dinero con el streaming, pero primero tendría que comprar el equipo adecuado.	*When I'm older I would like to earn money from streaming, but first I would need to buy the appropriate equipment.*

with a virtual reality headset — con un casco de realidad virtual

Practice Questions

Q1 *Write a blog post about how you use the Internet. You should aim to write 80-90 words. Write about:*

- *something you use the Internet for*
- *your opinion on Internet safety with reasons*
- *what you used the Internet for when you were younger*
- *something you will use the Internet for in the future.* *[18 marks]*

WRITING

Top Tip for Higher Students

✓ Use adverbs, e.g. 'actualmente', 'casi', 'incluso' or 'jamás' to give more detail about the time periods that you mention.

Higher

Q2 *Mario and Alba are talking about Internet usage. What do they say? Answer the following questions in English.*

LISTENING

Listening Track 15

a) **i)** What activity does Mario prefer to going on the Internet? *[1 mark]*

ii) What does Mario say is a great danger on the Internet? *[1 mark]*

b) **i)** What does Alba say is the best thing about the Internet? *[1 mark]*

ii) What is one thing Alba worries might happen? *[1 mark]*

Spiders love the Internet — they're always on the web...

There are lots of ways to say what you love or what annoys you, like 'me encanta comunicar con mis amigos en Gobbledegook'. OK, maybe not that exactly, but I'm sure you get the point... Just try to keep it varied.

Quick Quiz

Social Media

If you want something to break up the endless social media scrolling, these pages are just the ticket...

Las redes sociales — *Social networks*

Vocabulary

la red	*network*	el mensaje	*message*
social	*social*	chatear	*to chat (online)*
los medios	*media*		
la cuenta	*account*	mandar	*to send*
la actividad	*activity*	colgar (Higher)	*to post (on the Internet)*
el/la seguidor(a)	*follower*	enviar (Higher)	*to send*
compartir	*share*	contestar (Higher)	*to answer*
subir	*to upload*	el interés (Higher)	*interest*
el blog	*blog*	la amistad (Higher)	*friendship*
el comentario	*comment*		

Grammar (Higher only) — colgar (to post)

'Colgar' (to post) is a stem-changing verb (see p.126) that changes in the present tense:

Cuelgo las fotos que hago en mi blog.
I post the photos that I take on my blog.
Mis amigos cuelgan fotos en mi página.
My friends post photos on my page.

Hoy hay muchas aplicaciones de las redes sociales. Permiten al usuario hablar con otras personas y ver su actividad.

Nowadays there are many social networking apps. They allow the user to talk with others and to view their activity.

to gain followers — ganar seguidores

Las redes sociales están cambiando la forma en la que nos comunicamos. Por ejemplo, usamos imágenes para expresar cómo nos sentimos.

Social networks are changing the way in which we communicate. For example, we use images to express how we feel.

Uso las redes sociales para... — *I use social networks to...*

Q&A Audio

Question

¿Usas las redes sociales?
Do you use social networks?

Simple Answer

Sí, comparto fotos con mis amigos en las redes sociales.
Yes, I share photos with my friends on social networks.

Extended Answer

Sí, las uso para encontrar nuevos cantantes porque muchos suben sus canciones en ellas. Sin embargo, intento poner un límite al tiempo que paso en las redes sociales.
Yes, I use them to find new singers because many upload their songs on them. However, I try to put a limit on the time that I spend on social media.

Me encanta usar las redes sociales para hablar con mis amigos que viven lejos de mí.

I love using social networks to talk to my friends who live far away from me.

my cousins who live in Canada — mis primos que viven en Canadá

Uso mi cuenta para chatear con personas que comparten mis intereses. Además, cuelgo fotos de la comida que he preparado porque me gusta cocinar.

I use my account to chat with people who share my interests. Also, I post photos of food that I've prepared because I like cooking.

I've met in a game — he conocido en un juego

Paso demasiado tiempo en las redes sociales porque me pierdo leyendo comentarios.

I spend too much time on social media because I get lost reading comments.

when I could go out with my friends — cuando podría salir con mis amigos

Los problemas de las redes sociales — *The problems of social media*

Vocabulary

el contacto	*contact*	mental	*mental*	la crítica (Higher)	*criticism*
la actitud	*attitude*	solo/a	*alone*	la discusión (Higher)	*argument*
el/la joven	*young person*	la influencia	*influence*	la confianza (Higher)	*confidence*
la salud	*health*	la víctima	*victim*	el daño (Higher)	*harm*

Una red antisocial

Gracias a las redes sociales, puedo seguir noticias mundiales. Sin embargo, a veces es difícil apagar mi móvil.

Thanks to social networks, I can follow world news. However, sometimes it's difficult to switch off my phone.

I always have someone I can chat to — siempre tengo alguien con quien puedo chatear

Por un lado, puedo ver una variedad de vídeos en las redes sociales. Por otro lado, la mayoría tienen muchos anuncios.

On the one hand, I can watch a variety of videos on social media. On the other hand, the majority have many adverts.

I waste time looking at useless things — pierdo tiempo mirando cosas inútiles

'Pierdo' comes from 'perder', which is a stem-changing verb. See p.126.

Es importante no creer todo que lees en los medios sociales. Algunas páginas tienen mucha influencia pero lo que dicen es falso.

It's important to not believe all you read on social media. Some pages have a lot of influence but what they say is false.

Las redes sociales son útiles pero pueden ser preocupantes. Los comentarios negativos puede causar mucho daño a las víctimas.

Social networks are useful but they can be worrying. Negative comments can cause a lot of harm to victims.

cyberbullying — el ciberacoso

Practice Questions

Q1 *Answer these questions out loud in Spanish.* SPEAKING

a) ¿Cómo usas las redes sociales?

b) ¿Cuánto tiempo pasas en las redes sociales?

c) ¿Por qué es importante la tecnología? *[6 marks]*

Top Tip for Higher Students
✓ Use 'lo más útil es que...' or 'lo más divertido es que...' to describe why you like social media in extra detail.

Q2 *Toni has written a blog post about spending time on the Internet and social networks. Read their comments and then answer the questions below in English.* READING

Mucha gente dice que los jóvenes pasan demasiado tiempo en Internet, pero yo no estoy de acuerdo. En mi familia mis padres pasan mucho más tiempo en Internet que mis hermanos. Uso las redes sociales bastante. Como vivo lejos de mis amigos del colegio y no puedo verlos por las tardes, hablamos por nuestros móviles. Creo que tengo una relación malsana con mi móvil porque siempre estoy esperando mensajes nuevos.

a) In Toni's family, who spends the most time on the Internet? *[1 mark]*

b) What does Toni use social media for? *[1 mark]*

c) Why does Toni think they have an unhealthy relationship with their phone? *[1 mark]*

Update your status to 'revising' and give this vocab a like...

If you want to look really impressive, you can change the language settings on your social media apps to Spanish — you can keep your profiles updated and revise at the same time. Sounds like a win-win to me.

Social Media and Technology — Vocabulary

Sorry, your search for 'siesta' does not match any results here. You might find some of these other words useful, though...

Technology

la tecnología	*technology*
la versión	*version*
nuevo/a	*new*
moderno/a	*modern*
eléctrico/a	*electric*
el ordenador (portátil)	*(laptop) computer*
el móvil	*mobile phone*
el teléfono	*(tele)phone*
el número	*number*
llamar	*to phone*
la tableta	*tablet*
la radio	*radio*
el vídeo	*video*
funcionar	*to work*
apagar	*to turn off, shut down*
cargar	*to charge*

'El portátil' on its own can just mean 'laptop'.

positivo/a	*positive*
negativo/a	*negative*
servir	*to serve*

Higher

electrónico/a	*electronic*
el aparato	*device, apparatus*
los auriculares	*headphones, earbuds*
sonar	*to sound, ring*
colgar	*to hang (up)*
anunciar	*to announce, advertise*
la ventaja	*advantage, pro*
la desventaja	*disadvantage, con*

The Internet

el Internet	*Internet*
la web	*Internet, web*
en línea	*online*
la comunicación	*communication*
la aplicación	*application, app*
la página	*page*
el correo electrónico	*email*
personal	*personal*
la imagen	*image, picture*
la publicación	*publication*
publicar (en Internet)	*to post (online), publish*
bajar	*to download*
los datos	*data*
la información	*information*
privado/a	*private*
la seguridad	*security, safety*
seguro/a	*safe, secure*
proteger	*to protect*
la protección	*protection*
el virus	*virus*

el riesgo	*risk*
el peligro	*danger*
peligroso/a	*dangerous*

Higher

el/la usuario/a	*user*
práctico/a	*practical, convenient*
conectarse (a Internet)	*to connect (online)*
la búsqueda	*search*
comunicar	*to communicate*
comunicarse	*to communicate*
descubrir	*to discover*
el acceso	*access*
la contraseña	*password*
el daño	*damage*
robar	*to steal, rob*
desconocido/a	*unknown*

The verb 'comunicar' has a similar meaning to 'informar' ('to inform'). You use the reflexive verb 'comunicarse' to talk about who you communicate with and how, e.g. 'Me comunico con mis amigos por Internet.'

Streaming and Gaming

el streaming	*streaming*
directo/a	*direct*
el contenido	*content*
la música	*music*
la canción	*song*
la tele(visión)	*TV*
la serie	*series*
la realidad	*reality*
la videoconsola	*games console*
el equipo	*equipment*
caro/a	*expensive*
barato/a	*cheap*
el juego	*game*
el personaje	*character*
el primer plano	*foreground*
el segundo plano	*background*

In Spanish, you can use the phrase 'en directo' to mean 'live' (live streaming), e.g. 'Veo mi serie favorita en directo.'

la atención	*attention*
popular	*popular*
rápido/a	*fast, quick*
rápidamente	*quickly*

Higher

virtual	*virtual*
la pantalla	*screen, monitor*
el diseño	*design*
la memoria	*memory*
el sonido	*sound*
económico/a	*cheap, economic*

Social Media

la red	*network*
social	*social*
los medios	*media*
la cuenta	*account*
la actividad	*activity*
el/la seguidor(a)	*follower*
seguir	*to follow*
compartir	*to share*
subir	*to upload*
el blog	*blog*
la publicación	*post*
la conversación	*conversation*
el comentario	*comment*
el texto	*text*
el mensaje	*message*
chatear	*to chat (online)*
mandar	*to send*
el contacto	*contact*
la actitud	*attitude*
el/la joven	*young person*
la salud	*health*
mental	*mental*
la pena	*shame, sadness*
solo/a	*alone*

Doris doesn't know what to do with this many followers...

la influencia	*influence*
la víctima	*victim*

Higher

colgar	*to post (on the Internet)*
enviar	*to send*
contestar	*to answer*
guardar	*to keep, store, save*
grabar	*to record, film*
el interés	*interest*
la amistad	*friendship*
la belleza	*beauty*
la crítica	*criticism*
la discusión	*argument*
la confianza	*confidence, trust*
preocupar(se) (de/por)	*to worry*
el daño	*harm*

Revision Summary Test for Section Seven

Another test? I'm just going to try the 'turn it off and on again' trick on my brain...

- These questions are **hard**, but they'll really help you see **how well you know your stuff**.
- Tackle the **revision summary test** below, or scan the QR code to do it **online**. You can **track your progress** online and see **which areas need more work**.
- There are **sample answers** for the test here: www.cgpbooks.co.uk/GraciasExtras

Summary Test

Technology

1) How many words for technological devices and equipment can you remember from this section? There are 5 you need to know (plus 2 for Higher tier).
2) ¿Cómo y cuándo usas la tecnología?
3) Write the Spanish for:
   a) modern   b) electric   c) version   d) number   e) to phone   f) to charge
4) What's the technology like at your school? Write about it in Spanish.
5) In Spanish, give at least one positive and one negative of using technology.

Higher

6) Translate these sentences into English: 'Mi móvil sonó pero colgué rápidamente. Sólo era alguien que estaba intentando anunciar un producto que no quería.'
7) Translate these sentences into Spanish: 'I bought a new electronic device and it's the most recent version. It has more memory and I love the design and the sound quality.'

The Internet and Streaming

8) 'Uso la web para mirar páginas interesantes y uso mi correo electrónico para mandar tareas a mis profesores.' Translate this sentence into English.
9) In Spanish, give two ways that you use the Internet. Include as much detail as you can.
10) a) List as many nouns as you can think of that are related to Internet security. There are 7 you need to know (plus 3 for Higher tier).
    b) Use some of these words to write about potential dangers online.
11) 'I have a streaming app that allows me to watch music shows.' Say this in Spanish.
12) 'He encontrado un servicio del streaming barato para ver series de televisión.' Say this sentence in English.
13) Write the Spanish for: a) communication   b) character   c) foreground   d) background
14) What do you think about gaming? Write your answer in Spanish.

H

15) Translate this sentence into English: 'La semana pasada descubrí una nueva applicación de juegos. Baja juegos muy rápidamente, lo cual es excelente.'

Social Media

16) Dolores says: 'Having influence and lots of followers matters too much to young people.' Translate this sentence into Spanish. In Spanish, say whether you agree and why.
17) Which verbs can you think of from this section that would relate to sending messages and posting content online? There are 4 you need to know (plus 5 for Higher tier).
18) 'On my social media accounts I like to share videos with my online friends.' Say this in Spanish.
19) '¿Cómo usas las redes sociales?' Translate this question into English, then answer it in Spanish, giving as much detail as you can.

Higher

20) Marcos says: 'Creo que los jóvenes sufren presión para estar muy bellos. Las críticas de personas desconocidas pueden afectar tu confianza.' What has he said?
21) En español, escribe tu opinión sobre los medios sociales y cómo pueden afectar la salud mental.

School Subjects

Quick Quiz

On the subject of school, it's time for — yep, you guessed it, school subjects. It's important to learn them and be able to say what you think about them.

Remember there's also lots of online content here: www.cgpbooks.co.uk/Gracias

Las asignaturas — *Subjects*

Vocabulary

la educación	*education*	las matemáticas	*maths*	la educación física	*physical education*
el inglés	*English*	la(s) ciencia(s)	*science*	la música	*music*
el español	*Spanish*	la historia	*history*	H se me da bien / mal (+ subject)	*I am good / bad at (+ subject)*
la lengua	*language*	la religión	*religion (RE)*		

Mi asignatura favorita es... — *My favourite subject is...*

Q&A Audio

Question

¿Cuál es tu asignatura favorita?

What's your favourite subject?

Simple Answer

Mi asignatura favorita es la música. Me encanta tocar instrumentos diferentes.

My favourite subject is music. I love playing different instruments.

Extended Answer

El español es mi asignatura favorita porque es muy interesante. Será útil también porque espero ir a España el verano que viene.

Spanish is my favourite subject because it's very interesting. It will be useful too because I hope to go to Spain next summer.

To be fair, I never said I was any good...

Me gusta la historia. Es interesante aprender sobre el pasado. — *I like history. It's interesting to learn about the past.*

still relevant — todavía relevante

Gonzalo odia las ciencias pero los idiomas son más fáciles para él. — *Gonzalo hates science but languages are easier for him.*

biology — la biología
chemistry — la química
physics — la física

Se me da muy bien el inglés. Un día me gustaría escribir un libro. — *I'm very good at English. One day I would like to write a book.*

Nos encantan las matemáticas aunque para otros son una asignatura dura. — *We love maths even though for others it's a hard subject.*

difficult — difícil
complicated — complicado/a

Los deportes no me interesan mucho y se me da mal la educación física. — *Sports don't interest me much and I'm bad at PE.*

Practice Question

Q1 You are writing a blog post about your school subjects. You should write about 80-90 words in Spanish.

Write about:

- *which subject(s) you dislike and why*
- *which subject(s) you find hard or easy*
- *what your favourite subject is.* *[18 marks]*

WRITING

Top Tip for Higher Students

✓ Use the superlatives 'el/la mejor' or 'el/la peor' to say which subjects are the best or worst.

Subject yourself to learning all the asignaturas...

Remember — each subject has its own gender. Many are masculine and singular, while some are feminine and/or plural, e.g. 'las matemáticas'. Make sure you know the correct spelling and gender for each one.

Quick Quiz

School Life

If you have some time to spare in your busy timetable, I'd recommend going over these pages. You'll get to gush about all the things you love about school — or moan about what's rubbish...

El día escolar — *The school day*

Vocabulary

escolar (adj.)	*school*	terminar(se)	*to finish, end*
el club	*club, society*	durar	*to last, take (time)*
el curso	*school year*	el horario (H)	*timetable, schedule*
comenzar	*to start, begin*	empezar (H)	*to begin, start*
temprano	*early*		

Grammar — telling the time

If you're saying what time something is at, remember to put '<u>a</u>' first.

La hora de comer es <u>a la una</u>.
Lunchtime is <u>at one o'clock</u>.

For more about time, see p.5.

Mi colegio empieza a las nueve y el profesor pasa la lista a las nueve y cinco.	*My school starts at nine o'clock and the teacher reads the register at five past nine.*
Tengo cinco clases al día y cada clase dura cuarenta minutos.	*I have five lessons a day and each lesson lasts forty minutes.*
A las tres y media vuelvo a casa.	*At half past three I return home.*

at twenty to nine — a las nueve menos veinte
we go to the assembly room — vamos al salón de actos
the school day finishes — el día escolar termina

Q&A Audio

Question

¿Qué haces durante la hora de comer?
What do you do during lunchtime?

Simple Answer

Durante la hora de comer, juego al fútbol con mis amigas.
During lunchtime, I play football with my friends.

Extended Answer

Prefiero leer durante la hora de comer porque mis amigos van al club de tenis, que a mí no me gusta.
I prefer to read during lunchtime because my friends go to the tennis club, which I don't like.

En clase — *In class*

Vocabulary

la clase	*classroom, class, lesson*	el cuaderno	*notebook, workbook*
la sala	*room, hall*	el papel	*paper*
la puerta	*door*	la regla	*ruler*
la mesa	*table*	el bolígrafo	*pen*
la silla	*chair*	el/la compañero/a (Higher)	*classmate*
olvidar (+ noun)	*to forget*	prestar (Higher)	*to lend*
llevar	*to wear, carry, take*	la hoja (Higher)	*sheet (of paper)*
el libro	*book*	la pantalla (Higher)	*screen*

¿Me puedes prestar un bolígrafo para la prueba de geografía?	*Can you lend me a pen for the geography class test?*
Ayer, puse un estuche y varios libros en mi mochila.	*Yesterday, I put a pencil case and several books in my school bag.*
Me he olvidado de traer mi regla.	*I have forgotten to bring my ruler.*

a pencil — un lápiz
a calculator — una calculadora

'Olvidar' is usually followed by a noun, whereas 'olvidarse de' is usually followed by a verb.

¿Cómo es tu colegio? — *What's your school like?*

Vocabulary

el uniforme	*uniform*	internacional	*international*	el servicio	*toilet*
el colegio	*(high) school*	moderno/a	*modern*	la biblioteca	*library*
el instituto	*(high) school*	el patio	*playground, courtyard*	el equipo	*equipment*
la escuela	*school*			las instalaciones (Higher)	*facilities*
público/a	*public*	el campo	*field*	el gimnasio (Higher)	*gym*
privado/a	*private*	la piscina	*swimming pool*	el intercambio (Higher)	*exchange*

Hay quinientos alumnos en mi instituto y llevamos uniforme. — *There are 500 pupils at my school and we wear a uniform.*

we don't have to wear a uniform — no tenemos que llevar uniforme

Soy alumna aquí desde hace tres años. Me gusta este colegio y me llevo bien con los profesores. — *I've been a student here for three years. I like this school and I get on well with the teachers.*

the teachers are very nice — los profesores son muy simpáticos

La escuela de mi hermano tiene un campo de deportes grande donde pueden jugar al hockey. — *My brother's school has a big sports field where they can play hockey.*

a small gym where they can keep fit — un gimnasio pequeño donde pueden mantenerse en forma

En mi colegio, las clases no tienen suficientes sillas. — *In my school, the classrooms don't have enough chairs.*

the computers don't work well — los ordenadores no funcionan bien

Practice Questions

Q1 Juan, Marta and Álex are talking about their week at school. Choose the correct option from the times below to complete the sentences in English.

LISTENING

Listening Track 16

a) On Mondays, Juan has English at...
A. 8:30 **B.** 9:45 **C.** 9:20 *[1 mark]*

b) Marta has a history class on Thursdays at...
A. 10:15 **B.** 10:30 **C.** 11:15 *[1 mark]*

c) Álex prefers Wednesdays, when they have music at...
A. 11:45 **B.** 12:15 **C.** 13:30 *[1 mark]*

Higher

Q2 Read this message from Daraja about her school and answer the questions below in English.

READING

¡Hola! Soy Daraja. Voy a un colegio privado y hay ochocientos alumnos. En general, me encantan las instalaciones. Lo mejor es la biblioteca — hay muchos libros y estoy segura de que podrías encontrar todo lo que necesitas. Además, tenemos una piscina enorme y un campo deportivo. Lo malo es el gimnasio porque está muy sucio.

a) How many people go to Daraja's school? *[1 mark]*

b) Why does she think the library is the best facility? *[1 mark]*

c) How does Daraja describe the pool? *[1 mark]*

d) Why does Daraja dislike the gym? *[1 mark]*

What did one chair say to the other? *Silla* later...

Just like the school day itself, revision can be a slog. Splitting up your revision into manageable chunks will definitely help. As will scheduling a break to put your feet up and grab a snack — I'll take an apple, thanks...

Quick Quiz

School Pressures and Difficulties

I have difficulties remembering my left from my right — it's ruined my line-dancing classes...

Las reglas — *The rules*

Vocabulary

necesario/a	*necessary*	prohibir	*to forbid, ban*
hay que	*you must (general)*	pedir	*to ask for, order, request*
tener que	*to have to, must*	permitir (H)	*to allow*
deber	*to have to, must*	saltarse (H)	*to break (rule), skip (class)*
poder	*to be able to, can*		

Ernie wasn't very impressed with the new uniform rules...

No deberías gritar en clase. — *You should not shout in class.*

arrive late to — llegar tarde a

Hay que escribir claramente en el cuaderno. — *You must write clearly in your workbook.*

raise your hand before answering — levantar la mano antes de contestar

write in blue or black ink — escribir en tinta azul o negra

Las nuevas normas en nuestro instituto son muy estrictas. — *The new rules in our high school are very strict.*

Tenemos que llevar camisa blanca y zapatos negros. — *We have to wear a white shirt and black shoes.*

wear a tie — llevar corbata

Está prohibido usar el móvil en clase. — *It's forbidden to use your mobile phone in class.*

to run in the corridors — correr en los pasillos

to eat chewing gum — comer chicle

Las dificultades en el colegio — *Difficulties at school*

Vocabulary

aprender	*to learn*	el examen	*exam*	lograr (Higher)	*to achieve, succeed, manage*
estudiar	*to study*	aprobar	*to pass*	conseguir (Higher)	*to acquire, obtain, get*
escribir	*to write*	el resultado	*result*	equivocarse (Higher)	*to be wrong, make a mistake*
los deberes	*homework*	el error	*mistake, error*	la presión (Higher)	*pressure*

Me pongo nervioso antes de hacer una presentación delante de la clase. — *I get nervous before giving a presentation in front of the class.*

sitting an exam — presentarme a un examen

Se sienten bajo presión de sus padres para sacar buenas notas. — *They feel under pressure from their parents to get good grades.*

El conflicto entre alumnos es un problema grave en mi colegio. Creo que más gente debería pensar en el efecto que pueden tener sus palabras. — *Conflict between students is a serious problem in my school. I think more people should think about the effect their words can have.*

Bullying — El acoso

Tengo miedo de equivocarme en los exámenes y no aprobarlos. — *I'm afraid of making mistakes in the exams and not passing them.*

not being able to study the Baccalaureate — no poder estudiar el Bachillerato

La presión de grupo es difícil. Me gustaría hacer felices a mis amigos, pero no quiero saltarme las reglas. — *Peer pressure is difficult. I would like to make my friends happy, but I don't want to break the rules.*

Encontrar soluciones — *Finding solutions*

Tengo suerte porque mis amigos me apoyan mucho.	*I'm lucky because my friends support me a lot.*
Para reducir el estrés, intenta hacer deporte o algo divertido.	*To reduce stress, try to do sport or something amusing.*
Es importante respetar a todos tus compañeros.	*It's important to respect all your classmates.*
Necesito tener confianza en mi profesora para contarle mis problemas.	*I need to have confidence in my teacher in order to tell her my problems.*

my parents help me to study — mis padres me ayudan a estudiar

try to revise little by little — trata de repasar poco a poco

it's important to talk with someone — es importante hablar con alguien

other students — otros alumnos

not suffer in silence — no sufrir en silencio

Q&A Audio

Question

¿Cómo te preparas para un examen?

How do you prepare yourself for an exam?

Simple Answer

Para prepararme, voy a la biblioteca y estudio en silencio.

To prepare myself, I go to the library and study in silence.

Extended Answer

En mi opinión, estudiar con amigos es la mejor manera de prepararme para un examen. Nos ayudamos a pensar en soluciones prácticas a preguntas difíciles.

In my opinion, studying with friends is the best way to prepare myself for an exam. We help each other think of practical solutions to difficult questions.

Milo found his mallet was the practical solution to most everyday problems.

Practice Questions

Q1 *Choose one of the photos below. Talk in Spanish about what is in the photo. You should talk for about a minute and describe who is in the photo, where it takes place, and what is happening.*

SPEAKING

Top Tip for Higher Students
✓ Use tricky conjunctions like 'sino' to link your ideas together.

[8 marks]

Higher

Q2 *Omar is talking about pressures at school. What does he say?*
There are two correct statements in each list below.
Choose the correct options from each list.

LISTENING

Listening Track 17

a) Omar...

A. has to do homework on Mondays.
B. gets more homework than others.
C. gets anxious because of exams.
D. leaves it late to do his homework.

[2 marks]

b) His...

A. parents tell him to relax.
B. friends don't feel as pressured.
C. parents support him a lot.
D. friends compete with him.

[2 marks]

Problems at school are no laughing matter...

They say a problem shared is a problem halved. So if you're struggling with something or feeling stressed, you should definitely speak to someone. Just had to get that off my chest... I'll go back to being hilarious now.

School — Vocabulary

Learn all the vocab on these pages and I'm sure you'll be top of the class in no time at all...

School Subjects

la asignatura	*subject*
la educación	*education*
el inglés	*English*
el español	*Spanish*
el castellano	*(Castilian) Spanish*
la lengua	*language*
las matemáticas	*maths*
la(s) ciencia(s)	*science*
la historia	*history*
la religión	*religion*
la educación física	*physical education (PE)*
la música	*music*

favorito/a	*favourite*
útil	*useful*
fácil	*easy*
duro/a	*hard, harsh*
difícil	*difficult*
educativo/a	*educational*

Higher

el idioma	*language (specific language)*
se me da bien / mal + subject	*I am good / bad at + subject*
práctico/a	*practical, convenient*

You use 'durar' to say how much time something takes, or how long it lasts. E.g. 'La clase de inglés dura dos horas.'

School Life

el día	*day*
escolar (adj.)	*school*
la lista	*list*
el club	*club, society*
el curso	*school year*
comenzar	*to start, begin*
temprano	*early*
terminar(se)	*to finish, end*
durar	*to last, take (time)*
el/la director(a)	*headteacher*
el/la profesor(a)	*teacher, professor*
el/la estudiante	*student*
el/la alumno/a	*pupil, student*
la clase	*classroom, class, lesson*
la sala	*room, hall*
la puerta	*door*
la mesa	*table*
la silla	*chair*
olvidar (+ noun)	*to forget (something)*
llevar	*to wear, carry, take*
el libro	*book*
el cuaderno	*notebook, workbook*
el papel	*paper*
la regla	*ruler*
el bolígrafo	*pen*
el uniforme	*uniform*
la camisa	*shirt*
la corbata	*tie*
los pantalones	*trousers*
la falda	*skirt*
el zapato	*shoe*

el colegio	*(high) school*
el instituto	*(high) school, institute*
la escuela	*school*
público/a	*public*
privado/a	*private*
internacional	*international*
religioso/a	*religious*
moderno/a	*modern*
el patio	*playground, courtyard*
el campo	*field*
la piscina	*swimming pool*
el servicio	*toilet, service*
la biblioteca	*library*
el equipo	*equipment*
la tecnología	*technology*

Higher

el horario	*timetable, schedule*
empezar	*to begin, start*
el/la compañero/a	*classmate*
prestar	*to lend*
la cola	*glue*
la hoja	*sheet (of paper)*
la pantalla	*screen*
las instalaciones	*facilities*
el gimnasio	*gym*
el intercambio	*exchange*
desde hace (+ present tense)	*to have been + -ing + for + time*

School Pressures and Difficulties

la regla	*rule, regulation*
la norma	*rule*
estricto/a	*strict*
necesario/a	*necessary*
hay que	*you must (general), one must*
tener que	*to have to, must*
deber	*to have to, must*
poder	*to be able to, can*
prohibir	*to forbid, ban*
pedir	*to ask for, order, request*
preguntar	*to ask*
el silencio	*silence*
sentar(se)	*to sit down*
sentado/a	*sitting, seated*
de pie	*standing*
saber	*to know (how to)*
conocer	*to know (person, place)*
la responsabilidad	*responsibility*
responsable	*responsible*
la independencia	*independence*
independiente	*independent*
aprender	*to learn*
estudiar	*to study*
el estudio	*study*
escribir	*to write*
los deberes	*homework*
el proyecto	*project*
la presentación	*presentation*
el trabajo	*work, school assignment*
el nivel	*level*
preparar	*to prepare*
prepararse	*to prepare oneself, get ready*
mejorar	*to improve*
el éxito	*success*
la suerte	*luck*
el examen	*exam*
aprobar	*to pass*
sacar buenas / malas notas	*to get good / bad grades*
el resultado	*result, outcome*
el error	*mistake, error*
trabajar	*to work*
trabajador(a)	*hardworking*
cansado/a	*tired, tiring*
continuar	*to continue, carry on*
respetar	*to respect*
la palabra	*word*
causar	*to cause*
la violencia	*violence*

Higher

permitir	*to allow*
saltarse	*to break (rule), skip (class)*
gritar	*to shout*
callarse	*to be quiet, keep quiet*
lograr	*to achieve, succeed, manage*
conseguir	*to acquire, obtain, get*
contestar	*to answer*
expresar(se)	*to express (oneself)*
equivocarse	*to be wrong, make a mistake*
la capacidad	*ability*
capaz	*capable, able*
el conocimiento	*knowledge*
la confianza	*confidence, trust*
entregar	*to deliver, submit*
el control	*test*
la prueba	*class test*
la tarea	*task, homework*
el plazo	*deadline*
la presión	*pressure*
apoyar	*to support*
el consejo	*advice*
explicar	*to explain*
enseñar	*to teach, show*
la explicación	*explanation*
la enseñanza	*teaching*
reflejar	*to reflect*
la discusión	*discussion, argument*
consciente	*conscious, aware*
el comportamiento	*behaviour*

Marek loved studying history for the fancy dress opportunities.

Revision Summary Test for Section Eight

I haven't heard the bell ring yet, so it looks like you've still got time to try your hand at this test.

- These questions are **really tricky**, but they'll help you see **how well you know your stuff**.
- Tackle the **revision summary test** below, or scan the QR code to do it **online**. You can **keep track of your progress** online and see **which areas need more work**.
- There are **sample answers** here: www.cgpbooks.co.uk/GraciasExtras

Summary Test

School Subjects

1) List the 9 school subjects covered in this section in Spanish.
2) '¿Cuál es tu asignatura favorita y por qué?' Translate this question, then answer it in Spanish.
3) How would you say the words below in Spanish?
   a) education b) language c) useful d) difficult e) hard f) educational
4) (H) 'Se me da muy bien el español. Por lo tanto, me encanta estudiarlo y es muy práctico para viajar.' Translate these sentences into English.

School Life

5) How would you say the words and phrases below in English?
   a) una escuela moderna b) un colegio religioso c) el día escolar d) el curso
6) Cruz says: 'Durante la hora de comer, me gusta ir al club de tenis. ¿Qué te gusta hacer?' Translate what they said into English, then answer their question in Spanish.
7) How do you say the words below in Spanish?
   a) headteacher b) list c) to forget (something) d) toilet e) technology f) to start
8) Alex asks: '¿Qué uniforme llevas?' What is Alex's question? Answer it in Spanish.
9) Translate the words below into English:
   a) la sala b) la mesa c) la silla d) la puerta e) terminar(se) f) temprano g) público/a
10) '¿Qué equipo llevas al colegio?' Translate this question into English, then answer it in Spanish.

Higher

11) Obi says: 'I have been going to an international school for two years and the facilities are incredible.' Translate his sentence into Spanish, then write two sentences about your own school's facilities.
12) 'Mi profesora ha organizado un intercambio de escuelas. Se publicará el horario para la excursión en el sitio web del instituto la semana próxima.' Translate this into English.

School Pressures and Difficulties

13) How do you say the words below in English?
   a) la norma b) preguntar c) pedir d) saber e) conocer f) sentado/a g) la palabra
14) Give a school rule starting with each phrase: a) Es necesario b) Hay que c) Tengo que d) Debo
15) 'Siempre hago muchos errores cuando hago los deberes.' Translate this sentence into English.
16) How do you say the words below in Spanish?
   a) to sit down b) standing c) to get ready d) result e) to work f) hardworking g) to forbid
17) Antonio says: 'Preparar presentaciones y proyectos para el colegio es cansado.' What's he saying?
18) In your opinion, what do you need to do to get good grades in exams? Answer in Spanish.
19) In Spanish, suggest two different things that might help with school difficulties.

Higher

20) Write at least two sentences in Spanish about bad behaviour at your school and how to improve it.
21) You see these instructions on a piece of paper: 'Contesta a todas las preguntas de la prueba. Da explicaciones claras para cada punto que escribes.' What do they say?
22) What are two things that you would change about your school? Answer in Spanish.
23) How do you say the words below in English?
   a) saltarse b) gritar c) explicar d) lograr e) la capacidad f) el control

Education Post-16

Quick Quiz

It's time to spare a thought for your future self and all the things they could get up to.

Remember there's also lots of online content here: www.cgpbooks.co.uk/Gracias

¿Qué harás? — *What will you do?*

Vocabulary

estudiar	*to study*	aprobar	*to pass (test)*	el objetivo	*objective, goal*
la formación	*training, education*	el examen	*exam*	el título	*qualification*
el curso	*course*	el resultado	*result, outcome*	universitario/a	*university (adj.)*
la universidad	*university*			la prueba	*class test*
la carrera	*university degree*	el proyecto	*project, plan*	formarse (en, como)	*to train (as)*
la medicina	*medicine*			conseguir	*to obtain, get*

Higher: el objetivo, el título, universitario/a, la prueba, formarse (en, como), conseguir

See p.84 for more subjects.

Quiero formarme como fontanero porque espero trabajar con las manos. Me gusta mucho arreglar cosas.

I want to train as a plumber because I hope to work with my hands. I really like repairing things.

to do A levels — hacer el Bachillerato

to get a university degree — conseguir una carrera

Todo depende de mis exámenes. Si los apruebo, continuaré estudiando. Si los suspendo, haré un curso de formación profesional.

It all depends on my exams. If I pass them, I will continue studying. If I fail them, I will do a professional training course.

I will take a gap year — me tomaré un año sabático

Q&A Audio

Question

¿Cuáles son tus planes para el futuro?

What are your plans for the future?

Simple Answer

Quiero empezar a trabajar.

I want to start working.

Extended Answer

Me gustaría dejar de estudiar tan pronto como sea posible. Preferiría trabajar en una profesión para ganar experiencia laboral.

I would like to stop studying as soon as possible. I would prefer to work in a profession to gain work experience.

Grammar — conditional

To say that something could, should or would happen, use the conditional (p.133).

Me gustaría estudiar música.

I would like to study music.

'Quisiera' can also be used to say 'I would like' (p.134).

Practice Question

Q1 *Choose one of the photos below. Talk in Spanish about what is in the photo. You should talk for about a minute and describe who is in the photo, where it takes place, and what is happening.*

SPEAKING

Top Tip for Higher Students
✓ Use the passive voice accurately, e.g. 'los estudiantes son enseñados por un experto.'

[8 marks]

I think I'll study circus skills — I'm good at clowning around...

I also have an endless supply of terrible jokes, but we'll save those for later in the book. Seriously though, you'll really impress the examiner if you can confidently talk about what you want to do after your GCSEs.

Quick Quiz

Career Choices and Ambitions

My job is to make sure you know your way around careers vocab in Spanish, so let's get to it...

Los trabajos — *Jobs*

Vocabulary

trabajar	*to work*	el/la escritor(a)	*writer*	Higher	laboral	*work, working, labour*
el trabajo	*job*	el/la artista	*artist*		el empleo	*job, occupation*
la carrera	*career*	el actor	*actor (m)*		el/la médico/a	*doctor*
el/la policía	*police officer*	la actriz	*actress, actor (f)*		el/la capitán(a)	*captain*
la policía	*police (force)*	el/la cantante	*singer*		el/la empresario/a	*entrepreneur, manager, employer*
el/la doctor(a)	*doctor*	el/la modelo	*model*		el/la agente	*agent, officer*
el/la profesor(a)	*teacher, professor*	el sueño	*dream*		el negocio	*business, store*

Cuando era pequeño, mi padre era agente de un grupo musical. Viajábamos mucho. — *When I was little, my father was an agent for a band. We used to travel a lot.*

worked abroad a lot — trabajaba mucho en el extranjero

Me gustaría ser escritora de ficción porque me encanta escribir historias. — *I would like to be a fiction writer because I love writing stories.*

Me importa tener un trabajo bien pagado, como el de ingeniero. — *It's important to me to have a well-paid job, like an engineer.*

a job that would make me happy — un trabajo que me haría feliz

Q&A Audio

Question

¿Cuál sería el trabajo de tus sueños?
What would be your dream job?

Simple Answer

Quiero ser doctor.
I want to be a doctor.

Extended Answer

Siempre he querido ser médico, por eso voy a estudiar medicina en la universidad. Quisiera ayudar a otras personas.
I have always wanted to be a doctor, so I'm going to study medicine at university. I would like to help other people.

Grammar — I'm a...

You don't usually use the article 'un(a)' (p.103) when talking about jobs.

Soy pintor(a).
I'm a painter.

You do if you use an adjective.

Soy un buen jardinero.
I'm a good gardener.

Quisiera solicitar... — *I would like to apply for...*

Vocabulary

buscar	*to look for, search*	aceptar	*to accept*	Higher	solicitar	*to apply for, request*
la plaza	*vacancy*	el salario	*salary, wage*		el puesto	*position*
la experiencia	*experience*	ganar	*to earn*		la oportunidad	*opportunity, chance*
la oferta	*offer*	pagar	*to pay*		profesional	*professional*

You need to use the subjunctive (see p.140) here as the sentence refers to a hypothetical job rather than a job that you know exists.

Quisiera solicitar el puesto de cuidador que encontré en su sitio web. — *I would like to apply for the position of carer that I found on your website.*

Busco un trabajo en la construcción que tenga un salario muy competitivo y días de vacaciones suficientes. — *I am looking for a job in construction that has a very competitive salary and enough days off.*

En el mundo del trabajo... — *In the world of work...*

Vocabulary

la empresa	*company, firm*	el/la cliente	*customer*	hace falta (+ infinitive) [Higher]	*it's necessary (to)*
la compañía	*company, firm*	próximo/a	*next*	la reunión [Higher]	*meeting*
la oficina	*office*	el/la experto/a [Higher]	*expert*	atender [Higher]	*to assist (customer), serve*
el/la director(a)	*boss*	el/la compañero/a [Higher]	*colleague*		
el/la jefe/a	*boss, manager*	el traje [Higher]	*suit*		

La experiencia laboral — *Work experience*

Ayudo en una tienda de ropa en mi tiempo libre. Lo mejor es conversar con los clientes.

I help in a clothes shop in my free time. The best thing is chatting with customers.

No tengo empleo, pero a veces paseo al perro de mis vecinos y me pagan.

I don't have a job, but sometimes I walk my neighbours' dog and they pay me.

Trabajo en un restaurante los sábados. Me gusta el empleo, pero no gano mucho.

I work in a restaurant on Saturdays. I like the job, but I don't earn a lot.

that the employees get discounts — que los empleados reciben descuentos

a hairdresser's — una peluquería

I hope to find another job and earn more money — espero conseguir otro empleo y ganar más dinero

Practice Questions

Q1 *Tao has written about his future career plans.*

WRITING

> *Cuando era más pequeño, pensaba que me gustaría ser profesor. Mis padres son profesores y encuentran el trabajo interesante, pero mi padre dice que a veces es muy cansado. Ahora he decidido que estudiaré fotografía porque me encantaría tomar fotos de eventos.*

Top Tips for Higher Students

✓ Use the subjunctive to say what is important in a future job.

✓ Use impersonal verbs like 'hace falta' to say what is necessary.

Now it's your turn. Write an article about what you want to do in the future. You should write about 80-90 words in Spanish. Mention:

- *your dream job*
- *what you need to do to get your dream job*
- *what made you want your dream job.*

[18 marks]

Higher

Q2 *Read what Padma has written about her family and their jobs, then answer the following questions. Write **P** for Padma, **M** for madre and **H** for hermana.*

READING

> *Mi madre quería una familia en lugar de una carrera y eso era común para las mujeres de su generación. Hoy más mujeres deciden trabajar mientras su pareja cuida a los niños. Por ejemplo, mi hermana es empresaria y su marido se queda en casa con los niños. A mí, me gustaría trabajar y quiero ser policía. Sería un honor proteger mi ciudad y sentirme útil.*

a) Who didn't want a career? *[1 mark]*

b) Who is an entrepreneur? *[1 mark]*

c) Who wants to feel useful? *[1 mark]*

Interview Tip #101 — always dress to *empresa*...

It's perfectly fine to not know what you want to do yet — the examiner doesn't care whether what you say is true as long as it's correct in Spanish. You could tell them you want to be a fire-eater and they'd never know...

Future Opportunities — Vocabulary

Whether you want to be an astronaut or a pet food taster (yes, that's a real job), you still need to learn all this vocab...

Education Post-16

el futuro	*future*
continuar	*to continue, carry on*
estudiar	*to study*
el estudio	*study*
la formación	*training, education*
el curso	*course*
la universidad	*university*
la carrera	*university degree*
la medicina	*medicine*
aprobar	*to pass*
el examen	*exam*
sacar buenas / malas notas	*to get good / bad grades*
el resultado	*result, outcome*
el proyecto	*project, plan*

Higher

el objetivo	*objective, goal*
el título	*title, qualification*
universitario/a	*university (adj.)*
la prueba	*class test*
formarse (en, como)	*to train (as)*
conseguir	*to acquire, obtain, get*

For more vocabulary related to subjects you can study, flick back to p.79.

Career Choices and Ambitions

trabajar	*to work*
independiente	*independent*
el trabajo	*job*
la carrera	*career*
el/la policía	*police officer*
la policía	*police (force)*
el/la doctor(a)	*doctor*
el/la profesor(a)	*teacher, professor*
el/la escritor(a)	*writer*
el/la artista	*artist*
el actor	*actor (m)*
la actriz	*actress, actor (f)*
el/la cantante	*singer*
el/la modelo	*model*
el sueño	*dream*
buscar	*to look for, search*
llegar a (+ infinitive)	*to manage to*
la plaza	*vacancy*
la experiencia	*experience*
la oferta	*offer*
aceptar	*to accept*
el salario	*salary, wage*
ganar	*to earn*
pagar	*to pay*
la empresa	*company, firm*
la compañía	*company, firm*
la oficina	*office*
la mesa	*board (of company)*
el/la presidente/a	*president, chairperson*
el/la director(a)	*boss*
el/la jefe/a	*boss, manager*
el/la cliente	*customer*
próximo/a	*next*

Higher

laboral	*work, working, labour*
el empleo	*job, occupation*
el/la médico/a	*doctor*
el/la capitán(a)	*captain*
el/la empresario/a	*entrepreneur, manager, employer*
la agencia	*agency*
el/la agente	*agent, officer*
el negocio	*business, store*
el comercio	*trade, business (shop)*
solicitar	*to apply for, request*
el puesto	*position*
la oportunidad	*opportunity, chance*
profesional	*professional*
el/la experto/a	*expert*
el/la compañero/a	*colleague*
el traje	*suit*
hace falta (+ infinitive)	*it's necessary (to)*
la reunión	*meeting*
atender	*to assist (customer), serve*

Revision Summary Test for Section Nine

It might feel like it's all work and no play at the moment, but this test will help focus your revision.

- Yep, these questions are **hard** — they'll really help you see **how well you know your stuff**.
- Tackle the **revision summary test** below, or scan the QR code to do it **online**. Use the CGP RevisionHub to **track your progress** and see **which areas need more work**.
- You can find **sample answers** here: www.cgpbooks.co.uk/GraciasExtras

Summary Test

Education Post-16

1) How do you say the following words in Spanish?
   a) future b) to carry on c) course d) medicine e) project
2) How would you say the sentence below in English?
   'Para ir a la universidad, tengo que sacar buenas notas en mis exámenes.'
3) In Spanish, tell your parents that you want to study a university degree.
4) Carmen says: 'Preferiría buscar experiencia en una compañía y no continuar con mis estudios en la universidad.' Translate what she says into English.
5) Your friend doesn't want to go to university. What could they do instead? Tell them in Spanish and give two details.
6) Answer the following question in Spanish: ¿Qué quieres hacer después de los exámenes?
7) (H) Luis says: 'Aunque no aprobé mi primera prueba universitaria, conseguí un resultado muy bueno en mi última.' Translate what he says into English.

Career Choices and Ambitions

8) How many jobs and positions can you list in Spanish? There are 12 in this section (plus 5 for Higher tier). Make sure you list both the feminine and masculine forms.
9) Fernando says: 'Ser jefe de una empresa es mi sueño. Quiero llevar ropa de moda en la oficina.' Translate what he says into English.
10) What's the Spanish for...?
    a) independent b) police (force) c) to manage to d) vacancy e) offer f) to accept
11) 'In the future, my job will pay me well and I will be able to work with customers.' Say this sentence in Spanish.
12) Describe what a family member or friend does for a living in Spanish.
13) Your Colombian friend asks you: ¿En qué carrera te gustaría trabajar en el futuro? Answer them in Spanish and give at least one reason for your choice.
14) 'Me encanta leer y busco plazas para trabajar en una biblioteca.' Translate this into English.

Higher

15) Aldara says: 'Hizo falta ser estricta con mi compañero porque se negó a seguir las reglas en la reunión. Espero que sea más profesional en la próxima.' Translate what she says into English.
16) Rafael says: 'I'm going to work in my uncle's shop this summer. I think it will be a good opportunity to acquire experience serving customers.' Translate what he says into Spanish.
17) a) In Spanish, how would you ask someone if they have any work experience?
    b) What would be your answer to this question? Answer in Spanish and give at least one detail.
18) You're talking to a friend who has recently got a new job. They say: 'Solicité el puesto en este comercio porque el salario es más alto que el que gano ahora.' What does this mean in English?
19) ¿Cuáles son tus objetivos para el futuro? Answer this question in Spanish.
20) You see an advert that says the following: 'Acabamos de empezar un negocio y buscamos a gente con experiencia en la venta de trajes.' What is this advert saying?

Quick Quiz

Where to Go

Caution: reading the next few pages might just give you the travel bug.

Don't forget you can access your online content here: www.cgpbooks.co.uk/Gracias

Vamos de viaje — *We're going on a trip*

Vocabulary

las vacaciones	*holidays*	el cambio	*exchange (money)*	América Latina, Latinoamérica	*Latin America*
al/en el extranjero	*abroad*	el destino	*destination*	hispanohablante	*Spanish-speaking*
el viaje	*trip, journey*	el mundo	*world*	H recorrer	*to travel all over*
		España	*Spain*		

El próximo verano, quiero ir de vacaciones al extranjero. — *Next summer, I want to go on holiday abroad.*
(*to another country* — a otro país)

Todos querríamos ir de vacaciones juntos a Italia. — *We would all like to go on holiday together to Italy.*
(*France* — Francia, *Germany* — Alemania, *the USA* — los Estados Unidos)

Bashir va de viaje al otro lado del mundo. — *Bashir is going on a trip to the other side of the world.*

Me encantaría visitar España para recorrer sus regiones distintas. — *I would love to visit Spain to travel all over its different regions.*
(*to do an exchange year* — hacer un año de intercambio)

¿Cómo es el destino? — *What is the destination like?*

Vocabulary

el campo	*countryside*	el lago	*lake*	la playa	*beach*	el valle (Higher)	*valley*
tranquilo/a	*calm, tranquil*	la isla	*island*	el canal	*canal*	el río (Higher)	*river*
el bosque	*wood, forest*	la costa	*coast*	el calor	*heat, warmth*	la arena (Higher)	*sand*
la montaña	*mountain*	el mar	*sea*	H el paisaje	*landscape*	hermoso/a (Higher)	*beautiful*

Snowdonia es una región de Gales con muchas montañas. — *Snowdonia is a region of Wales with lots of mountains.*
(*a lot of countryside* — mucho campo)

Vamos a Menorca, una isla que tiene muchas playas de arena. — *We go to Menorca, an island that has many sandy beaches.*
(*beautiful views* — vistas preciosas)

Hay unos lagos hermosos en el norte de Inglaterra. — *There are some beautiful lakes in the north of England.*
(*large areas of forest* — grandes zonas de bosque)

Q&A Audio

Question

¿Adónde vas de vacaciones?
Where do you go on holiday?

Simple Answer

Voy de vacaciones a Irlanda del Norte.
I go on holiday to Northern Ireland.

Extended Answer

Voy de vacaciones a Irlanda del Norte para ver a mis abuelos. Solemos pasar unas semanas allí, en un pueblo cerca del mar.
I go on holiday to Northern Ireland to see my grandparents. We usually spend a few weeks there, in a village near the sea.

Tom didn't need a beach holiday — his living room worked just fine.

¿Por qué quieres ir allí? — *Why do you want to go there?*

Vocabulary

pasar	*to spend (time)*	histórico/a	*historic*
disfrutar (de)	*to enjoy*	hacer turismo	*to sightsee*
al aire libre	*outdoors*	conocido/a	*known, well-known*
el sitio	*place, site*	la arquitectura	*architecture*

(Higher: hacer turismo, conocido/a, la arquitectura)

Quiero ir a España porque tiene arquitectura hermosa.	*I want to go to Spain because it has beautiful architecture.*
Cada vez que he ido a Cádiz con mis amigos, lo hemos pasado muy bien.	*Every time I've been to Cádiz with my friends, we have had a really good time.*
Le gustaría ir a América Latina para ver una cultura diferente.	*She would like to go to Latin America in order to see a different culture.*
Espero ir a un sitio conocido como Machu Picchu algún día.	*I hope to go to a well-known site like Machu Picchu one day.*
Vamos a visitar Edimburgo porque es un sitio histórico.	*We are going to visit Edinburgh because it is a historic place.*
Preferiría ir de vacaciones a un país donde se puede pasar mucho tiempo al aire libre.	*I would prefer to go on holiday to a country where you can spend a lot of time outdoors.*

on holiday to Iceland — de vacaciones a Islandia

Rome — Roma
Berlin — Berlín
Athens — Atenas

enjoy the good weather — disfrutar del buen tiempo

Practice Questions

Q1 *Marina and Hugo are telling their Colombian friend about Barcelona. Choose the statement that is mentioned in each pair below.*

LISTENING

Listening Track 18

a) **A.** Barcelona is in the north of Spain.
B. Barcelona has millions of tourists. *[1 mark]*

b) **A.** It's surrounded by the Mediterranean Sea.
B. It's famous for its art and cuisine. *[1 mark]*

c) **A.** Marina thinks that there is lots to do outdoors.
B. In July and August, Marina loves spending all day on its beaches. *[1 mark]*

Q2 *Write an article about travel for a competition. You should aim to write 80-90 words in Spanish. Mention:*

WRITING

- *a place you like to visit on holiday*
- *your opinion of this place with reasons*
- *a recent holiday you went on*
- *what holiday plans you have for this year.* *[18 marks]*

Top Tip for Higher Students
✓ Use the 'we' form of the conditional to talk about what you and your family would like to do.

When do mountains like to go on holiday? Peak season...

I love a beach holiday — there's nothing better. Except the sand makes me feel icky when it gets in my toes. Oh, and I need options for shade too. I also hate getting wet, so I don't like getting too close to the sea...

Quick Quiz

Accommodation and Travel

Now you've chosen where you're going to visit, you need a place to stay and a way to get there...

Busco reservar una habitación... — *I'm looking to reserve a room...*

Vocabulary

reservar	*to reserve, book*	la vista (a)	*view (over, of)*	la tienda	*tent*
quedarse	*to stay*	la llave	*key*	el alojamiento (Higher)	*accommodation*
el hotel	*hotel*	el camping	*camping, campsite*	las instalaciones (Higher)	*facilities*
la habitación	*room*			el ascensor (Higher)	*lift, elevator*
individual	*single (room, bed)*				

Quisiera quedarme en un camping para cuatro noches. — *I would like to stay on a campsite for four nights.*

for a fortnight — para quince días

Siempre elegimos hoteles con excelentes críticas. — *We always choose hotels with excellent reviews.*

Es esencial encontrar una habitación que tenga cuarto de baño y una cama cómoda. — *It's essential to find a room that has a bathroom and a comfortable bed.*

Me gustaría quedarme en un albergue juvenil para conocer a gente nueva. — *I would like to stay in a youth hostel in order to meet new people.*

to save money — ahorrar dinero

Grammar (Higher only) — I need...

When talking about the features of something you require, use the subjunctive (p.140).

Busco un hotel que tenga piscina. ***I'm looking for a hotel that has a pool.***

Q&A Audio

Question

¿Qué tipo de habitación le gustaría a usted?

What type of room would you like?

Simple Answer

Me gustaría una habitación con vistas al mar.

I would like a room with sea views.

Extended Answer

Somos una familia de tres, así que necesitamos dos habitaciones — una individual y una doble.

We are a family of three, so we need two rooms — a single and a double.

¿Cuánto cuesta? — *How much does it cost?*

Vocabulary

costar	*to cost*	el euro	*euro*	caro/a	*expensive*
pagar	*to pay*	alto/a	*high*	barato/a	*cheap*
el precio	*price*	bajo/a	*low*	ahorrar (H)	*to save (money, time)*

Mi amigo y yo buscamos alojamiento barato. — *My friend and I are looking for cheap accommodation.*

have found a hotel with lower prices — hemos encontrado un hotel con precios más bajos

Una noche en este hotel cuesta ciento diez euros. — *One night in this hotel costs one hundred and ten euros.*

Preferiríamos pagar más para quedarnos en el centro de la ciudad. — *We would prefer to pay more to stay in the city centre.*

a room with modern facilities — una habitación con instalaciones modernas

Cómo llegar allí — *How to get there*

Vocabulary

viajar	*to travel*	el tren	*train*
llegar	*to arrive*	el billete	*ticket (transport)*
volver	*to return*	alquilar	*to rent, hire*
coger	*to take, catch*	el coche	*car*
el vuelo	*flight*	montar	*to ride*
el avión	*plane*	la bicicleta	*bicycle*
el barco	*boat, ship*	caminar	*to walk*
el equipaje	*luggage*	a pie	*on foot, walking*
el transporte público	*public transport(ation)*	tardar (Higher)	*to delay, take long*
		la frontera (Higher)	*border, frontier*
el autobús	*bus*	la maleta (Higher)	*suitcase*

Prefiero coger un vuelo directo porque puedo llegar a mi destino más pronto. — *I prefer to catch a direct flight because I can arrive at my destination sooner.*

Cogeré el autobús porque será la opción más barata y tardará menos tiempo. — *I will take the bus because it will be the cheapest option and it will take less time.*

Quieren viajar en barco, pero prefiero ir en tren porque es más rápido. — *They want to travel by boat, but I prefer to go by train because it's faster.*

Vamos a alquilar un coche y esperamos llegar a la frontera a las once. — *We are going to rent a car and we hope to arrive at the border at 11 o'clock.*

Cogí el metro hasta el hotel porque había mucho tráfico. — *I took the underground to the hotel because there was a lot of traffic.*

the high-speed train — el tren de alta velocidad

They hate the delays at the station — Odian los retrasos en la estación

I get seasick — me mareo

Practice Questions

Q1 *Read Lucía's diary entry about an upcoming trip and answer the questions below.*

En febrero voy de vacaciones a París. He organizado el transporte y dónde me voy a quedar. Voy a viajar en tren porque es más barato que viajar en avión y más cómodo que viajar en autobús. Una habitación en un hotel costaría mucho, entonces he reservado un piso pequeño por un precio mejor. Tiene una cocina y un balcón bonito. La estación está muy cerca también.*

*balcón — balcony

a) How will Lucía travel to Paris? *[1 mark]*

b) Why is Lucía going to use that type of transport? (1 detail) *[1 mark]*

c) What type of accommodation will she be staying in? *[1 mark]*

d) What is a feature of the accommodation? (1 detail) *[1 mark]*

(Higher) Q2 *Listen to these five sentences and write down **in Spanish** exactly what you hear. Use your knowledge of Spanish to make sure that what you have written is accurate.* *[10 marks]*

Listening Track 19

I stayed in a bird cage once — I like cheep accommodation...

At least if your flight gets delayed, there's plenty to do. Like eating all the snacks you were meant to save for the plane or having a nap on an uncomfortable seat. Or glancing at your boarding gate over... and over...

Quick Quiz

Tourist Attractions

Grab a guidebook because you're about to explore what there is to see and do, including festivals from around the Spanish-speaking world. I'm going to need a siesta after all this excitement...

¿Qué te gustaría hacer? — *What would you like to do?*

Vocabulary

el turismo	*tourism*	el museo	*museum*
el/la turista	*tourist*	el castillo	*castle*
el recuerdo	*souvenir*	el palacio	*palace*
la foto	*photo*	la exposición	*exhibition, display*
la plaza	*square*	H la excursión	*outing, trip*
el mercado	*market*	H el puesto	*stall (market)*

"It's supposed to be around here somewhere..."

No nos gusta nada más que dar un paseo por el mercado local. — *We like nothing more than to go for a stroll through the local market.*

visit historic monuments — visitar monumentos históricos

Vamos a hacer una excursión a las ruinas antiguas de un palacio. — *We are going to go on an excursion to the ancient ruins of a palace.*

El guía dice que hay que ver los tres grandes castillos. — *The guide says that you have to see the three great castles.*

explore the national park — explorar el parque nacional

Quiero ir a una exposición en la plaza mayor del pueblo. — *I want to go to an exhibition in the town's main square.*

Una actividad divertida es... — *An enjoyable activity is...*

Q&A Audio

Question

¿Qué hiciste durante tus vacaciones?

What did you do during your holiday?

Simple Answer

Fuimos a la playa y fue muy relajante.

We went to the beach and it was very relaxing.

Extended Answer

Pasamos mucho tiempo en la playa porque hacía sol. Tomé el sol y jugué con mis primos.

We spent a lot of time on the beach because it was sunny. I sunbathed and played with my cousins.

Grammar — la foto

Watch out for nouns that don't fit the masculine / feminine rule of ending with an '-o' or '-a' (p.101):

la foto	***the photo***
el agua	***the water***

('water' is actually a feminine noun, but it takes 'el' as its article because 'la agua' is too awkward to pronounce.)

Para mí, lo más importante es bañarme en el mar. — *For me, the most important thing is to go for a swim in the sea.*

to buy a souvenir — comprar un recuerdo
to do water sports — hacer deportes acuáticos

Mañana iré a un restaurante para probar la comida típica de la región. — *Tomorrow I will go to a restaurant to try the region's typical food.*

Muchos turistas aprovechan el calor tomando el sol. — *Many tourists take advantage of the heat by sunbathing.*

Cuando estoy de vacaciones, suelo tomar muchas fotos. — *When I'm on holiday, I usually take lots of photos.*

take my camera — llevar mi cámara
buy some guide books — comprar unas guías

Las experiencias culturales — *Cultural experiences*

Vocabulary

la cultura	*culture*	el Día de los Muertos	*Day of the Dead (Mexican celebration)*
la tradición	*tradition*	el Carnaval	*Carnival*
la fiesta	*party, festival*	la flor	*flower*
la Tomatina	*Tomatina festival*	la costumbre (H)	*custom, tradition*
Las Fallas (de Valencia)	*The Fallas festival*	el traje (H)	*costume*

En agosto voy a Buñol. Participaré en la Tomatina. Durante este evento, los participantes se tiran tomates unos a otros.

In August, I'm going to Buñol. I will participate in the Tomatina festival. During this event, the participants throw tomatoes at each other.

Visito Valencia cada marzo para ir a Las Fallas. Hay cinco días de fuegos artificiales y desfiles. La gente quema creaciones de papel maché también.

I visit Valencia each March to go to the Fallas Festival. There are five days of fireworks and parades. People burn papier mâché creations too.

Quiero visitar México durante las celebraciones del Día de los Muertos. Me gustaría disfrutar de la música Mariachi y experimentar la cocina local.

I want to visit Mexico during the Day of the Dead celebrations. I'd like to enjoy the Mexican folk music and experience the local cooking.

El febrero pasado vi el Carnaval de Cádiz. Hubo muchos desfiles y casi todo el mundo llevaba un traje divertido.

Last February I saw the Cádiz Carnival. There were lots of parades and almost everybody wore an amusing costume.

Practice Questions

Q1 Oleksii is discussing holiday activities with a friend.

SPEAKING

Cuando voy a un país extranjero, tengo ganas de hacer actividades al aire libre. Iré a Portugal el próximo año. Tomaré el sol y participaré en clases de baile en la playa.

Top Tip for Higher Students
✓ Use the subjunctive to express something you want to happen, e.g. 'Quiero que haga buen tiempo.'

Now it's your turn. Talk about what you like to do on holiday and what you'd like to see and do on your next one. Aim to talk for about two minutes. [4 marks]

Higher

Q2 You read this extract from a leaflet about Galicia, a region of Spain. Answer the questions below in English.

READING

La región hermosa de Galicia está en el norte de España. Aquí se puede conocer ciudades como Santiago de Compostela, la capital de la región. Si quieres explorar la ciudad, es posible coger el autobús o montar en bicicleta. Hay una catedral preciosa y varios museos que cuentan la historia de la región. Para disfrutar de la belleza de los edificios, es mejor hacer una gira por las calles.

a) Where is Galicia located? *[1 mark]*

b) Write down two things you can visit in Santiago de Compostela. *[2 marks]*

c) What's the best way to enjoy the architecture in Santiago de Compostela? *[1 mark]*

Time flies when you're on holiday...

If only it went as fast during revision... To help with this, I'd start with learning words that are similar to their English word. That way, you'll have already made a good bit of progress before you start on the trickier ones.

Travel and Tourism — Vocabulary

Welcome to a world of vocab about travel and tourism. There's lots to explore and we hope that you enjoy your stay...

Where to Go

las vacaciones	*holidays*
ir(se) de vacaciones	*to go on holiday*
al/en el extranjero	*abroad*
el viaje	*trip, journey*
la aventura	*adventure*
visitar	*to visit*
la visita	*visit*
el cambio	*exchange (money)*
la moneda	*coin (currency)*
extranjero/a	*foreign*
encontrarse	*to be located*
el destino	*destination*
el mundo	*world*
el continente	*continent*
el país	*country*
la región	*region*
la capital	*capital city*
África	*Africa*
Asia	*Asia*
Europa	*Europe*
el Reino Unido	*United Kingdom*
España	*Spain*
las Islas Baleares	*Balearic Islands*
las Islas Canarias	*Canary Islands*
Barcelona	*Barcelona*
Madrid	*Madrid*
América Latina, Latinoamérica	*Latin America*
Bolivia	*Bolivia*
Ecuador	*Ecuador*
Venezuela	*Venezuela*
Buenos Aires	*Buenos Aires*
Medellín	*Medellín*

hispanohablante	*Spanish-speaking*
el campo	*countryside*
tranquilo/a	*calm, tranquil*
el bosque	*wood, forest*
la montaña	*mountain*
el lago	*lake*
la isla	*island*
la costa	*coast*
el mar	*sea*
la playa	*beach*
el canal	*canal*
el calor	*heat, warmth, hot*
pasar	*to spend (time), pass by, happen*
disfrutar (de)	*to enjoy*
al aire libre	*outdoors*
el sitio	*place, site*
famoso/a	*well-known, famous*
histórico/a	*historic*

Higher

el intercambio	*exchange*
recorrer	*to travel all over*
hacer turismo	*to sightsee*
situar	*to locate*
situarse	*to be located*
el paisaje	*landscape*
el valle	*valley*
el río	*river*
la arena	*sand*
hermoso/a	*beautiful*
precioso/a	*beautiful*
conocido/a	*known, well-known*
la arquitectura	*architecture*

Accommodation

reservar	*to reserve, book*
organizar	*to organise*
quedarse	*to stay*
el hotel	*hotel*
la habitación	*room*
individual	*single (room, bed)*
la vista (a)	*view (over, of)*
la llave	*key*
cómodo/a	*comfortable*
moderno/a	*modern*
el camping	*camping, campsite*
la tienda	*tent*
costar	*to cost*
pagar	*to pay*

el precio	*price*
el euro	*euro*
el peso	*peso (currency)*
el dólar	*dollar*
alto/a	*high*
bajo/a	*low*
caro/a	*expensive*
barato/a	*cheap*

Higher

el alojamiento	*accommodation*
alojarse	*to stay (accommodation)*
las instalaciones	*facilities*
el ascensor	*lift*
ahorrar	*to save (money, time)*
quejarse	*to complain*

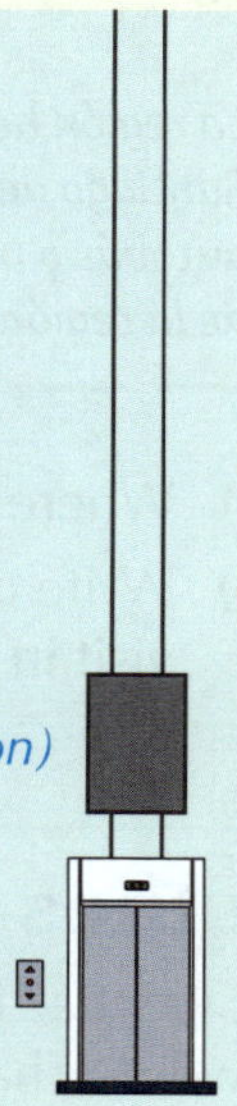

Travel

viajar	*to travel*
el viaje	*travel*
la distancia	*distance*
llegar	*to arrive*
salir	*to depart*
volver	*to return*
la vuelta	*return*
coger	*to take, catch*
perder	*to lose, miss*
el vuelo	*flight*
el avión	*plane*
el aeropuerto	*airport*
el puerto	*port, harbour*
el barco	*boat, ship*
el pasaporte	*passport*
el equipaje	*luggage*
directo/a	*direct, straight*
rápido/a	*fast, quick*
el transporte	*transport(ation)*
el transporte público	*public transport(ation)*
subir	*to get on (mode of transport)*
bajar	*to get off (mode of transport)*
el metro	*metro, underground*
el autobús, bus	*bus*
el tren	*train*
la estación	*station (train, bus...)*
el billete	*ticket (transport), note (money)*
el billete de ida	*single ticket*
el billete de ida y vuelta	*return ticket*
alquilar	*to rent, hire*
el coche	*car*
montar	*to ride*
la bicicleta	*bicycle*
caminar	*to walk*
a pie	*on foot, walking*

Higher

la llegada	*arrival*
la salida	*exit, departure*
regresar	*to return*
volar	*to fly*
tardar	*to delay, take long*
la frontera	*border, frontier*
el camino	*path, way, route*
el tráfico	*traffic*
la señal	*sign (road sign)*
la maleta	*suitcase*

Tourist Attractions

el turismo	*tourism*
el/la turista	*tourist*
perderse	*to get lost*
perdido/a	*lost*
tomar el sol	*to sunbathe*
el baño	*swim*
el recuerdo	*souvenir*
la cámara	*camera*
la foto	*photo*
el mapa	*map*
el edificio	*building*
el monumento	*monument*
la plaza	*square, place (available spot)*
el mercado	*market*
el museo	*museum*
el castillo	*castle*
el palacio	*palace*
real	*royal*
nacional	*national*
la exposición	*exhibition, display*
la cultura	*culture*
cultural	*cultural*
la tradición	*tradition*
tradicional	*traditional*
especial	*special*
la historia	*history, story*
el evento	*event*
la fiesta	*party, bank holiday, festival*
la feria	*fair, festival*
el festival	*festival*
la Tomatina	*Tomatina festival*
Las Fallas (de Valencia)	*The Fallas festival*
el Día de los Muertos	*Day of the Dead (Mexican celebration)*
el Carnaval	*Carnival*
el baile	*dance*
el flamenco	*flamenco (dance / music)*
el estilo	*elegance, manner*
la cocina	*cuisine, cooking*
tirar	*to throw, pull*
la flor	*flower*

Higher

observar	*to observe, watch*
aprovechar	*to take advantage of, make the most of*
la excursión	*outing, trip*
la gira	*tour*
el puesto	*stall, stand, place*
el plano	*map*
atraer	*to attract*
el interés	*interest*
el ambiente	*atmosphere*
la costumbre	*custom, tradition*
el desfile	*parade*
el traje	*costume*
anual	*annual*
el siglo	*century*

Revision Summary Test for Section Ten

Get in the holiday mood by trying out this section's summary test. Don't forget your suncream...

- These questions are **really tricky**, but they'll help you see **how well you know your stuff**.
- Tackle the **revision summary test** below, or scan the QR code to do it **online**. You can **keep track of your progress** online and see **which areas need more work**.
- There are **sample answers** here: www.cgpbooks.co.uk/GraciasExtras

Summary Test

Where to Go

1) Translate these sentences: 'I want to visit the capital of Spain. It is located in the centre of the country.'
2) Daniela says: 'Mucha gente va a Latinoamérica para disfrutar de los sitios históricos famosos.' How would you say this in English?
3) List the 15 holiday destinations in this section.
4) 'El mar estaba tranquilo durante mi viaje a la costa de la isla.' Translate this sentence into English.
5) Write the Spanish for: a) visit b) exchange (money) c) coin (currency) d) foreign
6) A guidebook says: 'Esta región hispanohablante tiene montañas altísimas. Además, uno de los canales más grandes del mundo corre por la zona.' Translate these sentences into English.
7) ¿Prefieres las vacaciones en el extranjero o dentro de tu propio país? ¿Por qué?

Higher

8) 'I have just done an exchange in Europe. The architecture was beautiful, but I didn't like the constant heat at all.' Translate these sentences into English.
9) ¿Qué aspectos de un paisaje te gustan más? ¿Por qué?

Accommodation and Travel

10) In Spanish, say you want to reserve a room for 4 nights. Say 2 features you want the room to have.
11) Julián says: 'En julio, me quedé en un camping en una tienda grande.' What is he saying?
12) List all the Spanish words in this section related to money and prices. There are 10 (plus 1 for Higher tier).
13) 'El autobús es el tipo de transporte más directo al aeropuerto.' How would you say this in English?
14) How would you say in Spanish that you need a return ticket to the train station?
15) Imagine you're going on holiday to Cuba. Say how you'll travel there and describe where you'll stay.
16) Pablo says: 'Para llegar al puerto a tiempo, debo alquilar un coche. Perderé el barco si voy a pie.' Translate what he is saying into English.
17) Give the Spanish for... a) distance b) to depart c) to return d) passport e) to get on f) single ticket

Higher

18) Translate these sentences into Spanish: 'I took the underground because there was a lot of traffic on the main route. Unfortunately, I forgot to pick up my suitcase because I was looking for the signs.'
19) Belén says: 'Las llegadas están tardando mucho tiempo porque las fronteras internacionales están cerradas. Espero que el vuelo no tenga que regresar a Madrid.' What does this mean in English?

Tourist Attractions

20) List all the places of interest from this section in Spanish. There are 7 you need to know.
21) ¿Cómo pasarías tus vacaciones perfectas? ¿Adónde irías y qué harías allí?
22) 'There are lots of photos from the exhibition on my camera.' Translate this sentence into Spanish.
23) Jia says: 'Voy a comprar un mapa de la ciudad porque estoy perdida.' What is she saying?
24) What's the English for...? a) la cultura b) la historia c) la feria d) el flamenco e) el estilo
25) a) Can you name the 4 festivals mentioned in this section? b) Imagine you're attending one of these festivals. In Spanish, describe what you might see there.

H

26) Translate this into English: 'Fui a Valencia para hacer turismo y observar la costumbre de Las Fallas.'

Nouns

Quick Quiz

Nouns are the words for people and objects — they're like the building blocks of a language.

Every Spanish noun is masculine or feminine...

1) Whether a word is masculine, feminine or plural affects lots of things.
2) Articles (words for 'the' and 'a') change depending on the noun's gender, and so do any adjectives which describe it.
3) If you see a word with 'el' or 'un' before it, it's usually masculine. 'La' or 'una' in front of a word means it's feminine.
4) If you don't have these clues, you can look at a word's ending to help you guess.

When you learn a new noun, learn its gender too.

el castillo alto (m) *the tall castle*
la casa alta (f) *the tall house*

Most masculine nouns end in:
-o -l -n -r -s -ta -aje -ma -pa

Most feminine nouns end in:
-a -ción -sión -tad -tud -dad -umbre

Languages, days of the week, months, rivers, seas and mountains are also masculine in Spanish.

5) You can't tell whether a noun ending in 'e', 'ista' or 'z' is masculine or feminine — you just have to learn them.

el coche *the car* la gente *the people*

...and some nouns can be both

1) Words for people often have a masculine and a feminine form. If the masculine noun ends in 'o', drop the 'o' and add 'a' to make it feminine.

Don't forget to change the article too.

el alumno → *la alumna (pupil)*

2) Nouns with other endings follow a different pattern. Here are a few examples:

Masc. ending	To make it feminine...	Example
-ante, -ente, -ista	no change	el turista *tourist (male)* → la turista *tourist (female)*
-or	add -a	el doctor *doctor (male)* → la doctora *doctor (female)*

Making nouns plural

1) Some nouns in Spanish end in a vowel. To make them plural, just add 's' — 'una cama' (*one bed*) becomes 'dos camas' (*two beds*).
2) There are some exceptions to this rule though:

Noun ending	To make it plural...	Example
consonant except 'z'	add 'es'	una flor (*one flower*) → dos flores (*two flowers*)
'z'	drop the 'z' and add 'ces'	una actriz (*one actress*) → dos actrices (*two actresses*)
'(i)ón'	drop the accent and add 'es'	un avión (*one plane*) → dos aviones (*two planes*)

Grammar Questions

Write 'el' or 'la' for each of these words. Then write each one in the plural form with 'los' or 'las'.

1. zapato **2.** camisa **3.** tradición **4.** color **5.** vez **6.** mitad
H [**7.** valle **8.** amistad **9.** ciudadano **10.** hoja **11.** impresión **12.** siglo] H

Some words are re-noun-ed for not playing by the rules...

It's annoying when Spanish breaks its own rules but you just have to learn the exceptions. Some nouns ending in 'a' are masculine, like 'el día' (day), and others ending in 'o' are feminine, like 'la foto' (photo).

Quick Quiz

Forming Nouns

In Spanish, you can make adjectives into nouns and even use the infinitive as a noun. Fancy stuff...

You can turn some adjectives into nouns

See p.115 for more on adjectives and their uses.

1) In English, adding the suffix '-ity' to an adjective can turn it into a noun. For example, 'secure' becomes 'security'.
2) You can form nouns from some adjectives in Spanish by adding the suffix '-idad'. For adjectives ending in a vowel, you often remove the ending and add '-idad'. If the adjective ends in a consonant, just add '-idad'.

diverso → divers- → la diversidad
diverse *diversity*

real → real- → la realidad
real *reality*

3) You can also form the Spanish words for languages by adding an article to the masculine form of nationality adjectives.

español *Spanish (person, object)* el español *Spanish (language)*

4) Adding an article also turns nationality adjectives into nationality nouns.

un inglés *an English person* los ingleses *the English (people)*

When a masculine singular nationality has an accent on its final syllable, it loses the accent in the feminine or plural form. See p.115 for more.

Verbs can be used as nouns too

1) In Spanish, the infinitive form of a verb can be used as a noun. It's usually equivalent to the '-ing' form in English.

The infinitive is the form of the verb you'd find in a dictionary, e.g. 'hablar' (to speak, talk).

Me encanta bailar por la tarde. *I love dancing in the evening.*

H Andar es bueno para la salud. *Walking is good for your health.*

2) When you use an infinitive as a noun, it's always masculine and usually singular. You'll need to make sure any adjectives you use agree.

Estudiar es necesario para aprobar la prueba. *Studying is necessary in order to pass the test.*

Add '-ito/a' to nouns to say 'little'

You can take off the final 'o' or 'a' from some nouns and add '-ito/a' instead to make something seem smaller or show affection.

Me encanta este pueblito.
I love this little town.

Grammar Questions

Translate the following sentences into **Spanish**.

1. I like eating Mexican food.
2. French is a cool subject.
3. Smoking is prohibited.
4. The Spanish are friendly.
H **5.** Being famous is complicated.
H **6.** Flying can be very expensive.

N'awww I love a tip-ito at the end of a page...

Nouns appear absolutely everywhere, so you need to be able to recognise all the weird and wonderful ways they're formed. You can also make nouns seem smaller with '-ito/a' — just make sure the gender agrees.

Quick Quiz

Articles

Articles are words like 'a' and 'the'. Where there's a noun, there's usually an article introducing it.

El, la, los, las — *the*

1) 'El', 'la', 'los' and 'las' are definite articles. They all mean 'the'.
2) The definite article changes depending on the gender of the noun, and whether it's singular or plural.

	Masculine	Feminine
Singular	el	la
Plural	los	las

3) Use 'el' before feminine nouns that start with a stressed 'a'.

El agua está fría. *The water is cold.*

4) When the masculine definite article 'el' is placed after the prepositions 'a' and 'de', it becomes 'al' and 'del'.

Al final del día... *At the end of the day...*

For more on prepositions, see p.108.

5) Sometimes you need a definite article in Spanish where you wouldn't use one in English:

a) With nouns used in a general sense:	No me gusta el café.	*I don't like coffee.*
b) In front of the days of the week and times:	los lunes a las seis	*Mondays at six o'clock*
c) In front of weights and measurements:	dos euros el kilo	*two euros a kilo*
d) When you use a person's title:	¿Cómo está el señor Gómez?	*How is Mr Gómez?*

Higher

6) There's a neuter article 'lo' for things that aren't masculine or feminine.

lo mejor / peor es que... *the best / worst thing is that...*

For more on 'lo' + adjective, have a look at p.115.

Un, una, unos, unas — *'a' and 'some'*

1) 'Un' and 'una' are indefinite articles. They both mean 'a'.
2) 'Un' is used for masculine words and 'una' is used for feminine words.

un gato *a cat*
una casa *a house*

3) When you make 'un' or 'una' plural, they become 'unos' and 'unas' — they mean 'some'.

unos gatos *some cats*
unas casas *some houses*

4) Watch out, though — 'a' is left out...

a) ...after the verb 'ser' when talking about someone's occupation or nationality:	Soy estudiante.	*I'm a student.*
b) ...after a negative verb:	No tengo perro.	*I haven't got a dog.*

Grammar Questions

Translate these sentences into **Spanish**.

1. I ate a cheese sandwich.
2. The water runs fast.
3. She is an English teacher.
4. He wants some chips.
5. I play basketball on Thursdays.
6. I don't have a ruler.

AHHHHHHHHHH — a stressed 'a'...

When you learn a noun, it's a really good idea to learn its gender at the same time because then you'll always know which articles you need. Now bear with me a second while I check on our ol' pal 'a' here...

Quick Quiz

Subject Pronouns

Subject pronouns are handy little words that save you from needing to repeat nouns all the time.

Yo, tú, él, ella — *I, you, he, she*

1) Pronouns are words that replace nouns — like 'you' or 'them'. You use them to avoid repeating nouns.
2) Subject pronouns replace the subject of a sentence. The subject is the noun doing the action.

Khadija went to the beach and she sat on the sand.

In English, the pronoun 'she' replaces Khadija's name. 'She' is a subject pronoun because it replaces the subject of the sentence — Khadija.

3) You don't normally include subject pronouns in Spanish sentences — but you still need to know them.

I	yo	**we**	nosotros/as
you (inf., sing.)	tú	**you (inf., pl.)**	vosotros/as
he/it	él	**they (masc.)**	ellos
she/it	ella	**they (fem.)**	ellas
you (form., sing.)	usted	**you (form., pl.)**	ustedes

The masculine 'they' form is also used for groups made up of masculine and feminine nouns.

There's also 'se' which means 'one'. It's used in phrases like 'se puede' (you (general) can, one can). It uses the third person singular form of the verb. See p.139 for more impersonal verbs.

Remember there are four ways to say 'you' in Spanish — see p.10 for more.

Fui a la playa y comí un helado. *I went to the beach and I ate an ice cream.*

You don't need the pronoun 'yo' here as the first person verb forms 'fui' and 'comí' show that the person speaking ('I') is doing the action.

4) You can use the indefinite pronoun 'alguien' (*someone*) to talk about an unidentified person.

Alguien cerró la puerta.
Someone closed the door.

¿Alguien dijo algo?
Did someone say something?

You can use subject pronouns for emphasis

Although you don't usually need subject pronouns in Spanish, they help emphasise exactly who does what:

¿Qué queréis hacer el fin de semana que viene? *What would you (inf., pl.) like to do next weekend?*

Yo quiero ir de compras, pero él quiere ir al cine.
*I want to go shopping, but **he** wants to go to the cinema.*

You include the pronouns here to emphasise who wants what. They're used in Spanish in cases when extra stress is put on pronouns in English.

¿Quieren visitar el museo? *Do they / you (form., pl.) want to visit the museum?*
Yo sí, pero ella no. *I do, but **she** doesn't.*

Remember that if you're using 'ustedes', you need the 'they' form of the verb.

Grammar Questions

Write down the Spanish subject pronoun you'd use to replace each of these subjects.

1. Mosi (m) y Jorge (m)
2. el señor Pérez y usted
3. Alberto (m) y Tania (f)
4. Tidam (m) y tú (m)
5. tu tío (m)
6. Biyu (f) y yo (f)
7. Miranda (f)
8. Nico (m)

Poor subject pronouns — they feel a bit left out in Spanish...

Not seeing subject pronouns is a bit unnatural at first, but if you get into the habit of checking the verb endings you'll be used to it in no time. Remember to only use them if you're emphasising who's doing the action.

Object Pronouns

Quick Quiz

Now you've got to grips with subject pronouns, it's time for object pronouns — what a treat.

Me, te, los, las — *me, you, them*

1) Object pronouns replace the object of a sentence. This is the thing having the action done to it.

2) Use direct object pronouns when you're talking about who or what an action is done to.

me	me
you (inf., sing.)	te
him/it/you (form., sing)	lo
her/it/you (form., sing)	la
them (m/f)/you (form., pl.)	los/las

H

us	nos
you (inf., pl.)	os

Cruz lava el coche. *Cruz washes the car.*

Cruz lo lava. *Cruz washes it.*

The pronoun usually goes before the verb and it needs to agree with the noun it replaces.

Me, te, les — *to me, to you, to them*

1) If you want to talk about doing something 'to' or 'for' someone, you need an indirect object pronoun.

El niño da la flor a su abuela. → El niño le da la flor.
The boy gives the flower to his grandmother. → *The boy gives the flower to her.*

2) These pronouns are the same ones you use with the verb 'gustar' when you say you like something. This is because 'me gusta el chocolate' literally means 'chocolate is pleasing to me'.

me	me
you (inf., sing.)	te
him/her/it/you (form., sing.)	le
them/you (form., pl.)	les

H

us	nos
you (inf., pl.)	os

Getting the order right

1) Object pronouns normally come before the verb, but they can go before or after the verb if it's an infinitive (p.125) or a present participle (p.136).

Lo quiero ver. **OR** Quiero verlo.
I want to see it.

Le estamos hablando. **OR** Estamos hablándole.
We're talking to him.

Often you need to add an accent to keep the right pronunciation.

2) With commands, the pronoun is tacked on to the end.

Escríbeme, por favor. *Write to me, please.*

Grammar Questions

Translate these sentences into **Spanish**, replacing the words in bold with the correct pronouns.

1. She breaks **the window**.
2. I drink **the water**.
3. He bought **her** a skirt.
4. I will send **them** an email.

H

5. I gave **you (inf., pl.)** the cat.
6. He told **us** the ending.

Getting the order right — most important for takeaways...

My ex-friend forgot to order poppadoms once. With ordering object pronouns, keep in mind that they usually go before the verb, but for infinitives, they can go before *or* after. For commands, just stick 'em on the end.

Quick Quiz

More Pronouns

I know, I know — it's another batch of pronouns. But it's the last two pages. I pinky promise.

Algo, alguno, ninguno — *something, one, none*

'Algo', 'alguno' and 'ninguno' are indefinite pronouns.

1) You can use the pronoun 'algo' to talk about an unidentified object.

¿Dijiste algo a alguien? *Did you (inf., sing.) say something to someone?*

'Alguien' ('someone') is another indefinite pronoun. See p.104 for more.

2) When you use 'alguno' to replace a singular noun, it can mean 'one' or 'any'. For plural nouns, it means 'some (of them)'. 'Ninguno' can mean 'none' or 'no one'.

Vi a algunos. *I saw some (of them).*

Ninguno de ellos lo tiene. *None of them has it.*

3) For feminine nouns, you need 'alguna(s)' or 'ninguna(s)'.

Que — *that, who*

1) 'Que' can mean 'that' or 'who' — it's a relative pronoun. You can use it to start a relative clause, which is a way of adding detail to a sentence.

2) 'Que' can be used to refer to the subject of a clause — the person or thing doing the action:

Allí está el hombre que vive en nuestra calle. *There's the man who lives on our street.*

Higher

3) 'Que' can also refer to the object of a clause — the person or thing something is done to:

¿Dónde está el pan que compré ayer? *Where's the bread that I bought yesterday?*

4) After prepositions, like 'con', 'a' and 'de', use 'el / la que' or 'el / la cual' for 'that / which'. When talking about plural nouns, you need to use 'los / las que' or 'los / las cuales' instead.

el mercado del cual compro flores
the market from which I buy flowers

los cafés a los que fui ayer
the cafés that I went to yesterday

5) If you're talking about a general idea instead of a specific subject, you need 'lo que'.

Van a venir, lo que es maravilloso. *They're going to come, which is wonderful.*

'Que' can refer to people or things, but 'quien' only refers to people.

6) You can also use 'cuando' (*when*), 'donde' (*where*) and 'quien' (*who*) as relative pronouns.

Voy a la playa cuando hace calor.
I go to the beach when it's hot.

la tienda donde compré el té
the shop where I bought the tea

el chico quien corre
the boy who runs

Some pronouns change after certain prepositions

Watch out — 'mí' needs an accent, but 'ti' doesn't.

Higher

1) The words for 'me' and 'you' (inf., sing.) become 'mí' and 'ti' after prepositions like 'a' (to), 'para' (for), and 'sobre' / 'de' (about).

me	mí	us	nosotros/as
you (inf., sing.)	ti	you (inf., pl.)	vosotros/as
him/her	él/ella	them (m/f)	ellos/as
you (form., sing.)	usted	you (form., pl.)	ustedes

Lo hice para ti. *I made it for you (inf., sing.).*

2) You can use these pronouns after the preposition 'a' to put extra emphasis on who you're talking about.

Me dio la pizza a mí. *He gave the pizza **to me**.*

3) You can't say 'con mí' or 'con ti' in Spanish — you need 'conmigo' and 'contigo' instead.

Está conmigo. *He's with me.*

Using pronouns to ask questions

Pronouns for asking questions are called 'interrogative pronouns'.

1) Normally, you can use '¿Qué...' to ask a question that starts with 'What...' in English.

¿Qué te gustaría hacer? *What would you (inf., sing.) like to do?*

2) Use '¿Cuál(es)...' when you'd use 'Which...' or 'Which one(s)...' in English. But remember — sometimes you need '¿Cuál...' when you'd actually use 'What...' in English — see p.8.

¿Cuál es mejor? *Which (one) is better?*

¿Cuál es su nombre? *What is his name?*

3) '¿Cuánto(s)/a(s)...' means 'How much...' or 'How many...'.

¿Cuánto cuesta la paella? *How much does the paella cost?*

4) '¿Quién...' means 'Who...'. It changes to 'Quiénes...' when you're referring to more than one person.

¿Quién es? *Who is it?*

Higher: You often use '¿Quién(es)...' with prepositions.

¿Con quién? *With whom?*

Esto, eso — *this, that*

If you don't know the gender of the noun you're replacing, or you want to talk about something more generally, you can use demonstrative pronouns like 'esto' and 'eso'.

'Esto' and 'eso' are invariable, which means they don't change to agree with a noun's gender.

No me gusta esto. *I don't like this.*

¿Qué es eso? *What's that?*

H: Use 'aquello' instead of 'eso' when the object is farther away.

¿Qué es aquello? *What's that (thing)?*

El mío, el tuyo — *mine, yours*

Higher

1) 'El mío', 'el tuyo', etc. are possessive pronouns. You use them to say 'mine' or 'yours'.

2) Possessive pronouns agree in gender and number with the noun they're replacing.

Possessive pronoun	Masc. sing.	Fem. sing.	Masc. pl.	Fem. pl.
mine	el mío	la mía	los míos	las mías
yours (inf., sing.)	el tuyo	la tuya	los tuyos	las tuyas
his/hers/its/yours (form., sing.)	el suyo	la suya	los suyos	las suyas
ours	el nuestro	la nuestra	los nuestros	las nuestras
yours (inf., pl.)	el vuestro	la vuestra	los vuestros	las vuestras
theirs/yours (form., pl.)	el suyo	la suya	los suyos	las suyas

Kwesi really didn't want to admit that the bread was his...

¿Es su casa? *Is it their house?*
No, la suya es más alta. *No, theirs is taller.*

¿Es tu pan? *Is it your (inf., sing.) bread?*
No, el mío está allí. *No, mine is there.*

Grammar Questions

Translate these sentences into **English**.

1. ¿Cuál es tu color favorito?
2. Leeré el libro que me dio.
3. ¿Has comido algo?
4. Eso no es verdad.

H:
5. La tuya está aquí.
6. Cociné para ti.
7. Irían contigo.
8. Querré aquello.

I gotta hand it *tuya* — you're a pro at pronouns...

I know it looked like the rest of the book was just going to be about pronouns, but I never break my promises. Now go and reward yourself with a quick break, then onwards and upwards with more delicious grammar.

Quick Quiz

Prepositions

Prepositions are very useful words that you can use to talk about direction, time or location.

Use these words to say where something is

Don't forget to use 'estar' (see p.128) to say where something is.

desde	*from, since*	al lado de	*next to*	fuera de	*outside of, away from*
entre	*between, among*	delante de	*in front of*	H dentro de	*within, inside*
encima de	*above*	(en) contra	*against*	H hacia	*toward(s)*

A — *to, at, away, on*

To say '<u>to</u>' in Spanish, you <u>normally</u> say '<u>a</u>'. But you can sometimes also use '<u>a</u>' to mean '<u>at</u>', '<u>away</u>' or '<u>on</u>'.

Va a Hull. *She's going to Hull.*

a las seis *at six o'clock*

Llegó a tiempo. *He arrived on time.*

En — *in, at, on*

You can <u>normally</u> use '<u>en</u>' to say '<u>in</u>'. You can also use '<u>en</u>' to say '<u>at</u>' or '<u>on</u>'.

En Leeds... *In Leeds...*

Estoy en casa. *I'm at home.*

Lo vi en la tele. *I saw it on TV.*

De — *of, from*

'<u>De</u>' usually means '<u>of</u>' or '<u>from</u>'. You can also use '<u>de</u>' to say what something's <u>made of</u> or <u>who</u> something <u>belongs to</u>.

un vaso de agua *a glass of water*

Es de oro. *It's made of gold.*

la casa de Xavi *Xavi's house*

Hasta — *until, up to*

You can use '<u>hasta</u>' to say '<u>until</u>' or '<u>up to</u>'.

Solo va hasta Kent. *It only goes up to Kent.*

Está abierto hasta las dos. *It's open until two o'clock.*

Sobre — *on, on top of, about*

'<u>Sobre</u>' means '<u>on</u>' in the sense of physically '<u>on top of</u>'. You can also use '<u>sobre</u>' to say '<u>about</u>'.

Está sobre el armario. *It's on top of the wardrobe.*

Está sobre la mesa. *It's on the table.*

Discuten sobre sus planes. *They argue about their plans.*

Grammar Questions

Use what you know about prepositions to translate these sentences into **Spanish**.

1. We talked about the weather.
2. The café is closed until Monday.
3. I saw it on the wall.
4. They're from Valencia.
H **5.** The dog ran towards me.
H **6.** I live within the city.

Not a *de* goes by where I don't use a preposition...

You can add 'de' to some adverbs to make useful location prepositions, e.g. 'cerca' (*close, near, nearby*) can become 'cerca de' (*close to, near to*). You also have 'detrás de' (*behind*), which is perfect for pantomimes.

Prepositions with Verbs and Nouns

Quick Quiz

Prepositions aren't just for describing where something is — you'll often see them before an infinitive or noun and after certain verbs. When they follow a verb, they can change its meaning.

Some prepositions are followed by an infinitive...

1) 'Para' followed by an infinitive means 'to' or 'in order to'.

   Veo la tele para descansar. *I watch TV to relax.*

2) The preposition 'sin' means 'without'. Use it with an infinitive when you want to say 'without -ing'.

   Salió sin decir una palabra más. *He left without saying another word.*

Higher

3) You can use 'antes de' + infinitive to say 'before -ing'.

   Compré la entrada antes de llegar al cine. *I bought the ticket before arriving at the cinema.*

4) If you want to say 'after -ing', use 'después de' + infinitive.

   Después de terminar el examen, iré a una fiesta. *After finishing the exam, I will go to a party.*

...and some are followed by a noun

In some verb phrases, the preposition is followed by a noun.

Voy de vacaciones en julio. *I'm going on holiday in July.*

H Se parece a su abuela. *She looks like her grandmother.*

Verb phrase	Meaning
ir de vacaciones	to go on holiday
estar de acuerdo	to be in agreement
depender de	to depend on
disfrutar de	to enjoy
parecerse a (H)	to look like
confiar en (H)	to rely on

Some verbs are followed by a preposition

1) Sometimes you need to use a preposition after the verb. The preposition can change the verb's meaning:

Verb	Verb + preposition	Example sentence
llegar (*to arrive*)	llegar a (*to manage to*)	Llegué a encontrarlo. (*I managed to find it.*)
dejar (*to let, leave*)	dejar de (*to stop -ing*)	He dejado de leerlos. (*I've stopped reading them.*)
H tratar (*to treat, deal with*)	tratar de (*to try to*)	Trataré de hacerlo rápido. (*I'll try to do it quickly.*)

2) The verb that comes after the preposition is always an infinitive.

Grammar Questions

Translate these sentences into **English**.

1. Hablé sin pensar.
2. Llegaste a aprobarlo.
3. Ha dejado de fumar.
4. Juego para ganar.
H **5.** Cerraré la puerta antes de salir.
H **6.** Trato de beber más agua.

Let's pretend there's a joke about prepositions here...

I enjoyed writing the last one so much that I think my creative juices might have run dry. While I grab a top up, try learning these verb phrases with specific examples — they'll be easier to remember in a sentence.

Quick Quiz

'Por', 'Para' and the Personal 'a'

'Por' and 'para' each have multiple uses. But don't fret — they're listed below to help you.

Use 'por' to...

1) ...say 'by'. — Fue pintada por un artista famoso. *It was painted by a famous artist.*

2) ...say 'for' or 'per'. — Vivió allí por un año. *He lived there for a year.* — seis meses por año *six months per year*

3) ...say 'through', 'in' or 'at'. — Entré por la puerta. *I came through the door.*

Higher

4) ...say 'around'. — El museo está por aquí. *The museum is around here.*

5) ...say 'because of'. — No salí por el mal tiempo. *I didn't go out because of the bad weather.*

You usually use 'por' to talk about the past, but sometimes you need it for the future, e.g. 'Estaré en Galicia por dos años'.

Use 'para' instead...

Using 'para' with an infinitive helps you say 'in order to' (see p.109).

1) ...in future time phrases like 'for X number of days' or 'for / by X time'. — Quiero el coche para un día. *I want the car for one day.*

2) ...when you're talking about destinations. — el tren para Bilbao *the train for Bilbao*

3) ...to say who something is for. — El artista la pintó para su cliente. *The artist painted it for his client.*

H

4) ...to give your opinion. — Para mí, es importante. *For me, it's important.*

The personal 'a'

You need an extra 'a' before the word for any human being or pet after almost every verb.

Estoy buscando a Ozan.
I'm looking for Ozan.

BUT

Estoy buscando un libro.
I'm looking for a book.

You don't usually use the personal 'a' after 'tener' or 'ser'.

Grammar Questions

Translate these sentences into **English**.

1. Ahora llega el tren para París.
2. Lo haré para mañana.
3. Vi la tele por tres horas.
4. Camino por el campo.
H
5. Lo guardaban para sus hijos.
6. Salían raramente por el calor.

Decide whether you need a personal 'a' in each of these sentences.

7. Vieron ___ la película ayer.
8. Conocía ___ mucha gente.
9. Sacará ___ buenas notas.
10. Visito ___ mi abuelo.
H
11. Iban a ver ___ sus pájaros.
12. Eso destruye ___ las plantas.

Don't confuse the personal 'a' with the preposition 'a'...

The preposition 'a' is used in sentences with an indirect object, like 'doy el sombrero al caballo' (I give the hat to the horse). The personal 'a' is used when the human being or pet you're talking about is a direct object.

Conjunctions

Quick Quiz

Conjunctions help you link your ideas together to make longer, more complex sentences.

Y — *and*

1) 'Y' means 'and' — you use it just like you would in English.

Me gusta jugar al fútbol. *I like playing football.*	AND	Me gusta jugar al rugby. *I like playing rugby.*	=	Me gusta jugar al fútbol y al rugby. *I like playing football and rugby.*

2) 'Y' changes to 'e' before a word starting with 'i' or 'hi'.

Hablo español e inglés. *I speak Spanish and English.*

O — *or*

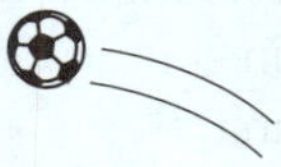

1) 'O' means 'or'.

Juego al fútbol los sábados. *I play football on Saturdays.*	OR	Juego al rugby los sábados. *I play rugby on Saturdays.*	=	Juego al fútbol o al rugby los sábados. *I play football or rugby on Saturdays.*

2) When 'o' comes just before a word starting with 'o' or 'ho', it changes to 'u'.

Cuesta siete u ocho euros. *It costs seven or eight euros.*

Pero — *but*

1) 'Pero' means 'but'.

Me gusta el fútbol. *I like football.*	BUT	No me gusta el rugby. *I don't like rugby.*	=	Me gusta el fútbol, pero no me gusta el rugby. *I like football, but I don't like rugby.*

H 2) When 'but' means 'but rather', it becomes 'sino'.

No es español, sino francés. *He isn't Spanish, but (rather) French.*

Porque — *because*

There's more about 'porque' and opinions on p.12.

'Porque' means 'because'. It helps you give opinions:

Me gusta esta comida porque está rica. *I like this food because it's tasty.*

Other conjunctions you need to know

You usually use 'ni' with a negative verb to say 'neither...nor...'. See p.138 for more on negatives.

que	*that, than*	ya que	*since*	mientras (Higher)	*while, whereas*
si	*if, whether*	sin embargo (H)	*however, nevertheless*	(no) ni... (ni)... (Higher)	*nor, neither ... nor*
como	*like, as*	aunque (H)	*although*	para que (Higher)	*so that, in order to*

Grammar Questions

Translate these sentences into **Spanish**, deciding which conjunctions you need to use.

1. PE is exciting, but it's hard.
2. I like history because it's easy.
3. As I'm ill, I'll stay at home.
4. If it's hot, I go to the beach.
5. I have art and English classes.
6. Do you prefer blue or green?

You don't want to sound like a robot, so start using conjunctions...

I don't want to stop you from doing it in your free time, but an exam is probably the wrong place to start.

Nouns, Articles & Linking Words — Grammar List

There's a lot to take in from this section so I've popped the essentials on these next two pages — I'm nice like that.

Nouns

Common endings for masculine nouns are:
-o, -l, -n, -r, -s, -ta, -aje

Common endings for feminine nouns are:
-a, -ción, -sión, -tad, -tud, -dad, -umbre

For nouns ending in 'e' or 'ista', see p.101.

Some masculine nouns can be made feminine:

el amigo → **la** amig**a**	*friend (m/f)*
el escrit**or** → **la** escrit**ora**	*writer (m/f)*
un ingl**és** → **una** ingl**esa**	*English person (m/f)*
el artista → **la** artista	*artist (m/f)*
el cantante → **la** cantante	*singer (m/f)*
el cliente → **la** cliente	*client, customer (m/f)*

There are different ways to make singular nouns plural:

el gato → **los** gato**s**	*cat(s)*
el canal → **los** canal**es**	*channel(s)*
la voz → **las** vo**ces**	*voice(s)*
la estaci**ón** → **las** estaci**ones**	*station(s)*
el coraz**ón** → **los** coraz**ones**	*heart(s)*

Some nouns can be formed from adjectives:

activo → la activi**dad**	*activity*
español → **el** español	*Spanish (language)*

You can also use the infinitive of a verb as a noun:
Reciclar es importante. — *Recycling is important.*

Add -ito/a to make a noun seem smaller:
la cosa → la cos**ita** — *thing → little thing*

Articles

Articles (words like 'the' and 'a') introduce nouns. They change depending on the noun's gender and whether it's singular or plural.

Definite articles:

el	*the (m, sing.)*
la	*the (f, sing.)*
los	*the (m, pl.)*
las	*the (f, pl.)*

Indefinite articles:

un	*a, an (m, sing.)*
una	*a, an (f, sing.)*
unos	*some (m, pl.)*
unas	*some (f, pl.)*

The masculine singular article 'el' changes when combined with the prepositions 'a' or 'de':

a + el → al
de + el → del

H: The article 'lo' can be used to talk about general things, e.g. 'lo bueno' (*the good thing*).

Subject Pronouns

Subject pronouns replace the subject of the sentence.

yo	*I*
tú	*you (inf., sing.)*
él	*he, it (m)*
ella	*she, it (f)*
usted	*you (form., sing.)*
nosotros/as	*we*
vosotros/as	*you (inf., pl.)*
ellos	*they (m)*
ellas	*they (f)*
ustedes	*you (form., pl.)*

Higher: Some subject pronouns change after certain prepositions.

con + mí → conmigo	*with me*
con + ti → contigo	*with you (inf., sing.)*

Emphatic Pronouns

Use subject pronouns after the preposition 'a' for emphasis.

Higher:

(a) mí	*(to) me*
(a) ti	*(to) you (inf., sing.)*
(a) él / ella	*(to) him / her*
(a) usted / ustedes	*(to) you (form., sing./pl.)*
(a) nosotros/as	*(to) us*
(a) vosotros/as	*(to) you (inf., pl.)*
(a) ellos / ellas	*(to) them (m/f)*

Direct Object Pronouns

Direct object pronouns replace the person or thing the action is being done to.

me	*me*
te	*you (inf., sing.)*
lo	*him, it (m), you (form., sing.)*
la	*her, it (f), you (form., sing.)*
los	*them, you (form., pl.) (m)*
las	*them, you (form., pl.) (f)*
nos (H)	*us*
os (H)	*you (inf., pl.)*

Indirect Object Pronouns

Indirect object pronouns replace the person or thing being indirectly affected by the action.

me	*(to) me*
te	*(to) you (inf., sing.)*
le	*(to) him, her, it, you (form., sing.)*
les	*(to) them, you (form., pl.)*
nos (H)	*(to) us*
os (H)	*(to) you (inf., pl.)*

Indefinite Pronouns

Indefinite pronouns refer to nouns that are general and unspecific.

alguien	*someone*
algo	*something*
alguno	*one*
algunos	*some (of them)*
ninguno	*no one, none*
todo	*everything, all*
todos	*everyone, all of them*

Demonstrative Pronouns

These demonstrative pronouns replace things in a sentence that are unspecific. They don't have to agree in gender or number.

	esto	*this*
	eso	*that*
H	aquello	*that (thing)*

Prepositions with Verbs and Nouns

Some prepositions are followed by an infinitive:

	para (+ infinitive)	*in order to (+ verb)*
	sin (+ infinitive)	*without (+ -ing)*
H	antes de (+ infinitive)	*before (+ -ing)*
H	después de (+ infinitive)	*after (+ -ing)*

Some verb phrases use a preposition + noun:

	ir de vacaciones	*to go on holiday*
	estar de acuerdo	*to be in agreement*
	disfrutar de (+ noun)	*to enjoy*
H	parecerse a (+ noun)	*to look like*
H	confiar en (+ noun)	*to rely on*

The meaning of some verbs changes when they're followed by a preposition:

E.g. llegar → llegar a
to arrive → *to manage to*

Relative Pronouns

Relative pronouns introduce extra information to a sentence. 'Que' can mean 'who' (if you're referring to someone) or 'that' (if you're referring to something).

que *who, that*

E.g. Es el vecino que cuidó a mi gato.
He's the neighbour who took care of my cat.

Higher

After prepositions, you use 'el/la que', 'los/las que', 'el/la cual' or 'los/las cuales' to say 'that / which'.

el/la que — los/las que — *that / which*
el/la cual — los/las cuales

E.g Lo vi durante el evento al que asistí.
I saw it during the event that I attended.

If you're talking about a general idea, you need 'lo que'.

lo que *what, that which*

E.g. La carta nunca llegó, lo que era una sorpresa.
The letter never arrived, which was a surprise.

'Cuando', 'donde' and 'quien' can also be relative pronouns.

cuando *when* — donde *where* — quien *who*

Possessive Pronouns

Possessive pronouns show what belongs to who.

Higher	el/la mío/a, los/las míos/as	*mine*
Higher	el/la tuyo/a, los/las tuyos/as	*yours (inf., sing.)*
Higher	el/la suyo/a, los/las suyos/as	*his, hers, its, yours (form., sing./pl.), theirs*
Higher	el/la nuestro/a, los/las nuestros/as	*ours*
Higher	el/la vuestro/a, los/las vuestros/as	*yours (inf., pl.)*

Remember — the personal 'a' is different to the preposition 'a'. See p.110 for more.

Prepositions

a	*to, at, away, on*		debajo de	*underneath, below, under*
al	*(to) the (m, sing.)*		encima de	*above*
en	*in, at, on*		al lado de	*next to*
de	*of, from*		delante de	*in front of*
del	*of the (m, sing.)*		(en) contra	*against*
hasta	*until, up to*		fuera de	*outside of, away from*
desde	*from, since*		durante	*during*
sobre	*on, on top of, about*		menos	*except, minus*
con	*with*	Higher	por	*around, because of*
sin	*without*	Higher	dentro de	*within, inside*
por	*by, for, through, in, at, per*	Higher	hacia	*toward(s)*
		Higher	(a) través (de)	*through, across*
para	*for*	Higher	según	*according to*
entre	*between, among*	Higher	salvo	*except for, but*
bajo	*under, underneath*	Higher	a pesar de	*despite, in spite of*

Conjunctions

	y, e	*and*
	o, u	*or*
	pero	*but*
	porque	*because*
	que	*that, than*
	si	*if, whether*
	como	*like, as*
	ya que	*since*
	pues	*so, well, well then*
Higher	sin embargo	*however, nevertheless*
Higher	no obstante	*however, nevertheless*
Higher	aunque	*although*
Higher	mientras	*while, whereas*
Higher	(no) ni...(ni)...	*nor, no (after negative verb), neither...nor...*
Higher	para que	*so that, in order to*
Higher	dado (que)	*given (that)*
Higher	sino	*but, rather*
Higher	por lo tanto	*therefore*

Revision Summary Test for Section Eleven

If more grammar ar-tickles your fancy, this test will let you show off everything you've learnt.

- These questions are **hard**, but they'll really help you see **how well you know your stuff**.
- Tackle the **revision summary test** below, or scan the QR code to do it **online**. You can **track your progress** online and see **which areas need more work**.
- There are **sample answers** for the test here: www.cgpbooks.co.uk/GraciasExtras

Summary Test

Nouns and Articles

1) Write either 'm' or 'f' to show whether each noun is masculine or feminine.
   a) azúcar b) canción c) conejo d) papel e) playa f) hotel g) falda h) clase
2) Make these nouns feminine: a) el estudiante b) el vecino c) un chileno d) el director
3) Make each of these nouns plural — don't forget to include 'los' or 'las':
   a) examen b) mes c) sábado d) comunidad e) habitación f) nariz g) camisa
4) Translate these sentences into Spanish: a) Reading is interesting. b) Singing is really boring.
5) Choose the correct article in bold to complete each of these sentences: a) **El** / **La** agua está limpia.
   b) **Los** / **Las** chicas juegan al fútbol. c) Dame **un** / **una** bolígrafo, por favor.
6) Fill in the gaps with 'a' or 'de' combined with the correct definite article ('el' or 'la'):
   a) Voy ...... parque. b) Salió ...... biblioteca. c) Le gustaría ir ...... fiesta. d) al lado ...... banco
7) Translate the following into Spanish: a) I'm a teacher. b) I don't have a cat. c) Are you Spanish?

Pronouns

8) List all the Spanish subject pronouns in this section. There are 12 you need to know.
9) Rewrite these sentences, replacing the words in bold with the correct direct object pronoun.
   a) Buscaba **la caja**. b) Estudio **las ciencias**. c) Vi **al actor**. d) He encontrado **mis zapatos**.
10) Now rewrite these sentences, replacing the words in bold with the correct indirect object pronoun.
   a) Di los libros **a los alumnos**. b) Envié la carta **a mi tía**. c) Hablará **a sus amigos** mañana.
11) Translate these sentences into Spanish using the correct indefinite pronouns.
   a) I have something in my eye. b) Did they buy some (of them)? c) None of them made dinner.
12) What type of pronoun is the word 'que'? How would you say 'que' in English?
13) Translate these sentences into Spanish using the correct interrogative pronouns.
   a) Who called you (inf., sing.)? b) What did they do yesterday? c) Which one is worse?
14) Translate these sentences into Spanish using the correct demonstrative pronouns.
   a) I never wanted this. b) I'd like to do that. c) Have you read this? d) That isn't fair.

Higher

15) Complete each sentence by circling the correct option:
   a) Ese pan es para **tú** / **ti**. c) Pensaba en **ella** / **suya**. e) ¿Los churros son para **me** / **mí**?
   b) A **ellos** / **él** le gustan mucho. d) ¿Vamos **contigo** / **con tú**? f) Hablábamos de **ti** / **tú**.
16) Translate these sentences into English: a) ¿Es la tuya o la mía? b) Puse el vuestro en la cocina.

Prepositions and Conjunctions

17) Fill in the gaps with the correct preposition in Spanish: a) Queremos las bicicletas ...... una semana.
   b) Pagué treinta euros ...... el vestido. c) La vi ...... la tele. d) Me preguntaron ...... este tema.
18) Translate these sentences into English: a) Entré en la casa por la ventana. b) Fui al café de Diego.
   c) Leí el libro sin terminarlo. d) Van a quedarse hasta noviembre. e) Bailé mucho durante la fiesta.
19) What do these verbs mean in English? a) dejar de b) llegar a c) depender de
20) Choose the correct conjunction in bold, then translate these sentences into English:
   a) Es una fiesta tradicional **y** / **e** importante. b) Comí esos bocadillos **porque** / **pero** me encantan.

H

21) Translate these sentences into English: a) Leo antes de acostarme. b) Lo haré después de comer.
22) Say what the conjunction 'sino' means in English, then give a sentence in Spanish that uses it.

Quick Quiz

Adjectives

Jazz up your work with some flashy describing words — and collect more marks while you're at it.

Adjectives describe things

Spanish adjectives will be in the masculine singular form in the dictionary.

1) In Spanish, adjectives have to agree with the noun they refer to, even if they aren't right next to it.
2) This means the adjective changes depending on the gender of the noun and whether it's singular or plural.
3) Adjectives that end in 'o' in the masculine singular form change the 'o' to 'a' in the feminine form. When plural, the adjective ends in 'os' (masculine) or 'as' (feminine).

el chico alto — *the tall boy*

la chica alta — *the tall girl*

los chicos altos — *the tall boys*

las chicas altas — *the tall girls*

4) Adjectives with certain endings follow different rules:

Ending	Example	Masc. sing.	Fem. sing.	Masc. pl.	Fem. pl.
-e	triste (*sad*)	triste	triste	tristes	tristes
-ista	optimista (*optimistic*)	optimista	optimista	optimistas	optimistas
most consonants	habitual (*usual*)	habitual	habitual	habituales	habituales
-z	feliz (*happy*)	feliz	feliz	felices	felices
-és	inglés (*English*)	inglés	inglesa	ingleses	inglesas
-ol	español (*Spanish*)	español	española	españoles	españolas

Nationality adjectives ending in consonants add an ending in the feminine and the plural. If they have an accent in the masculine singular, they drop it in the feminine and plural.

5) Some adjectives don't change to agree — most of these are colours.

tres coches naranja — *three orange cars*

siete trenes rosa — *seven pink trains*

You can add -able to some verb stems to make adjectives

For some verbs that end in '-ar', you can add the suffix '-able' to the verb stem to form an adjective.

aceptar (*to accept*) ⟶ aceptable (*acceptable*)

Spanish adjectives with this ending often end in '-able' in English too.

Lo bueno, lo malo — *the good thing, the bad thing*

Higher

1) In Spanish, you can say 'the good thing' or 'the bad thing' by using 'lo' followed by 'bueno' or 'malo'.
2) You can do this with any adjective. To say 'the most... thing', just add 'más' before the adjective.

Lo peor es que... — *The worst thing is that...*

Lo más útil es que... — *The most useful thing is that...*

Grammar Questions

Translate these phrases into **Spanish**, making sure the adjectives agree.

1. the happy dog
2. a vegan dessert
3. the orange trousers
4. a recyclable bottle
5. the English sister
6. a comparable number
H **7.** the dangerous thing
H **8.** the funniest thing

Adjectives agree (and I'm sure you do too) that this page is great...

Don't let unfamiliar adjectives catch you out — learn how different endings change depending on the noun.

Quick Quiz

More Adjectives

Adjectives are really useful for saying what's yours and for pointing things out. For example, this is *my* delicious muffin and it is certainly not *yours*... Sorry. I'm just protective of my snacks.

Most adjectives go after the word they describe

1) In Spanish, most adjectives go after the noun (the word they describe).
2) But that's not always the case — some adjectives always go in front of the noun they're describing, like these ones:

Es un vestido bonito.
It's a nice dress.

mucho/a	*much, a lot of*	alguno/a	*a/an, some*	demasiados/as	*too many*	último/a	*last, latest*
muchos/as	*many, lots of*	ninguno/a	*no, not...any*	primero/a	*first*	cada	*each, every*
otro/a	*other, another*	poco/a	*a few, not much*	segundo/a	*second*		
otros/as	*other*	pocos/as	*a few, not many*	tercero/a	*third*		
		demasiado/a	*too much*	próximo/a	*next*		

algunos parques — *some parks*

pocas casas — *a few houses*

demasiada lluvia — *too much rain*

Some adjectives change before masculine nouns...

primer	*first (m) (pre-noun)*	mal	*bad (m) (pre-noun)*	gran	*big, great (pre-noun)*
tercer	*third (m) (pre-noun)*	algún	*a/an, any (m) (pre-noun)*		
buen	*good (m) (pre-noun)*	ningún	*no, not...any (m) (pre-noun)*		

1) Some adjectives lose the final 'o' when they go in front of a masculine noun.

el tercer libro — *the third book*

un buen día — *a good day*

2) 'Alguno' and 'ninguno' drop the final 'o' and add an accent.

No hay ningún taxi libre. — *There's no taxi free.*

3) 'Grande' is the only adjective that drops 'de' in front of both masculine and feminine words.

el gran plan — *the great plan*

una gran señora — *a great lady*

...and some change their meaning depending on their position

Adjective	Before the noun...	After the noun...
grande	un gran hombre *a great man*	un hombre grande *a big man*
único	el único edificio *the only building*	el edificio único *the unique building*
nuevo	un nuevo coche *a new (to owner) car*	un coche nuevo *a newly-made car*
viejo	un viejo amigo *an old (long-standing) friend*	un amigo viejo *an old (aged) friend*
antiguo	un antiguo castillo *a former castle*	un castillo antiguo *an old castle*
pobre	un pobre chico *a poor (unfortunate) boy*	un chico pobre *a poor (not rich) boy*

"I should've checked that advert more carefully..."

Mi, tu, nuestro — *my, your, our*

'Mi', 'tu', 'nuestro' etc. are possessive adjectives.

1) Words like 'my' and 'your' show possession. In Spanish they go before the noun and have to agree with the noun they're describing — not the owner. You only need to learn the forms in brackets if you're doing Higher tier (see below).

Possessive	Masc. sing.	Fem. sing.	Masc. pl.	Fem. pl.
my	mi (mío)	mi (mía)	mis (míos)	mis (mías)
your (inf., sing.)	tu (tuyo)	tu (tuya)	tus (tuyos)	tus (tuyas)
his/her/its/your (form., sing.)	su (suyo)	su (suya)	sus (suyos)	sus (suyas)
our	nuestro	nuestra	nuestros	nuestras
your (inf., pl.)	vuestro	vuestra	vuestros	vuestras
their/your (form., pl.)	su (suyo)	su (suya)	sus (suyos)	sus (suyas)

'Su(s)' can mean 'his', 'her', 'its', 'their' and 'your' (formal). Use the rest of the sentence to work out which of these it is.

mi libro — *my book*
su perro — *his dog*

H

2) The forms in brackets are long-form adjectives. You use them for emphasis and put them after the noun:

el gato nuestro — *our cat*

The 'our' and 'your (inf., pl.)' forms are the same in the short and long forms.

Este, ese — *this, that*

'Este', 'ese' and 'aquel' are demonstrative adjectives.

1) Use 'este' to say 'this'. It's an adjective, so it changes to agree with the noun. When the noun is feminine, use 'esta', and when it's plural, use 'estos' (masculine) or 'estas' (feminine).

este tigre *this tiger* — esta leche *this milk* — estos huevos *these eggs* — estas mesas *these tables*

2) Use 'ese' to say 'that' in English. Use 'esa' for feminine nouns, and 'esos' or 'esas' for plural nouns.

ese tigre *that tiger* — esa leche *that milk* — esos huevos *those eggs* — esas mesas *those tables*

Higher

3) 'Aquel' also means that. It's used for things that are further away — in English, you might say 'that over there'.

4) 'Aquel' changes to 'aquella' in the feminine form and 'aquellos' and 'aquellas' for the plural forms.

aquel tigre	*that tiger (over there)*
aquella leche	*that milk (over there)*
aquellos huevos	*those eggs (over there)*
aquellas mesas	*those tables (over there)*

Indefinite adjectives describe words in a more general way

1) 'Otro' (*other, another*), 'todo' (*all, the whole*), 'alguno' (*some*), 'ninguno' (*no, not any*) and 'mismo' (*same*) are all examples of indefinite adjectives. They change to agree with the noun.

2) 'Cada' (*each, every*), is also an indefinite adjective, but it never changes to agree with what it's describing.

otro tigre	*another tiger*
algunos tigres	*some tigers*
cada tigre	*each tiger*

Grammar Questions

Translate these phrases into **Spanish**, making sure the adjectives go in the right place.

1. the first day
2. few shops
3. each family
4. no ice cream
5. their books
6. those films
H **7.** my pen (long form)
8. that sock over there H

Someone must really like tigers...

Possessive adjectives show who something belongs to, and demonstrative adjectives show where something is compared to where you are. Indefinite adjectives generally describe how much of something there is.

Quick Quiz

Comparative and Superlative Adjectives

Comparative and superlative adjectives help you compare one thing to another. Marvellous.

Más, menos — *more, less*

'More' is a comparative. 'The most' (Higher only) is a superlative.

1) In Spanish you can't say 'cheaper' or 'cheapest' — you have to say '<u>more cheap</u>' or '<u>the most cheap</u>'.

Este piso es barato. *This flat is cheap.* → Este piso es más barato. *This flat is cheaper.* → [H] Este piso es el más barato. *This flat is the cheapest.*

2) To say '<u>less cheap</u>' or '<u>the least cheap</u>', use '<u>menos</u>'.

Este piso es barato. *This flat is cheap.* → Este piso es menos barato. *This flat is less cheap.* → [H] Este piso es el menos barato. *This flat is the least cheap.*

[H] 3) To say 'the most / least' if the word you're describing is <u>feminine</u>, use 'la más / menos'. For <u>plural</u> words, use 'los/las más / menos'.

Zeynab es la más baja. *Zeynab is the shortest.*

Más / menos ... que — *more / less ... than*

1) Use '<u>más</u> ... <u>que</u>' (more ... than) and '<u>menos</u> ... <u>que</u>' (less ... than) to <u>compare</u> two things <u>directly</u>.
2) To say two things are <u>as</u> young or old or brilliant <u>as</u> each other, use '<u>tan</u> ... <u>como</u>' (as ... as).

Catalina es más tranquila que Minho, pero ella es tan tranquila como Daniel.
Catalina is more calm than Minho, but she is as calm as Daniel.

There are some exceptions...

All these comparatives and superlatives add 'es' for the plural forms.

					Higher	
bueno	*good*	→	mejor	*better*	→ el mejor	*the best*
malo	*bad*	→	peor	*worse*	→ el peor	*the worst*
viejo	*old (people only)*	→	mayor	*older*	→ el mayor	*the oldest*
joven	*young (people only)*	→	menor	*younger*	→ el menor	*the youngest*

If the noun is feminine or plural, you'll need to change the 'el' to 'la', 'los' or 'las'.

Sara es mayor que Javier. *Sara is older than Javier.*

[H] Aya es la mayor. *Aya is the oldest.*

Grammar Questions

Translate these sentences into **Spanish** — watch out for the irregular adjectives though.

1. This page is easier.
2. I am as tall as my father.
3. Faiza is older than Emilio.
4. Books are better than films.
[H] **5.** Today is the worst day.
[H] **6.** She is the youngest.

Making comparisons is the best thing ever...

Comparatives have to agree with what they're describing. So to say 'The horse and the cat are angrier' in Spanish, you say 'El caballo y el gato están más enfadad<u>os</u>' because 'the horse and the cat' is a plural phrase.

Adverbs

Quick Quiz

Adverbs describe how you do something, like cooking terribly — even my toast gets incinerated...

Adverbs describe how actions are done

1) If you wanted to describe how you run, you could say 'I run slowly' — 'slowly' is an adverb of manner.
2) In English, you add '-ly' to the adjective 'slow' to make 'slowly'.
3) It's similar in Spanish — to form an adverb of manner, you add '-mente' to the end of the adjective. However, you need to make sure the adjective is in the feminine form first.

lento (*slow*) ⟶ lenta *(feminine form of 'slow')* + -mente ⟶ lentamente *(slowly)*

4) With adjectives that don't end in 'o', you can just add '-mente'.

fácil (*easy*) + -mente ⟶ fácilmente *(easily)*

5) Unlike with adjectives (see p.115), adverbs don't need to agree. This is because they're describing an action, not the person doing the action.
6) Adverbs of manner come after the verb.

Comemos rápidamente.	*We eat quickly.*
Habla alegremente.	*She speaks happily.*
Estudio tranquilamente.	*I study calmly.*
Responden claramente.	*They answer clearly.*

Some adverbs are formed differently

You don't say 'I sing goodly' in English, and you can't say 'buenamente' in Spanish either.

bueno/a	*good*	⟶	bien	*well*
malo/a	*bad*	⟶	mal	*badly*

Canto bien.	*I sing well.*
Canto mal.	*I sing badly.*

Letting Andrea choose the music was a big mistake...

Some adverbs describe possibility

Adverbs of certainty describe how possible something is. They normally come before the verb.

probablemente	*probably*
completamente	*completely*
H quizá(s)	*perhaps, maybe*

Probablemente seré profesor.
I will probably be a teacher.

Higher

Quizás visitaré.
I'll maybe visit.

Grammar Questions

Turn these adjectives into adverbs, then translate the **adverb** into **English**.

1. positivo **2.** directo **3.** social **4.** diferente **5.** exacto **6.** perfecto **7.** posible **8.** tradicional

H: **9.** evidente **10.** suave **11.** auténtico **12.** anual

Adverbs are stubborn — they never agree with anything...

Though I guess that makes them a bit easier than adjectives. Just remember to use the adjective's feminine form if you're forming an adverb with an adjective and '-mente' and you'll be an adverbs expert in no time.

Quick Quiz

Adverbs and Adverbial Phrases

And here's another page on adverbs — these ones say where or when something is happening.

Adverbs can tell you where something is done...

Adverbs of place say where things happen. They come after the verb in a phrase or sentence.

aquí	*here*	cerca	*close, near*	dentro (Higher)	*inside*
acá	*here*	lejos (de)	*far (away, off)*	fuera (Higher)	*out, outside, away*
allí	*there, over there*	detrás	*behind, at the back*	abajo (Higher)	*downstairs, down, below*
ahí	*there*	delante	*in front*	arriba (Higher)	*upstairs, up there*
allá	*there*				

Mi tía trabaja aquí. *My aunt works here.* (*there* — allí)

Está muy cerca. *It's very near.* (*far away* — lejos)

...or when it's happening

Adverbs of time say when or how often something is done. They can come at the beginning or end of a sentence, or after the verb they describe.

ya	*already*	luego	*later, afterwards*	pronto	*soon, early*
todavía	*still*	siempre	*always, forever*	temprano	*early*
ahora	*now*	nunca	*never*	tarde	*late*
antes	*before, beforehand*	a veces	*sometimes*	jamás (H)	*never*
después	*after, afterwards*	a menudo	*often*	aún (H)	*still, yet*

Ya tengo un sombrero. *I already have a hat.*

Siempre veo la tele. *I always watch TV.*

Adverbial phrases work like adverbs

Adverbial phrases can often be used like adverbs and describe how, when or where something is happening. They are placed at the beginning or end of a sentence, or after the verb they describe.

en línea	*online*	al aire libre	*outdoors*	(H) por todas partes	*everywhere*

Hago compras en línea. *I do shopping online.*

Paso tiempo al aire libre. *I spend time outdoors.*

Grammar Questions

Translate these phrases into **Spanish**.

1. My shoes are here.
2. I want to leave now.
3. Sometimes I travel.
4. We live far away.
5. The shop is over there.
6. (H) There are birds everywhere. (H)

I want a tip about adverb placement, and I want it ahora...

Adverbs of manner and adverbs of place come after the verb they describe, while adverbs of certainty usually come before the verb. Adverbs of time can go at the beginning or end of a sentence, or come after the verb.

Comparative and Superlative Adverbs

Quick Quiz

You can use similar techniques to those you learned on p.118 to compare how people do things.

Comparative adverbs compare how people do actions

1) To say that something is done 'more ...ly', use 'más ... que'.

Pilar trabaja más alegremente que Hani. *Pilar works more happily than Hani.*

2) If you want to say that something is done 'less ...ly', use 'menos ... que'.

Hani trabaja menos alegremente que Pilar. *Hani works less happily than Pilar.*

3) To say that someone does something 'as ... as' someone else, use 'tan ... como'.

Pilar trabaja tan alegremente como Hani. *Pilar works as happily as Hani.*

Paula and Alazne found that pizza always helped them work more happily.

Superlative adverbs say who does something the 'most ...ly'

Higher

To say someone does something 'the most ...ly', follow this pattern. Remember to change 'el' to 'la' if the subject is feminine, 'los' if it's a masculine plural subject, and 'las' for a feminine plural subject.

Ligaya es la que trabaja más alegremente. *Ligaya is the one who works the most happily.*
Juan es el que baila menos rápidamente. *Juan is the one who dances the least quickly.*

Watch out for irregulars...

bien	*well*	→	mejor	*better*	→ (H) el que mejor...	*the one who ... the best*
mal	*badly*	→	peor	*worse*	→ (H) el que peor...	*the one who ... the worst*

Juego mejor que él. *I play better than him.*

Escribo peor que Lin. *I write worse than Lin.*

Higher

Él es el que peor cocina. *He's the one who cooks the worst.*
Ellas son las que mejor actúan. *They are the ones who act the best.*

In Spanish, irregular superlative adverbs come straight after the 'que' and before the verb.

Grammar Questions

Complete the sentences in **Spanish** so that they match the words in the brackets.

1. Wafa come .... yo. (more quickly than)
2. Yo pinto .... ella. (better than)
3. Luis baila .... tú. (as well as)

Higher

4. Alba (f) es .... habla .... (the most calmly)
5. Ellos son .... estudian. (the best)
6. Inoke (m) es .... corre. (the worst)

Superlative Simon — the ultimate superhero...

For regular comparative adverb structures, remember to sandwich the adverb in between 'más / menos / tan' and 'como / que'. For irregular comparative adverb structures, just stick the adverb straight before the 'que'.

Quick Quiz

Quantifiers and Intensifiers

You can use this page to say you've had enough of Spanish adjectives and adverbs...

Quantifiers say how many or how much

1) Just saying 'I have apples' is boring. Use quantifiers to say you have lots of apples — or too many. You can use quantifiers as adjectives with a noun or as adverbs with a verb.

mucho	*a lot (of), much*	demasiado	*too much*
(un) poco	*not much, little*	H tanto	*so much*

These quantifiers are adverbs, but they also have adjective forms. See p.116 for these.

2) When quantifiers are adjectives, they go before the noun, and most change their endings to agree with it.

Tengo muchos planes. *I have a lot of plans.*

pocas personas *not many people*

3) When you use quantifiers with verbs, they work like adverbs, so they go after the verb and don't change their endings.

Hablas demasiado. *You (inf., sing.) talk too much.*

Comen mucho. *They eat a lot.*

4) To say something is 'more than...' followed by a number, use 'más de'.

Intensifiers strengthen what you're saying

1) You can use intensifiers like 'very' and 'quite' to add detail to what you're saying.

2) Intensifiers go before the word they're modifying, but their endings don't change at all.

muy	*very*	bastante	*rather, quite, enough*

Simón está muy feliz. *Simón is very happy.*

Comemos bastante bien. *We eat quite well.*

Adding 'ísimo' makes adjectives stronger

1) If you add 'ísimo/a/os/as' to an adjective, it's like adding 'very' — it makes the meaning stronger.

2) The ending of 'ísimo' changes like other regular adjectives to agree with the noun it describes.

Su voz es hermosísima. *Her voice is very beautiful.*

Él es divertidísimo. *He is very funny.*

Grammar Questions

Rewrite each sentence, changing the quantifier or intensifier so it's used correctly.

1. Hay demasiado gatos aquí.
2. Es interesante bastante.
3. Tengo muchas amigos.
4. Un poca cantan.
5. Es un libro mucho bueno.
6. Hay una playa buenísimo.

I personally can't get enough of quantifiers and intensifiers...

But I think I've got too many apples. Remember — you only need to change a quantifier to agree if it's used with a noun. Quantifiers that are used with verbs don't need to agree and intensifiers don't change either.

Adjectives and Adverbs — Grammar List

If you've been thinking 'my nouns and verbs need extra details', then this list of adjectives and adverbs is a real treat.

Adjectives

Adjectives often change to match the gender and number of what they describe. Many feminine adjectives change an '-o' to '-a'.

bueno/a	*good*	propio/a	*own*
malo/a	*bad*	H ambos/as	*both*

Other adjectives only change as plurals.

grande *big, large (post-noun)*

Some adjectives change when they go in front of a masculine singular noun.

buen	*good (pre-noun)*	gran	*big, great (pre-noun)*
mal	*bad (pre-noun)*		

Their position can change their meaning.

único/a	*only (pre-noun), unique (post-noun)*
nuevo/a	*new (pre-noun), newly-made (post-noun)*
viejo/a	*old (long-standing) (pre-noun), old, aged (post-noun)*
antiguo/a	*former (pre-noun), old (pre- and post-noun), antique (post-noun)*

Possessive Adjectives

mi	*my*	nuestro/a/os/as	*our*
tu	*your (inf., sing.)*	vuestro/a/os/as	*your (inf., pl.)*
su	*his, her, its, your (form.), their*		

Higher:

mío/a/os/as	*mine*
tuyo/a/os/as	*your (inf., sing.)*
suyo/a/os/as	*his, her, its, your (form.), their*
nuestro/a/os/as	*our*
vuestro/a/os/as	*your (form., pl.)*

These Higher words are long-form possessive adjectives.

Demonstrative Adjectives

este/a	*this*	ese/a	*that*	H aquel/la	*that*
estos/as	*these*	esos/as	*those*	H aquellos/as	*those*

Indefinite Adjectives

cada	*each, every*	alguno/a	*a/an, any*
otro/a	*other, another*	ningún	*no, not...any (m, pre-noun)*
todo/a	*all, the whole (+ noun)*	ninguno/a	*no, not...any*
mismo/a	*same*		
algún	*a/an, any (m, pre-noun)*		

Adverbs

For most adverbs, add '-mente' to the feminine form of an adjective.

absolutamente	*absolutely*	simplemente	*simply*
directamente	*directly, straight away*	normalmente	*normally*
exactamente	*exactly*	generalmente	*generally*
inmediatamente	*immediately*	especialmente	*mainly, especially*
solamente	*only*	finalmente	*finally*
perfectamente	*perfectly*	H aproximadamente	*approximately*
verdaderamente	*truly*	H actualmente	*currently, at present*
desafortunadamente	*unfortunately*		
recientemente	*recently*		

Others don't follow this pattern.

también	*also*	H aún	*still, yet*
H además	*also, besides, as well*	H incluso	*including, even*

Adverbs of manner describe how something is done.

bien *well, good* mal *badly* así *like this/that*

Adverbs of certainty describe how likely something is.

probablemente *probably* H quizá(s) *perhaps, maybe*

Adverbs of place describe where something happens.

acá	*here*	arriba	*upstairs, up there*	H dentro	*inside*
ahí, allá	*there*	H abajo	*downstairs, down, below*	H por todas partes	*everywhere*
detrás	*behind*				

Adverbs of time show when or how often something occurs.

ya	*already*	siempre	*always, forever*	Higher: casi	*almost, nearly*
sólo	*only, just*	todavía	*still*	Higher: jamás	*never*
pronto	*soon, early*	a menudo	*often*	Higher: primero	*firstly*
temprano	*early*				
entonces	*then, so*				

Comparatives

más (...que)	*more (...than), adj. / adv. + er (...than)*
menos (...que)	*less (...than), fewer (...than)*
tan...como	*as...as*
mejor	*better*
peor	*worse*

Superlatives

Higher:

el/la/los/las mejor(es)	*the best*
el/la/los/las peor(es)	*the worst*
el/la/los/las menor(es)	*the youngest*
el/la/los/las mayor(es)	*the oldest*

Quantifiers & Intensifiers

Quantifiers say how much of something there is.

mucho	*a lot (of), much*
(un) poco	*not much, little*
demasiado	*too much*
H tanto	*so much*

Intensifiers add details.

muy	*very*
bastante	*rather, quite, enough*

Revision Summary Test for Section Twelve

Ah, another section down. You know what that means — a lovely summary test to have a crack at.

- These questions are **really tricky**, but they'll help you see **how well you know your stuff**.
- Tackle the **revision summary test** below, or scan the QR code to do it **online**. You can **keep track of your progress** online and see **which areas need more work**.
- There are **sample answers** here: www.cgpbooks.co.uk/GraciasExtras

Summary Test

Adjectives

1) Add the adjective in brackets to each phrase so that it agrees with the noun.
   a) las chicas (feliz) b) el hombre (optimista) c) los exámenes (difícil) d) un calcetín (rosa)
2) Turn these verbs into adjectives using '-able': a) lavar b) olvidar c) salvar
3) Rewrite each sentence, putting the adjective in brackets into the right position.
   a) Quiero pantalones. (esos) c) Es una casa. (gran) e) Es mi móvil. (primer)
   b) Es la película. (tercera) d) Es una casa. (grande) f) Hay tiendas. (muchas)
4) Say the following phrases in Spanish:
   a) each horse b) another hamburger c) all night d) the same pen e) any eggs
5) (H) Translate these sentences into Spanish using long-form possessive adjectives.
   a) The best thing about my dress is the colour. b) Her shoes are in that box over there.

Adverbs

6) Turn these adjectives into adverbs: a) extraordinario b) duro c) malo d) fácil e) bueno
7) Choose the adverb or adverbial phrase in these sentences, then translate each sentence into English.
   a) Ya he terminado el libro. c) A veces voy al teatro. e) Probablemente beberé café.
   b) Me encantaría estudiar allí. d) El coche llegó finalmente. f) Hago ejercicio al aire libre.
8) Rewrite each sentence so that the adverbs are in the correct position.
   a) Es guay independientemente viajar. b) Lejos vivo de mi colegio. c) Está ahora trabajando.
9) (H) Fill in the gaps by choosing the most appropriate adverb from each list.
   a) .... veré a mi amigo mañana. (Quizás / Aún / Jamás)
   b) Han limpiado todos los cuartos, ... el baño. (incluso / ya / sólo)

Comparatives and Superlatives

10) Correct the mistakes in these sentences.
    a) Carmen habla más rápidamente como Dani. c) Odio estudiar. Estudio más mal que tú.
    b) Mi prima es tan directa que mi tía. d) Monika puede cantar mayor que yo.
11) Translate each sentence into Spanish: a) Raúl is older than his sister. b) We write better than them.
12) (H) Translate these sentences into Spanish:
    a) Jorge (m) is the proudest. c) Those girls are the youngest of the class.
    b) Paula (f) is the one who paints the worst. d) They are the ones who run the slowest.

Quantifiers and Intensifiers

13) Complete each sentence by adding the quantifier or intensifier in brackets.
    a) Es una asignatura .... divertida. (quite) c) Mi amigo estudia .... (too much)
    b) Tengo .... cuadernos. (many) d) .... gente vive en este pueblo. (a few)
14) For each sentence, say if the part in bold is a quantifier (Q) or intensifier (I), then translate the sentence.
    a) La fiesta fue **muy** emocionante. c) Ayer dormí **poco**.
    b) Este verano voy a viajar **mucho**. d) Has bebido **bastante** leche.
15) Translate these sentences into Spanish, adding the ending in brackets to form the adjective.
    a) Paella is very good. (-ísima) b) The castle is very big. (-ísimo)

Verbs in the Present Tense

Quick Quiz

As a reward for all your hard work, I've bought you a present in the form of a tense. You lucky thing.

Verbs are actions

1) A verb is an action word like 'speak', 'eat' and 'live'.
2) Verbs can be put into different tenses, such as the future or past. For example, 'Yesterday, I ate a pie'.
3) To use a verb, you need to know its infinitive — the form you find in a dictionary, e.g. 'hablar' (*to speak*).

Forming the present tense

1) Regular verbs in Spanish end in '-ar', '-er' or '-ir'. To form the present tense of these regular verbs, you need to find the stem. To do this, remove the last two letters from the infinitive.

Infinitive	Remove last two letters	Stem
hablar	-ar	habl-

2) Then add the endings below to the stem.

-ar verbs

I speak	hablo	hablamos	we speak
you (inf., sing.) speak	hablas	habláis	you (inf., pl.) speak
he/she/it/you (form., sing.) speak(s)	habla	hablan	they/you (form., pl.) speak

Cantan. *They sing.*

Camina. *He walks.*

-er verbs

I eat	como	comemos	we eat
you (inf., sing.) eat	comes	coméis	you (inf., pl.) eat
he/she/it/you (form., sing.) eat(s)	come	comen	they/you (form., pl.) eat

Creo. *I believe.*

Depende. *It depends.*

-ir verbs

I live	vivo	vivimos	we live
you (inf., sing.) live	vives	vivís	you (inf., pl.) live
he/she/it/you (form., sing.) live(s)	vive	viven	they/you (form., pl.) live

Abren. *They open.*

Escribe. *She writes.*

H 3) Some verb forms change the spelling in their stem to avoid changing the pronunciation.

coger (*to catch*) ⟶ Cojo. *I catch.*

When to use the present tense

For another way to say what you're doing now, see p.136-137.

1) Use the present tense for actions taking place now...

Hablo español. *I speak / I'm speaking* Spanish.

2) ...or for things that take place regularly.

Canto todos los días. *I sing* every day.

3) You can also use it for things that are about to happen.

Mañana voy al cine. *Tomorrow I'm going* to the cinema.

Grammar Questions

Put each of these infinitives into the present tense. The form of the verb is given in brackets.

1. bailar (yo)
2. beber (nosotros)
3. discutir (ustedes)
4. romper (ellas)
5. aprender (él)
6. mandar (vosotros)
7. escribir (tú)
8. visitar (ellos)

As the old saying goes, there's no tense like the present...

If you want full marks, you'll need to know the present tense inside out, back to front and top to bottom.

Quick Quiz

Irregular Verbs in the Present Tense

My irregular verb senses are tingling... It must be time to look at some rule breakers.

Some verbs are stem-changing

These are also called 'radical-changing verbs'.

Adva was excited about all types of stem changes.

1) A stem-changing verb is a verb that changes its spelling in the present tense.
2) Usually, the 'e' in the stem changes to 'ie', or the 'o' or 'u' changes to 'ue'. Some verbs change the 'e' in their stem to 'i'.
3) The stem changes in every form apart from the 'we' and 'you (inf. pl.)' forms.

pensar — to think (e to ie)	
I think	pienso
you (inf., sing.) think	piensas
he/she/it/you (form., sing.) think(s)	piensa
we think	pensamos
you (inf., pl.) think	pensáis
they/you (form., pl.) think	piensan

Even though their stems change, their endings are regular.

These verbs also change their 'e' to 'ie'...

cerrar	*to close*	despertar(se)	*to wake up*
comenzar	*to start*	querer	*to want, love*
preferir	*to prefer*	H empezar	*to start*

encontrar — to find (o to ue)	
I find	encuentro
you (inf., sing.) find	encuentras
he/she/it/you (form., sing.) find(s)	encuentra
we find	encontramos
you (inf., pl.) find	encontráis
they/you (form., pl.) find	encuentran

These verbs also change their 'o' or 'u' to 'ue'...

doler	*to hurt*	jugar	*to play*
dormir	*to sleep*	llover	*to rain*
poder	*to be able to*	volver	*to return*

pedir — to ask for (e to i)	
I ask for	pido
you (inf., sing.) ask for	pides
he/she/it/you (form., sing.) ask(s) for	pide
we ask for	pedimos
you (inf., pl.) ask for	pedís
they/you (form., pl.) ask for	piden

These verbs also change their 'e' to 'i'...

You also drop the 'u' in the present tense 'I' form of seguir — 'sigo'.

decir	*to say, tell*	servir	*to serve*
repetir	*to repeat*	seguir	*to follow*
vestirse	*to get dressed*	H elegir	*to choose*

Some stem-changing verbs follow a different pattern

1) In some stem-changing verbs, the stem only changes its spelling in the 'I' form. All the other forms of the verb follow the same pattern as regular verbs in the present tense.

poner — to put (add g)	
I put	pongo

Pongo mis dibujos sobre la mesa. *I put my drawings on the table.*

conocer — to know (c to zc)	
I know	conozco

Conozco a unas personas aquí. *I know a few people here.*

2) Here are a couple of examples of verbs that follow a similar pattern to 'poner'...

salir — to leave, go out	salgo	*I leave, I go out*
traer — to bring	traigo	*I bring*

'Traer' is a little different — the 'e' changes to 'i' as well.

3) ...and here are some that follow a similar pattern to 'conocer':

reducir — to reduce	reduzco	*I reduce*
H ofrecer — to offer	ofrezco	*I offer*

'Hacer', 'ir' and 'tener'

In Spanish, the verbs 'to do / make', 'to go' and 'to have' are irregular.

hacer — to do, make

I do, make	hago
you (inf., sing.) do, make	haces
he/she/it/you (form., sing.) do(es), make(s)	hace
we do, make	hacemos
you (inf., pl.) do, make	hacéis
they/you (form., pl.) do, make	hacen

Only the 'I' form is irregular in the present tense.

Hago mis deberes. *I do my homework.*

Lo hago sonreír. *I make him smile.*

ir — to go

All of the present tense forms of 'ir' are irregular.

I go	voy
you (inf., sing.) go	vas
he/she/it/you (form., sing.) go(es)	va
we go	vamos
you (inf., pl.) go	vais
they/you (form., pl.) go	van

The verb 'dar' (to give) follows the same pattern as 'ir' in the present tense — 'I give' is 'doy', 'you give' is 'das', etc.

Va al concierto. *He's going to the concert.*

Siempre van allí. *They always go there.*

tener — to have

I have	tengo
you (inf., sing.) have	tienes
he/she/it/you (form., sing.) has/have	tiene
we have	tenemos
you (inf., pl.) have	tenéis
they/you (form., pl.) have	tienen

'Venir' (to come) follows a similar pattern to 'tener'. It also has an irregular 'I' form — 'vengo'.

Tengo cinco primos. *I have five cousins.*

Tiene mucho papel. *She has a lot of paper.*

'Tener' can also sometimes mean 'to be'

You can sometimes use 'tener' + noun to mean 'to be' + adjective.

You don't need an article for the nouns when you use them in this way with 'tener'.

Tienen hambre. *They are hungry.*

¿Tiene sed? *Is she thirsty?*

Tengo miedo. *I'm afraid.*

Tiene quince años. *He is fifteen.*

Tenemos calor. *We are hot.*

¿Tienen frío? *Are they cold?*

Grammar Questions

Correct the spelling mistake in each of these sentences.

1. Comenza a las tres.
2. Quieremos leche.
3. Yo do el libro a Lola.
4. Podes entrar.
5. Repeten las direcciones.
6. Penso que es importante.

Translate these sentences into **Spanish**, making sure the stem of each verb is spelt correctly.

7. I'm also coming to the party.
8. We're going there tomorrow.
9. I get dressed quickly.
10. I don't have a pen.
11. The students are hungry.
12. I recognise her from the film.

Irregular verbs are a regular pain...

Just like the neighbour's cat, Pickles, who insists on leaving perfumed presents in my flowerbeds. I will stop you, Pickles, even if it's the last thing I do... Ahem. Sorry — I got a bit carried away there. As you were...

Quick Quiz

'Ser' and 'Estar' in the Present Tense

The verbs 'ser' and 'estar' both mean 'to be'. If that isn't confusing enough, they're used in different situations *and* they're both irregular. I'm starting to feel a bit dizzy...

Use 'ser' for permanent things

The verb 'ser' means 'to be'. It's used for permanent things. You need it to...

ser — to be	
I am	soy
you are (inf., sing.)	eres
he/she/it/you (form., sing.) is/are	es
we are	somos
you are (inf., pl.)	sois
they/you (form., pl.) are	son

1) ...talk about nationalities.

Somos ingleses. *We are English.*

2) ...talk about someone's job.

Mi tío es profesor. *My uncle is a teacher.*

3) ...say someone's name or say who someone is in relation to you.

Nerea y Sabina son mis primas. *Nerea and Sabina are my cousins.*

4) ...describe the physical characteristics of a person or thing.

Es largo. *It is long.*

Eres muy alto. *You (inf., sing.) are very tall.*

5) ...describe someone's personality.

Sois amables. *You (inf., pl.) are kind.*

Son felices. *They are happy.*

Juma was ser-tain he wasn't that tall...

Use 'estar' for temporary things and locations

'Estar' also means 'to be'. You use it to...

estar — to be	
I am	estoy
you are (inf., sing.)	estás
he/she/it/you (form., sing.) is/are	está
we are	estamos
you are (inf., pl.)	estáis
they/you (form., pl.) are	están

1) ...talk about things that might change in the future.

Estoy bastante enfermo. *I'm quite ill.*
(But you might not be ill next week.)

Estás muy triste hoy. *You (inf., sing.) are very sad today.*
(But you might not be sad tomorrow.)

2) ...talk about where someone or something is.

Madrid está en España. *Madrid is in Spain.*

Estamos en casa. *We are at home.*

Grammar Questions

Decide whether you need 'ser' or 'estar' in each of these sentences.

1. Es / Está muy enfadado hoy.
2. Siempre es / está trabajador.
3. Somos / Estamos de Hull.
4. Soy / Estoy en Bradford.
5. Es / Está mi hermano.
6. Mi padre es / está doctor.

To be or to be — that's a question worth asking...

'Ser' and 'estar' are two of the most important verbs in Spanish — you'll need them all the time. It might take a while to get your head around when to use each one, but the more you practise, the easier it'll become.

The Preterite Tense

Quick Quiz

Fun fact: 'entire pester teeth' is an anagram of 'the preterite tense'. You heard it here first.

I went — *The preterite tense*

To form the preterite tense of regular verbs, find the stem (see p.125) and then add these endings...

-ar verb endings

I	-é	-amos	we
you (inf., sing.)	-aste	-asteis	you (inf., pl.)
he/she/it/ you (form., sing.)	-ó	-aron	they/ you (form., pl.)

-er and -ir verb endings

I	-í	-imos	we
you (inf., sing.)	-iste	-isteis	you (inf., pl.)
he/she/it/ you (form., sing.)	-ió	-ieron	they/ you (form., pl.)

Don't forget the accent — without it, you'd be saying 'I speak to Sonal'.

Habló con Sonal. *He spoke to Sonal.*

Some verbs are irregular in the preterite tense

1) Here are three important irregular verbs in the preterite tense. Watch out — 'ser' and 'ir' are the same.

ser — to be; ir — to go	
I was / went	fui
you (inf., sing.) were / went	fuiste
he/she/it/you (form., sing.) was (were) / went	fue
we were / went	fuimos
you (inf., pl.) were / went	fuisteis
they/you (form., pl.) were / went	fueron

dar — to give	
I gave	di
you (inf., sing.) gave	diste
he/she/it/you (form., sing.) gave	dio
we gave	dimos
you (inf., pl.) gave	disteis
they/you (form., pl.) gave	dieron

2) Some verbs change their stem in the preterite tense. If you know what the stem change is, you can predict what the verb is going to be in its other forms.

Infinitive	I	he/she/it/you (form., sing.)	Infinitive	I	he/she/it/you (form., sing.)
decir (*to say*)	dije	dijo	tener (*to have*)	tuve	tuvo
poder (*to be able to*)	pude	pudo	estar (*to be*)	estuve	estuvo
poner (*to put*)	puse	puso	hacer (*to do, make*)	hice	hizo
querer (*to want*)	quise	quiso	venir (*to come*)	vine	vino
traer (*to bring*)	traje	trajo			

The 'he/she/it/ you (form., sing.)' form is sometimes different to what you might expect.

Higher

3) Verbs ending in '-aer' and '-eer' add 'y' in the third person forms, e.g. 'cayó' (*she fell*), 'leyeron' (*they read*).

4) Other verbs only have stem changes in the 'he/she/it' and 'they' forms. Some change their 'e' to 'i' ('pedir' becomes 'pidió' / 'pidieron'). Some change their 'o' to 'u' ('dormir' becomes 'durmió' / 'durmieron').

5) Some verbs have spelling changes in the 'I' form of the preterite tense. Verbs ending in '-car' change from 'c' to 'qu' ('tocar' becomes 'toqué'). Verbs ending in '-zar' change from 'z' to 'c' ('cruzar' becomes 'crucé'). Verbs ending in '-gar' change from 'g' to 'gu' ('llegar' becomes 'llegué').

Grammar Questions

Put these verbs into the preterite tense. The subject is given in brackets.

1. venir (tú) **2.** cargar (ellos) **3.** dar (yo) **4.** ir (él) H **5.** pedir (usted) **6.** jugar (yo) H

Wanted: two irregular verbs masquerading as each other...

Don't panic —the context of a sentence should help you work out whether you're looking at 'ser' or 'ir'.

Quick Quiz

The Imperfect Tense

If you wanted to talk about what you 'were doing' before you turned the page, this is how you'd do it...

I was going / I used to go — *The imperfect tense*

1) To form the imperfect tense, find the stem (see p.125) and then add these endings. The 'I' form and the 'he/she/it/you (form., sing.)' form look the same, so you'll have to use the context to tell which is which.

-ar verb endings

I	-aba
you (inf., sing.)	-abas
he/she/it/you (form., sing.)	-aba

Higher

we	-ábamos
you (inf., pl.)	-abais
they/you (form., pl.)	-aban

Compraba zapatos.
I was buying / used to buy shoes.

-er and -ir verb endings

I	-ía
you (inf., sing.)	-ías
he/she/it/you (form., sing.)	-ía

Higher

we	-íamos
you (inf., pl.)	-íais
they/you (form., pl.)	-ían

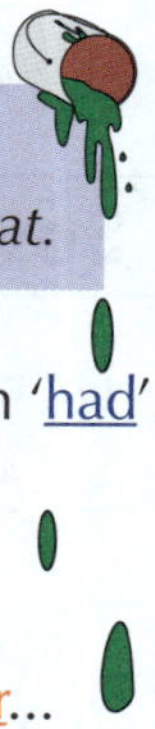

Comía carne.
I was eating / used to eat meat.

2) Some verbs have slightly different translations too — 'estar' can mean 'was/were' and 'tener' can mean 'had'.

There are three irregular verbs in the imperfect tense

1) 'Ser', 'ir' and 'ver' are the only three verbs which don't follow the pattern. 'Ser' and 'ir' are irregular...

ser — to be

I	era
you (inf., sing.)	eras
he/she/it/you (form., sing.)	era

Higher

we	éramos
you (inf., pl.)	erais
they/you (form., pl.)	eran

Era rubio.
He was / used to be blonde.

ir — to go

I	iba
you (inf., sing.)	ibas
he/she/it/you (form., sing.)	iba

Higher

we	íbamos
you (inf., pl.)	ibais
they/you (form., pl.)	iban

Iba de compras.
I was going / used to go shopping.

2) ...but 'ver' is almost regular — just add the '-er' endings onto 've-', e.g. 'veía'.

Veía la tele. *I was watching / used to watch TV.*

Había — *There was / There were*

'Hay' and 'había' come from the verb 'haber'.

In the present tense, 'hay' means 'there is' or 'there are'. The imperfect form of 'hay' is 'había', which means 'there was' or 'there were' — it stays the same, regardless of whether the noun is singular or plural.

Había mucho ruido. *There was a lot of noise.*

Había nubes. *There were clouds.*

Grammar Questions

Put these verbs into the imperfect tense. The subject is given in brackets.

1. cantar (tú) **2.** decir (él) **3.** aprender (usted) **4.** pagar (ella) **5.** estar (yo) **6.** tener (tú)

H: **7.** volver (ustedes) **8.** seguir (vosotros) **9.** ser (nosotros) **10.** ir (ellos)

Learning the imperfect — a perfect way to spend your time...

Everyone has to learn the singular imperfect forms, but only Higher tier students need to learn the plural forms.

Using the Past Tenses

Quick Quiz

Choosing which past tense to use isn't always easy, but I'm here to help you crack it.

Learn when to use the preterite tense vs. the imperfect tense

1) Use the preterite tense to talk about a single completed action in the past or an event that happened during a set period of time.

Fui al cine el jueves. *I went to the cinema on Thursday.*

Ayer hizo calor. *Yesterday it was hot.*

2) Use the imperfect tense to talk about what you used to do repeatedly or to describe something in the past.

Hacía calor. *It was hot.*

Iba al cine cada jueves. *I used to go to the cinema every Thursday.*

3) You can also use the imperfect tense to talk about something that was happening when something else happened. You need to use the preterite tense for the action that interrupts the imperfect.

Cuando caminaba a Correos, vi a mi amigo. *When I was walking to the post office, I saw my friend.*

I have done — *The present perfect tense*

1) You use the present perfect tense to say 'have done' or to talk about something that happened recently. To form it, you need the present tense of the verb 'haber' and the past participle.

haber — to have...

I	he	hemos	we
you (inf., sing.)	has	habéis	you (inf., pl.)
he/she/it/you (form., sing.)	ha	han	they/you (form., pl.)

Han jugado al tenis.
They have played tennis.

'Jugado' is a past participle.

2) To form a past participle, you remove the 'ar' from '-ar' verbs and add '-ado'.

3) For '-er' and '-ir' verbs, you remove the 'er' or 'ir' and add '-ido'.

ayudar *(to help)* ⟶ ayudado *(helped)*

comer *(to eat)* ⟶ comido *(eaten)*

The past participle always stays the same — you don't need to make it feminine or plural.

4) There are some irregular participles that don't follow these rules. You'll just have to learn them.

Infinitive	Past participle
ver	visto *(seen, watched)*
hacer	hecho *(done, made)*
decir	dicho *(said, told)*

Infinitive	Past participle
poner	puesto *(put)*
volver	vuelto *(returned)*
romper(se)	roto *(broken)*

Infinitive	Past participle
escribir	escrito *(written)*
abrir	abierto *(opened)*
H descubrir	descubierto *(discovered)*

Grammar Questions

Translate these sentences into **Spanish**.

1. He has travelled to Spain.
2. She has run 500 metres.
3. They have finished the exam.
4. Have you (tú) eaten already?
5. We have written a letter.
6. They have returned home.

Preterite or imperfect? It's a very tense business...

To say what 'has happened' very recently, use the present perfect tense. To say what 'happened' once or over a set time period, use the preterite. For descriptions or repeated actions in the past, use the imperfect tense.

Quick Quiz

The Future Tenses

You'll need to talk about things that are going to happen at some point in the future. There are two ways you can do it — and the first one's a piece of cake...

I'm going to... — *The immediate future tense*

This tense is also known as the 'periphrastic future'.

1) The immediate future tense can be used to talk about something that's about to happen, as well as something further on in the future.
2) To form the immediate future, take the present tense of 'ir' (*to go*) that goes with the person you're talking about.
3) Then, add 'a' and a verb in the infinitive.

ir — to go	
I am going	voy
you (inf., sing.) are going	vas
he/she/it/you (form., sing.) is/are going	va
we are going	vamos
you (inf., pl.) are going	vais
they/you (form., pl.) are going	van

voy
I am going
This is the present tense of 'ir'.
\+ a +
comer
to eat
This is another verb in the infinitive.
=
Voy a comer.
I am going to / will eat.
This is a sentence about the future.

I will... — *The proper future tense*

This tense is also known as the 'inflectional future'.

1) Use the proper future tense to say what will happen.
2) To form it, take the 'future stem' of the verb — for most verbs, this is the infinitive.
3) Add the ending that matches the person you're talking about (the endings are the same for all verbs).

hablar *infinitive* + é *future ending* = hablaré *I will talk.*

Future endings	
I	-é
you (inf., sing.)	-ás
he/she/it/you (form., sing.)	-á
we	-emos
you (inf., pl.)	-éis
they/you (form., pl.)	-án

Higher (we, you (inf., pl.), they/you (form., pl.))

4) There are a few verbs that have a special future stem, so you just have to learn them off by heart. These are the most important ones.

Infinitive	'I' form
tener *(to have)*	tendré
hacer *(to do, make)*	haré
poder *(to be able to)*	podré
poner *(to put)*	pondré

Infinitive	'he/she/it' form
haber *(to have...)*	habrá

'Haber' is a bit different to other verbs — you only really need to use it in the 'he/she/it' form.

Higher

Infinitive	'I' form
saber *(to know)*	sabré
querer *(to want)*	querré
venir *(to come)*	vendré
decir *(to say)*	diré
salir *(to go out)*	saldré

Grammar Questions

Put these present tense verbs into the immediate and proper future tenses, keeping the subject the same.

1. haces
2. tiene
3. baila
4. doy
5. puedes
6. juego
H **7.** ponen
H **8.** venimos
9. queremos
10. vivís
H **11.** dice
H **12.** sabéis

Predicting the future might be tough, but talking about it isn't...

Use the immediate future tense to talk about something that's going to happen soon, e.g. scoffing a slice of cherry pie. Use the proper future tense to talk about things that 'will happen' further ahead in the future.

The Conditional

Quick Quiz

You could gloss over this page, but I would advise against it...

Future stem + imperfect -er / -ir endings — *The conditional*

1) The conditional can be used for saying 'would'. It uses the same stems as the proper future tense (see p.132) and adds these endings:

Pepe would eat the whole bowlful — if only Isuri would put it down...

Conditional endings

I	-ía
you (inf., sing.)	-ías
he/she/it/you (form., sing.)	-ía

Higher

we	-íamos
you (inf., pl.)	-íais
they/you (form., pl.)	-ían

comer
to eat
This is the infinitive. Not all verbs use the same future stem though (see p.132).

\+

comía
I was eating.
This is the -er / -ir ending of the imperfect tense.

=

comería
I would eat.
This is a sentence in the conditional.

2) You can combine the conditional with other tenses to make more complicated sentences:

Bailaría, pero me duelen los pies. *I would dance, but my feet hurt.*

Le gustaría ir a la playa, pero no puede ir porque está lloviendo.
She would like to go to the beach, but she can't go because it's raining.

For more on conjunctions, check out p.111.

Irregular verbs in the conditional

The stems for irregular verbs are the same ones you use for the proper future tense (see p.132). You just add the conditional endings instead:

Infinitive	'I' form
tener *(to have)*	tendría
hacer *(to do, make)*	haría
poder *(to be able to)*	podría
poner *(to put)*	pondría

Infinitive	'he/she/it' form
haber *(to have...)*	habría

Higher

Infinitive	'I' form
saber *(to know)*	sabría
querer *(to want)*	querría
venir *(to come)*	vendría
decir *(to say)*	diría
salir *(to go out)*	saldría

Saldría de la casa, pero estoy cansado.
I would leave the house, but I'm tired.

¿Podría ayudarme? *Could you (form., sing.) help me?*

Using 'poder' (to be able to) in the conditional lets you say 'could'.

Grammar Questions

Write these verbs in the conditional. The subject has been given to you in brackets.

1. ir (yo)
2. cantar (él)
3. poner (tú)
4. hablar (usted)
5. hacer (ella)
6. pedir (yo)

H
7. decir (vosotros)
8. venir (nosotros)
9. querer (ustedes)
10. saber (ellos)

I'll hand over the pizza on one condition...

You recite all those irregular stems while patting your head, rubbing your stomach and standing on one leg. I'll have a go too. Don't forget that regular and irregular verbs use the same endings in the conditional.

Quick Quiz

Modal Verbs

Modal verbs help you express desire, ability or obligation, so you might find this page rather useful...

Deber, poder, querer, tener que, saber

1) Modal verbs are usually followed by an infinitive.

Debo terminar el proyecto ahora.
I must finish the project now.

Deben llevar una corbata para la fiesta.
They have to wear a tie for the party.

Using 'deber' in the conditional helps you say 'should'.

2) As well as 'deber' (*to have to, must*), there are four other modal verbs you need to know:

a) Use 'poder' to say 'can' or 'could'.

No puedo ir al cine. *I can't go to the cinema.*

Scary films are better at home anyway...

b) Use 'querer' to say 'want to'.

Quiero viajar a más países. *I want to travel to more countries.*

c) You can also use 'tener que' when you want to say 'have to' or 'must'.

Tengo que volver a casa a las seis. *I have to return home at six o'clock.*

'Tener' by itself isn't a modal verb. You need to add the 'que' to show the action that you have to do.

d) You can use 'saber' to say 'know how to'.

Sabe montar en bicicleta. *She knows how to ride a bicycle.*

You could also translate this sentence as 'She can ride a bicycle.'

Quisiera, me gustaría — *I would like*

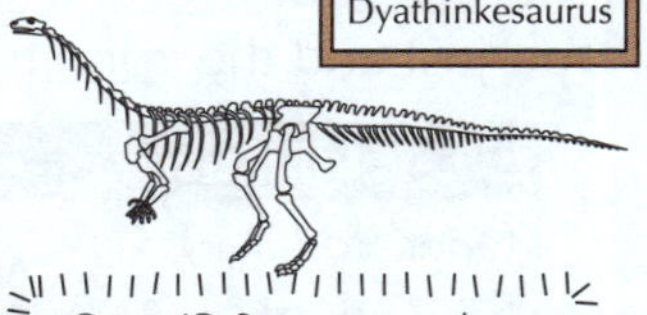

1) 'Quisiera' and 'me gustaría' are two common ways of saying 'I would like'.
Just like other modal verbs, they are followed by an infinitive.

Quisiera / Me gustaría visitar el museo. *I would like to visit the museum.*

See p.12 for more on how to use verbs like 'gustar'.

2) You can use 'quisiera' and 'me gustaría' in polite requests.

Quisiera / Me gustaría reservar una mesa para tres personas. *I would like to reserve a table for three.*

3) Using other pronouns with 'gustar' in the conditional helps you say what other people 'would like'.

¿Te gustaría leer? *Would you (inf., sing.) like to read?*

Le gustaría comer. *She would like to eat.*

Grammar Questions

Translate these sentences into **English**.

1. Debes estudiar para el examen.
2. Juanjo no sabe hablar español.
3. ¿Pueden venir a la fiesta?
4. Tenemos que escuchar bien.
5. No quiero volver a casa.
6. Quisiera pagar la cuenta.

What do verbs say in the mountains? Modalay hee hoo!

Don't be put off by their fancy-schmancy name — modal verbs are really useful for talking about things you 'can' or 'have to' do. Using them confidently in your exams will get you top marks, so show off your skills.

Reflexive Verbs and Pronouns

Quick Quiz

Sometimes you'll have to talk about things you do to yourself — like 'washing yourself' or 'getting yourself up' in the morning. It sounds weird in English, but in Spanish they do it all the time.

Me, te, se... — *Reflexive pronouns*

1) Reflexive pronouns usually mean 'self'. They change form depending on who's doing the action:

myself	me
yourself (inf., sing.)	te
himself/herself/oneself/ yourself (form., sing.)	se

Higher

ourselves	nos
yourselves (inf., pl.)	os
themselves/ yourselves (form., pl.)	se

You can tell which verbs are reflexive by checking in the dictionary. If you look up 'to wake up', it'll say 'despertarse'.

2) When you use a reflexive verb on its own, the pronoun goes before it.

Me despierto. *I wake up.*

3) If you have a verb followed by a reflexive infinitive, the reflexive pronoun goes before the first verb or at the end of the infinitive.

Me debo levantar. *I have to get up.*

Debes levantarte. *You (inf., sing.) have to get up.*

Higher

4) You can also use reflexive pronouns for reciprocal actions where two people do something to each other.

Nos hablamos. *We talk to each other.*

¿Os visteis? *Did you (inf., pl.) see each other?*

Lavarse, despertarse, levantarse... — *Reflexive verbs*

1) Reflexive verbs follow a straightforward pattern, e.g. 'lavarse' = to have a wash (literally 'to wash oneself'). You can use them in any tense as well — they take the same endings as their non-reflexive forms.

I have a wash	me lavo
you (inf., sing.) have a wash	te lavas
he/she/it/you (form., sing.) has/have a wash	se lava

Higher

we have a wash	nos lavamos
you (inf., pl.) have a wash	os laváis
they/you (form., pl.) have a wash	se lavan

Me llevo bien con él. *I get on well with him.*

H

¿Os sentís mal? *Do you (inf., pl.) feel ill?*

2) There are lots of these verbs, but here are the ones you really should know:

despertarse	*to wake up*
levantarse	*to get up*
llamarse	*to be called*
vestirse	*to get dressed*
ponerse	*to get, become (+ adjective)*
dormirse	*to fall asleep*
sentirse (H)	*to feel*
acostarse (H)	*to go to bed*

'despertarse', 'sentirse', 'vestirse' and 'acostarse' are all stem-changing verbs (see p.126).

Se puso triste. *She became sad.*

Me despierto tarde. *I wake up late.*

Grammar Questions

Write these reflexive verbs in the present tense. The subject has been given to you in brackets.

1. llamarse (yo) **3.** vestirse (él) **5.** acostarse (yo) **7.** sentirse (nosotros)

2. llevarse (tú) **4.** despertarse (usted) **6.** levantarse (ellos) **8.** ponerse (vosotros)

H (5–8)

Just me, myself and I revising reflexive verbs...

The verbs on this page will be really handy in the exam. Now, where did I put that reflexive pronoun...

Quick Quiz

Verbs with '-ing' and 'Just Done'

The continuous tenses help you specify that something is ongoing at a particular moment.

Use the present continuous for what's happening right now

1) Most of the time you'd translate 'I am doing' with the present tense, e.g. 'hago'.
2) If you want to stress that something is happening at the moment, you use the present continuous.

   Estoy cocinando. *I'm cooking.*

3) To form the present continuous, you need the correct part of 'estar' (*to be*) in the present tense...

estar — to be

I am	estoy
you (inf., sing.) are	estás
he/she/it is you (form., sing.) are	está
we are	estamos
you (inf., pl.) are	estáis
they/you (form., pl.) are	están

4) ...and the '-ing' part — also called the present participle or gerund.
5) It's made up of the stem of the verb (p.125), plus the correct ending.

   a) If it's an -ar verb, add '-ando'.

   estoy *present of 'estar'* + habl- *'hablar' stem* + -ando *-ar ending* = estoy hablando *I am speaking*

   b) If it's an -er or -ir verb, add '-iendo'.

   estás *present of 'estar'* + com- *'comer' stem* + -iendo *-er ending* = estás comiendo *you (inf., sing.) are eating*

6) There are a few stem-changing present participles. For example, in verbs like 'pedir', the 'e' changes to 'i'.

   pedir (*to ask for*) → pidiendo

   decir (*to say*) → diciendo

   The 'o' changes to 'u' in the stem of verbs like 'dormir'.

   dormir (*to sleep*) → durmiendo

   morir (*to die*) → muriendo

   If the verb's stem ends in a vowel, you add '-yendo' instead of '-iendo'.

   leer (*to read*) → leyendo

   construir (*to build*) → construyendo

The imperfect continuous is for saying what was happening

1) If you want to stress that something was happening in the past, use the imperfect continuous.
2) The imperfect continuous is similar to the present continuous, except 'estar' has to be in the imperfect tense (see p.130). You only need to know the 'I', 'you (form., sing.)' and 'he/she/it' forms for this tense.

   estaba *imperfect of 'estar'* + habl- *'hablar' stem* + -ando *-ar ending* = estaba hablando *I was speaking*

   Estaba buscando mis llaves. *I was looking for my keys.*

   Se estaba cayendo, pero lo cogí. *It was falling, but I caught it.*

   Estaba durmiendo cuando llegaron. *He was sleeping when they arrived.*

   The preterite tense is used here to show that a sudden action — the people arriving — interrupted an ongoing action in the imperfect continuous — i.e. the person sleeping.

Pavel wasn't letting a falling *fruta* block his *ruta*.

There are a few other ways to say '-ing'

Higher

1) If you want to say you continue to do something or you'll still be doing something, you can use the present tense of the verbs 'seguir' or 'continuar' with a present participle.

Ron and Sue should have checked the forecast...

sigo / continúo *present of 'seguir' / 'continuar'*	+	habl- *'hablar' stem*	+	-ando *-ar ending*	=	sigo / continúo hablando *I am still speaking*

Siguen / Continúan andando. *They continue to walk.*

Sigue / Continúa lloviendo. *It's still raining.*

In the present tense, 'continuar' has an accent on the 'u' in all its forms except the 'we' and 'you (inf., pl.)' forms.

2) To say you have been doing something for a certain amount of time, you can use the present tense of the verb 'llevar', followed by a time period and a present participle.

llevo *present of 'llevar'*	+	dos horas *time period*	+	escribiendo *present participle*	=	Llevo dos horas escribiendo. *I have been writing for two hours.*

Lleva treinta minutos limpiando su habitación. *He's been cleaning his bedroom for thirty minutes.*

Llevamos casi cinco horas chateando. *We've been chatting for almost five hours.*

3) You can also use the present tense with 'desde hace' to say how long you've been doing something.

Toco la guitarra desde hace cuatro años. *I've been playing the guitar for four years.*

'Acabar de' — *to say that something's just happened*

Higher

To say what's just happened, use the present tense of 'acabar', followed by 'de' and a verb in the infinitive.

'Acabar' is a regular '-ar' verb.

acabar de... — to have just...	
I have just...	acabo de...
you (inf., sing.) have just...	acabas de...
he/she/it/you (form., sing.) has/have just...	acaba de...
we have just...	acabamos de...
you (inf., pl.) have just...	acabáis de...
they/you (form., pl.) have just...	acaban de...

Acabo de llegar. *I have just arrived.*

Acaba de salir. *She has just left.*

Acabamos de verla. *We have just seen her.*

Grammar Questions

Put these verbs into the present continuous. The subject has been given to you in brackets.

1. traer (tú) **3.** decir (ellos) **5.** bailar (nosotros) **7.** servir (ustedes)

2. abrir (usted) **4.** correr (vosotros) **6.** leer (yo) **8.** seguir (ella)

Translate these sentences into **Spanish**.

9. He was asking for a menu. **11.** The cat was sleeping. H **13.** They have just seen the film.

10. I was studying in my room. **12.** She was working well. H **14.** We have just had breakfast.

The present continuous just goes on and on and on...

Careful, though — it isn't used as much in Spanish as it is in English, so don't be tempted to put it absolutely everywhere. Treat it like salt on chips — use sparingly for the best results. Then get it down the hatch ASAP.

Quick Quiz

Negative Forms

No, I won't write anything here about negatives. Nothing at all... except that they're pretty useful.

'No' in front of the verb means 'not'

1) To change a sentence to mean the opposite in Spanish, you have to put 'no' in front of the verb:

   Hablo español. *I speak Spanish.* → No hablo español. *I don't speak Spanish.*

2) You can do the same with all the tenses: No fui al parque. *I didn't go to the park.*

3) Sometimes you have to say 'no' twice. This is because 'no' in Spanish means both 'no' and 'not'.

   No, no quiero paella, gracias.
   No, I don't want paella, thanks.

4) You can also put 'nada' (*not anything, nothing*), 'nunca' (*never*) or 'nadie' (*nobody, no one*) before a verb to make it negative.

   Nunca canta. *She never sings.*

5) These words can be used with 'no' too. The 'no' goes before the verb and the other negative word goes after it.

   No vi a nadie. *I didn't see anybody.*

'nadie' can also mean 'anybody' or 'anyone' after a negative verb.

There are some tricky negatives to learn too

There are more negatives you need to understand — for top marks you should use them too.

(no) ... ningún / ninguna	*no, not ... any (pre-noun)*
(no) ... ninguno / ninguna	*no one, none, one (after a negative verb), anyone (after a negative verb)*
no ... todavía / todavía no ...	*not ... yet*
ya no	*no longer, no more*
(no) ... tampoco	*neither, either (after a negative verb)*
(no) ... ni ... (ni ...)	*nor, or (after a negative verb), neither ... nor ...*

Higher

See p.116 for more information on 'ningún'.

No hay ningún cuarto. *There aren't any rooms.*

No queda ninguno. *There are none left.*

No ha salido todavía. *She hasn't left yet.*

Todavía no ha llegado. *He hasn't arrived yet.*

Higher

Tampoco hay camas. *Neither are there beds.*

No me gusta tampoco. *I don't like it either.*

Ya no voy a Sevilla.
I no longer go to Seville.

No van ni a Londres ni a Madrid ni a Barcelona.
They go to neither London, nor Madrid nor Barcelona.

In negative lists, you need a 'ni' before each item.

Grammar Questions

Translate these sentences into **Spanish** using negative forms.

1. We didn't go to the library.
2. They don't have any cakes.
3. There's nothing here.
4. Nobody is in the car.
H **5.** It's neither red nor green.
H **6.** We no longer go to the gym.

On a positive note, you've nearly finished another page...

Sometimes you don't need 'no' — just put the negative word before the verb to make the sentence negative.

Impersonal Verbs and the Passive

Quick Quiz

Quick — do your best impression of a sponge and soak up all the information on this page...

Impersonal verbs use a generic subject

You can make any Spanish verb impersonal by using its 'he/she/it' form and adding 'se' before it.

1) Impersonal verbs don't have a specific subject — they use a general one like 'it' or 'one'.
2) You can use 'se puede' to say 'you (general) / one can' and 'se necesita' to say 'you (general) / one needs to'.

Se puede comer. *You (general) can eat.*

¿Se necesita salir? *Does one need to leave?*

3) Use 'hace' and a noun to talk about the weather. See p.59 for more.

Hace calor. *It is hot.*

4) Here are some more important impersonal verbs you need to know:

Impersonal verb	Meaning	Example sentence
hay	there is / there are	Hay libros en esta caja. (*There are books in this box.*)
hay que	you (general) / one must	Hay que reciclar. (*One must recycle.*)
parece	it seems	Parece un poco diferente. (*It seems a little different.*)
basta + infinitive	it's enough to + verb	Basta hacerlo una vez. (*It's enough to do it once.*)
falta (+ infinitive)	it's/is still to be (+ past participle)	Falta descubrirlo. (*It's still to be discovered.*)
hace falta (+ infinitive)	it's necessary (to)	Hace falta trabajar. (*It's necessary to work.*)
vale la pena (+ infinitive)	it's worth it (to)	Vale la pena esperar. (*It's worth it to wait.*)

Higher

There are two forms of the passive

For the passive voice, past participles must agree with the subject. So 'escrita' is used because 'la carta' is feminine.

Higher

1) In an active sentence, the subject does something. In the passive voice, something is done to the subject.

Escribió la carta. *He wrote the letter.*

Fue escrita por él. *It was written by him.*

2) The passive is formed using 'ser' (*to be*), a past participle (see p.131) and 'por' (*by*).

fueron — *they were* — This part changes depending on the tense and subject.
\+ limpiado — *cleaned* — past participle of the verb 'limpiar'
\+ por — *by*
= Las mesas fueron limpiadas por ellos. *The tables were cleaned by them.* A sentence in the passive voice. The past participle has to agree with the subject.

3) You can also form the passive with 'se' and the third-person forms of any verb. Use the 'he/she/it' form for a single subject, and the 'they' form for a plural subject:

El arroz se cocina por diez minutos. *The rice is cooked for ten minutes.*

Las puertas se abren a las nueve. *The doors are opened at nine.*

Grammar Questions

Translate these sentences into **Spanish** using impersonal verbs.

1. You can rest now.
2. One must do exercise.
3. You need to go to class.
4. There are many parks.
5. It's worth it to learn this content. (H)
6. It seems like a marvellous idea. (H)

One has to learn this — it's nothing personal...

These topics are plain sailing as long as you remember to use the 'he/she/it' or 'they' forms of the verb.

Quick Quiz

The Subjunctive

Oh yes, you're in for a treat — it's time to learn about the Spanish subjunctive...

Forming the present subjunctive

Higher

1) Sometimes, the present subjunctive is needed instead of the normal present tense.
2) To form the present subjunctive of 'hacer', 'tener' and 'venir', take the stem from the 'I' form of the normal present tense and add the '-ar' verb endings.

hago → hag- + -a = haga

3) You'll need to learn the subjunctive forms for 'ir' and 'ser' by heart — they are completely irregular.

You only need to know the singular forms of these verbs in the present subjunctive.

Verb	I	you (inf., sing.)	he/she/it/ you (form., sing.)
hacer (*to do, make*)	haga	hagas	haga
tener (*to have*)	tenga	tengas	tenga
venir (*to come*)	venga	vengas	venga
ir (*to go*)	vaya	vayas	vaya
ser (*to be*)	sea	seas	sea

Use the present subjunctive...

Higher

1) ...after 'cuando' (*when*) when talking about the future:

Cuando sea mayor, viviré en Italia. *When I am older, I will live in Italy.*

2) ...to request or command someone else does something:

Vyvan quiere que yo haga la cena. *Vyvan wants me to make dinner.*

3) ...to express a wish or desire:

Espero que Noor tenga los billetes. *I hope that Noor has the tickets.*

4) ...after expressing an emotion:

Es triste que no vayas de vacaciones. *It's sad that you (inf., sing.) don't go on holiday.*

5) ...after 'para que' (*so that*) to express purpose:

Mejoramos el sitio para que sea más fácil usarlo. *We're improving the site so that it's easier to use it.*

6) ...after 'que' (*that*) to express possibility or necessity:

Es posible que venga a la fiesta.
It's possible that he'll come to the party.

Es importante que hagas los ejercicios.
It's important that you (inf., sing.) do the exercises.

It looks like Vyvan and Greg will be having a takeaway...

You normally only use the subjunctive when there's a different person doing the second verb.

Grammar Questions

Decide whether you need the present subjunctive or normal present tense in each of these sentences.

Higher

1. Piensan que Charvi ____ a su clase. (venir)
2. Lo explico para que ____ más claro. (ser)
3. Ya sé que ella ____ más hijos que yo. (tener)
4. Me preocupa que el libro no ____ bueno. (ser)
5. Llamo a mi novio cuando él ____ al café. (ir)
6. Es necesario que yo ____ mis deberes. (hacer)

Higher

It's sad that you're nearly finished with grammar *sob*...

If Spanish grammar were a video game (a truly frightening thought...), the subjunctive would be the final level. It can be a pretty tricky topic, so don't be afraid to revisit this page whenever you're feeling unsure.

The Imperative

Quick Quiz

Imperatives are words that give a command. They change depending on whether you're talking to one person or a group. So learn what's on this page and you'll be giving out orders in no time...

Singular informal commands

1) To form a singular informal command, take the 'tú' part of the present tense verb and take off the 's'.

das *you give* → ¡Da! *Give!*

escribes *you write* → ¡Escribe! *Write!*

2) With commands, pronouns (e.g. me, them, it) are placed at the end of the word and you need to add an accent to show where the stress is.

¡Cómelo! *Eat it!*

¡Llámame! *Call me!*

3) There are a few common irregular imperatives you need to know.

¡Ven aquí, por favor! *Come here, please!*

¡Dime! *Tell me!*

¡Hazlo! *Do it!*

You don't need an accent when you use pronouns with the irregular imperatives.

Infinitive	Informal singular
ser (*to be*)	¡Sé!
ir (*to go*)	¡Ve!
tener (*to have*)	¡Ten!
venir (*to come*)	¡Ven!
hacer (*to do, make*)	¡Haz!
decir (*to say, tell*)	¡Di!
poner (*to put (on)*)	¡Pon!
salir (*to go out, leave*)	¡Sal!

Plural informal commands

Higher

1) To tell two or more people what to do in an informal way, take the infinitive and change the final 'r' to 'd'.

hablar *(to speak, talk)* → ¡Hablad! *Speak!*

dormir *(to sleep)* → ¡Dormid! *Sleep!*

mirar *(to look, watch)* → ¡Mirad! *Look!*

leer *(to read)* → ¡Leed! *Read!*

2) The verbs that are irregular in singular informal commands follow the same rules as regular verbs in the you (inf., pl.) form.

salir *(to go out)* → ¡Salid! *Go out!*

ir *(to go)* → ¡Id! *Go!*

poner *(to put (on))* → ¡Poned la caja allí! *Put the box there!*

Laura was sure she could make space for more boxes...

Grammar Questions

Translate these sentences into **Spanish** using informal singular commands.

1. Sing this song!
2. Go to your room!
3. Write the message!
4. Take it!
5. Say something!
6. Drink the water!

Translate these sentences into **Spanish** using informal plural commands.

H
7. Learn these words!
8. Watch this video!
9. Wait here, please!
10. Buy that now!
11. Make your beds!
12. Cross the street!
H

Learn how to use the imperative... Go on...

Commands are far handier than you probably realise — you can order someone to tap dance, tell a really annoying person to go away, or request a llama to be delivered to your house... The possibilities are endless.

Verbs and Tenses — Grammar List

Regular Verbs

All regular verbs that end in '-ar', '-er' or '-ir' can be conjugated like these three examples.

-ar verbs, e.g. hablar (to speak)

Subject	Present	Preterite	Imperfect	Proper Future	Conditional
yo	habl**o**	habl**é**	habl**aba**	habl**aré**	habl**aría**
tú	habl**as**	habl**aste**	habl**abas**	habl**arás**	habl**arías**
él / ella / usted	habl**a**	habl**ó**	habl**aba**	habl**ará**	habl**aría**
nosotros/as	habl**amos**	habl**amos**	habl**ábamos**	habl**aremos**	habl**aríamos**
vosotros/as	habl**áis**	habl**asteis**	habl**abais**	habl**aréis**	habl**aríais**
ellos / ellas / ustedes	habl**an**	habl**aron**	habl**aban**	habl**arán**	habl**arían**

-er verbs, e.g. comer (to eat)

Subject	Present	Preterite	Imperfect	Proper Future	Conditional
yo	com**o**	com**í**	com**ía**	com**eré**	com**ería**
tú	com**es**	com**iste**	com**ías**	com**erás**	com**erías**
él / ella / usted	com**e**	com**ió**	com**ía**	com**erá**	com**ería**
nosotros/as	com**emos**	com**imos**	com**íamos**	com**eremos**	com**eríamos**
vosotros/as	com**éis**	com**isteis**	com**íais**	com**eréis**	com**eríais**
ellos / ellas / ustedes	com**en**	com**ieron**	com**ían**	com**erán**	com**erían**

-ir verbs, e.g. vivir (to live)

Subject	Present	Preterite	Imperfect	Proper Future	Conditional
yo	viv**o**	viv**í**	viv**ía**	viv**iré**	viv**iría**
tú	viv**es**	viv**iste**	viv**ías**	viv**irás**	viv**irías**
él / ella / usted	viv**e**	viv**ió**	viv**ía**	viv**irá**	viv**iría**
nosotros/as	viv**imos**	viv**imos**	viv**íamos**	viv**iremos**	viv**iríamos**
vosotros/as	viv**ís**	viv**isteis**	viv**íais**	viv**iréis**	viv**iríais**
ellos / ellas / ustedes	viv**en**	viv**ieron**	viv**ían**	viv**irán**	viv**irían**

Important Irregular Verbs

You only need to know the subjunctive forms for ser, ir, tener, hacer and venir.

ser (to be)

Subject	Present	Preterite	Imperfect	Proper Future	Conditional	Subjunctive
yo	soy	fui	era	seré	sería	sea
tú	eres	fuiste	eras	serás	serías	seas
él / ella / usted	es	fue	era	será	sería	sea
nosotros/as	somos	fuimos	éramos	seremos	seríamos	
vosotros/as	sois	fuisteis	erais	seréis	seríais	
ellos / ellas / ustedes	son	fueron	eran	serán	serían	

Imperative
tú ¡Sé!

You need the present tense forms of 'ir' to make the immediate future tense (see p.132).

ir (to go); irse (de) (to leave)

Subject	Pronoun	Present	Preterite	Imperfect	Proper Future	Conditional	Subjunctive
yo	me	voy	fui	iba	iré	iría	vaya
tú	te	vas	fuiste	ibas	irás	irías	vayas
él / ella / usted	se	va	fue	iba	irá	iría	vaya
nosotros/as	nos	vamos	fuimos	íbamos	iremos	iríamos	
vosotros/as	os	vais	fuisteis	ibais	iréis	iríais	
ellos / ellas / ustedes	se	van	fueron	iban	irán	irían	

Imperative
tú ¡Ve!
¡Vete (de)!

tener (to have)

Subject	Present	Preterite	Imperfect	Proper Future	Conditional	Subjunctive
yo	tengo	tuve	tenía	tendré	tendría	tenga
tú	tienes	tuviste	tenías	tendrás	tendrías	H tengas
él / ella / usted	tiene	tuvo	tenía	tendrá	tendría	tenga
nosotros/as	tenemos	tuvimos	teníamos	tendremos	tendríamos	
vosotros/as	tenéis	tuvisteis	H teníais	H tendréis	H tendríais	**Imperative**
ellos / ellas / ustedes	tienen	tuvieron	tenían	tendrán	tendrían	tú ¡Ten!

Irregular imperatives are included on these pages. You can find out how to form regular imperatives in the 'tú' and 'vosotros' forms on p.141.

hacer (to do, make)

Subject	Present	Preterite	Imperfect	Proper Future	Conditional	Subjunctive
yo	hago	hice	hacía	haré	haría	haga
tú	haces	hiciste	hacías	harás	harías	H hagas
él / ella / usted	hace	hizo	hacía	hará	haría	haga
nosotros/as	hacemos	hicimos	hacíamos	haremos	haríamos	
vosotros/as	hacéis	hicisteis	H hacíais	H haréis	H haríais	**Imperative**
ellos / ellas / ustedes	hacen	hicieron	hacían	harán	harían	tú ¡Haz!

venir (to come)

Subject	Present	Preterite	Imperfect	Proper Future (Higher)	Conditional (Higher)	Subjunctive
yo	vengo	vine	venía	vendré	vendría	venga
tú	vienes	viniste	venías	vendrás	vendrías	H vengas
él / ella / usted	viene	vino	venía	vendrá	vendría	venga
nosotros/as	venimos	vinimos	veníamos	vendremos	vendríamos	
vosotros/as	venís	vinisteis	H veníais	vendréis	vendríais	**Imperative**
ellos / ellas / ustedes	vienen	vinieron	venían	vendrán	vendrían	tú ¡Ven!

poner (to put (on)); ponerse (to get, become (+ adjective))

Subject	Pronoun	Present	Preterite	Imperfect	Proper Future	Conditional	Subjunctive
yo	me	pongo	puse	ponía	pondré	pondría	ponga
tú	te	pones	pusiste	ponías	pondrás	pondrías	H pongas
él / ella / usted	se	pone	puso	ponía	pondrá	pondría	ponga
nosotros/as	nos	ponemos	pusimos	poníamos	pondremos	pondríamos	**Imperative**
vosotros/as	H os	ponéis	pusisteis	H poníais	H pondréis	H pondríais	tú ¡Pon!
ellos / ellas / ustedes	se	ponen	pusieron	ponían	pondrán	pondrían	¡Ponte!

You also need to know the future and conditional forms of 'estar', but they are regular — you can use the '-ar verbs' table on the previous page to form them.

estar (to be)

Subject	Present	Preterite	Imperfect
yo	estoy	estuve	estaba
tú	estás	estuviste	estabas
él / ella / usted	está	estuvo	estaba
nosotros/as	estamos	estuvimos	estábamos
vosotros/as	estáis	estuvisteis	H estabais
ellos / ellas / ustedes	están	estuvieron	estaban

haber (to have done something)

You need these forms of 'haber' to form the present perfect tense.

Subject	Present
yo	he
tú	has
él / ella / usted	ha
nosotros/as	hemos
vosotros/as	habéis
ellos / ellas / ustedes	han

Verbs and Tenses — Grammar List

Other Common Verbs

The stems of these verbs change their spellings in certain tenses. See p.126 for more on stem-changing verbs.

decir (to say, tell)

Subject	Present	Preterite	Future (Higher)	Conditional (Higher)
yo	digo	dije	diré	diría
tú	dices	dijiste	dirás	dirías
él / ella / usted	dice	dijo	dirá	diría
nosotros/as	decimos	dijimos	diremos	diríamos
vosotros/as	decís	dijisteis	diréis	diríais
ellos / ellas / ustedes	dicen	dijeron	dirán	dirían

Imperative tú ¡Di!

oír (to hear)

Subject	Present
yo	oigo
tú	oyes
él / ella / usted	oye

traer (to bring)

Subject	Preterite
yo	traje
tú	trajiste
él / ella / usted	trajo
nosotros/as	trajimos
vosotros/as	trajisteis
ellos / ellas / ustedes	trajeron

salir (to leave, go out)

Subject	Future (Higher)	Conditional (Higher)
yo	saldré	saldría
tú	saldrás	saldrías
él / ella / usted	saldrá	saldría
nosotros/as	saldremos	saldríamos
vosotros/as	saldréis	saldríais
ellos / ellas / ustedes	saldrán	saldrían

Imperative tú ¡Sal!

In the present tense, 'salir' is only irregular in its 'yo' form ('salgo').

dar (to give)

Subject	Present	Preterite
yo	doy	di
tú	das	diste
él / ella / usted	da	dio
nosotros/as	damos	dimos
vosotros/as	dais	disteis
ellos / ellas / ustedes	dan	dieron

Imperative tú ¡Da!

You'd usually use '¡Da!' with a pronoun, e.g. '¡Dame ese libro!'. See p.141 for more on the imperative.

ver (to see, watch)

Subject	Present	Imperfect
yo	veo	veía
tú	ves	veías
él / ella / usted	ve	veía
nosotros/as	vemos	veíamos (H)
vosotros/as	veis	veíais (H)
ellos / ellas / ustedes	ven	veían (H)

Reflexive Verbs and Pronouns

Reflexive verbs are useful for talking about things you do to yourself — they use reflexive pronouns.

Reflexive Pronoun		llamarse (to be called)
me	*myself*	me llamo
te	*yourself (inf., sing.)*	te llamas
se	*himself, herself, itself, oneself, yourself (form., sing.)*	se llama
nos (H)	*ourselves*	nos llamamos
os (H)	*yourselves (inf., pl.)*	os llamáis
se (H)	*themselves, yourselves (form., pl.)*	se llaman

For more on reflexive pronouns and where to put them in a sentence, see p.135.

Impersonal Verbs

These are the impersonal forms of 'haber':

Present	hay	*there is / are*
Imperfect	había	*there was / were / used to be*
Proper Future	habrá	*there will be / is going to be*
Conditional	habría	*there would be*

se puede	*you (general) / one can*
se necesita	*you (general) / one needs to*
hace + weather noun	*it is...*
hay que	*you (general) / one must*
parece (Higher)	*it seems*
basta + infinitive (Higher)	*it's enough to + verb*
falta + infinitive (Higher)	*it's, is still to be (+ past participle)*
hace falta (+ infinitive) (Higher)	*it's necessary (to)*
vale la pena (+ infinitive) (Higher)	*it's worth it (to)*

Modal Verbs

See p.134 for more information about modal verbs.

querer (to want, love)

Subject	Present	Preterite	Imperfect	Proper Future	Conditional
yo	quiero	quise	quería	querré	querría
tú	quieres	quisiste	querías	querrás	querrías
él / ella / usted	quiere	quiso	quería	querrá	querría
nosotros/as	queremos	quisimos	queríamos	Higher querremos	Higher querríamos
vosotros/as	queréis	quisisteis	H queríais	querréis	querríais
ellos / ellas / ustedes	quieren	quisieron	querían	querrán	querrían

poder (to be able to, can)

Subject	Present	Preterite	Imperfect	Proper Future	Conditional
yo	puedo	pude	podía	podré	podría
tú	puedes	pudiste	podías	podrás	podrías
él / ella / usted	puede	pudo	podía	podrá	podría
nosotros/as	podemos	pudimos	podíamos	podremos	podríamos
vosotros/as	podéis	pudisteis	H podíais	H podréis	H podríais
ellos / ellas / ustedes	pueden	pudieron	podían	podrán	podrían

saber (to know (how to))

Subject	Present	Imperfect	Proper Future	Conditional
yo	sé	sabía	sabré	sabría
tú	sabes	sabías	sabrás	sabrías
él / ella / usted	sabe	sabía	sabrá	sabría
nosotros/as	sabemos	sabíamos	Higher sabremos	Higher sabríamos
vosotros/as	sabéis	H sabíais	sabréis	sabríais
ellos / ellas / ustedes	saben	sabían	sabrán	sabrían

Hilde reckons she's nearly finished revising for her GCSE Spanish exams.

Past Participles

Use past participles with the verb 'haber' to form the perfect tense ('I have done').

Regular endings for past participles:

-ar verbs	-er / -ir verbs
-ado, e.g. habl**ado**	**-ido**, e.g. viv**ido**

These past participles are irregular:

Verb	Past participle	
abrir	abierto	*opened*
decir	dicho	*said, told*
escribir	escrito	*written*
hacer	hecho	*done, made*
poner	puesto	*put*
romper	roto	*broken*
ver	visto	*seen*
volver	vuelto	*returned*
H descubrir	descubierto	*discovered*

To say what's just happened use this phrase:

Higher

acabar de + infinitive	*to have just (+ past participle)*

Present Participles

Use present participles with the verb 'estar' to form the present and imperfect continuous ('I am/was doing').

Regular endings for present participles:

-ar verbs	-er / -ir verbs
-ando, e.g. habl**ando**	**-iendo**, e.g. viv**iendo**

These present participles change the spellings of their stems:

Verb	Present participle	
pedir	pidiendo	*asking for, ordering, requesting*
decir	diciendo	*saying, telling*
dormir	durmiendo	*sleeping*
morir	muriendo	*dying*
leer	leyendo	*reading*
H construir	construyendo	*building*

Some set phrases in Spanish need a present participle:

Higher

seguir / continuar + present participle	*(to) continue to, still be + -ing*
llevar + time period + present participle	*(to) have been + -ing for X time*

Revision Summary Test for Section Thirteen

Here it is — the final revision summary. Test yourself if you dare. *Plays suspenseful music*

- Yep, these questions are **hard** — they'll really help you see **how well you know your stuff**.
- Tackle the **revision summary test** below, or scan the QR code to do it **online**. Use the CGP RevisionHub to **track your progress** and see **which areas need more work**.
- You can find **sample answers** here: www.cgpbooks.co.uk/GraciasExtras

Summary Test

The Present Tense

1) List all the present tense forms of these verbs: a) preparar b) beber c) recibir
2) Explain how the verb stem changes its spelling in the present tense for: a) jugar b) servir c) doler d) preferir e) repetir f) conocer g) salir h) comenzar
3) Give a sentence in the present tense using these verbs: a) hacer b) ir c) ser d) estar e) tener

The Preterite, Imperfect and Present Perfect Tenses

4) List all the preterite tense endings for '-ar' verbs and '-er' and '-ir' verbs.
5) Give the 'I' form of the preterite tense for: a) ser b) dar c) traer d) poner e) querer f) decir
6) List all the singular imperfect tense endings for regular '-ar' verbs and '-er' and '-ir' verbs.
7) Translate these sentences into Spanish: a) She has danced. b) I have learnt. c) They have left.
8) Explain when you'd use the preterite, imperfect and present perfect tenses.
9) (H) Give the correct imperfect tense form for each of the verbs below. The subject is given in brackets. a) ser (vosotros) b) ir (nosotros) c) ver (ustedes) d) estar (ellos) e) tener (Luisa y yo)

The Future Tenses and the Conditional

10) Translate these sentences into Spanish using the immediate future tense: a) I am going to go to Spain. b) We are going to arrive this evening. c) He is not going to get lost.
11) Using the proper future tense, say that you will buy a present for your sister.
12) 'En un mundo perfecto, comería patatas fritas todos los días.' Translate this sentence into English.
13) (H) Translate these sentences into Spanish, using the proper future tense or the conditional: a) I would come. b) They will tell you. c) She would know the way. d) We will go.

Modal Verbs, Reflexives and -ing Verbs

14) List all the modal verbs and phrases in this section. There are 7 you need to know.
15) Translate these sentences into Spanish: a) She falls asleep early. b) Are you (inf., sing.) staying here?
16) What are the present participles of these verbs? a) pasar b) volver c) pedir d) dormir e) caer
17) (H) Describe two ways to say how long you 'have been doing' something. Give an example of each one.
18) (H) 'We have just found your (inf., pl.) keys.' How would say this in Spanish?

Negative Forms, Impersonal Verbs and the Passive

19) Write a sentence using each of these negatives: a) (no) nunca b) (no) nada c) (no) nadie
20) List all the impersonal verbs in this section. There are 5 you need to know (plus 5 for Higher tier).
21) (H) Say these sentences in Spanish: a) I no longer live there. b) I wear neither skirts nor dresses.
22) (H) Give a sentence using the passive voice with: a) 'ser' + past participle b) 'se' + a third-person form

The Subjunctive and the Imperative

23) What are the singular informal imperatives for these verbs? a) correr b) decir c) salir d) tomar
24) (Higher) In Spanish, use an imperative to tell two of your friends to open the door.
25) (Higher) Translate this sentence into Spanish: 'I hope that Dídac comes to my party.'
26) (Higher) List all the singular forms of the present subjunctive for: a) hacer b) tener c) ir d) ser

Spelling and Pronunciation

Spanish pronunciation can be tricky, so use this page to help if you're unsure how to pronounce a word. You can scan the QR code to hear the sounds and words in the tables spoken aloud. → Listening Track 20

Spanish pronunciation is quite different to English

The table below shows some of the main ways of spelling common sounds in Spanish.

Listen to the audio and practise pronouncing each sound out loud as you hear it.

Spelling	Example 1	Example 2
a	antiguo	abrir
o	bolsa	perro
e	esquina	viejo
i	idea	instituto
u	comunidad	usar
ll	llevar	calle
ch	noche	mucho
ca	campo	chica
co	comer	contacto
cu	discutir	recursos
cu + vowel	cuando	cuenta
ce	excelente	hace
ci	estación	medicina
z	zapato	cruzar
que	parque	quedar
qui	quisiera	equipo
ga	cargar	gafas
go	luego	agosto
gu	gustar	segundo
ge	general	argentino
gi	página	religión
gue	hamburguesa	sigue
gui	seguidor	alguien
j	jugar	bajo
ñ	sueño	mañana
v	varios	ver
-r-, -r	querer	pasar
rr, r-, -r-	error	sonreír
silent h	hermano	hora

In some Spanish-speaking countries, these (ce, ci, z) sound more like 's' than 'th' in English.

This is the 'he / she / it / you (form., sing.)' form of seguir. It's a stem-changing verb (see p.126 for more). (sigue)

'-r-' sounds like it's being rolled more when it comes after 'n', 'l' or 's'. (sonreír)

In Spanish, you don't pronounce the 'h' at the beginning of words. (silent h)

"Knock knock."
"Who's there?"
"Sí."
"Sí who?"
"Sí what a bad pronunciation joke I've made!"

Some Spanish words have an accent to show you which vowel you need to stress when you say them.

á	rápido	matemáticas
é	éxito	inglés
í	increíble	típico
ó	corazón	avión
ú	autobús	útil

It's useful to know how accents change the pronunciation of a word, but you'll only be tested on these if you're taking Higher tier.

The Speaking Exam

'But what will my exams be like?' I hear you cry. Well, you'll find your answer on the next four pages...

There are four exams for GCSE Spanish

1) Your Edexcel Spanish GCSE is assessed by four separate exams — Speaking, Listening, Reading and Writing.
2) Each exam is worth 25% of your final mark. You'll get a grade between 1 and 9 (with 9 being the highest).
3) You'll probably have your speaking exam a couple of weeks before the rest of your exams.

The speaking exam has three parts

During your preparation time, you can make notes to use at any point during the exam.

1) Your speaking exam will be conducted and recorded by your teacher.
2) The exam is in three parts. Before you start, you'll get 15 minutes of preparation time.
The time allowed for the exam is 10-12 minutes at Higher tier and 7-9 minutes at Foundation tier.

1 Read aloud

You'll get a card with several sentences on it, in Spanish. You'll read the sentences out loud, then your teacher will ask you two questions in Spanish related to the topic of the sentences.

2 Role play

You'll get a card with a scenario on it. At Higher tier, there are three questions for you to answer and two to ask. At Foundation tier, you'll have four questions to answer and one to ask.

3 Picture task

Before the exam, you'll get a card with two photos on it. You'll describe one photo and answer questions on it, and then you'll have a discussion on the same theme.

Try to be imaginative with your answers

You need to find ways to show off the full extent of your Spanish knowledge. You should try to:

1) Use a range of tenses — e.g. for a question on daily routine, think of when something different happens.

Pero mañana jugaré al fútbol. *But tomorrow I will play football.*

2) Talk about other people, as well as yourself — it's fine to make people up if that helps.

Me gusta el rugby, pero mi primo lo odia. *I like rugby, but my cousin hates it.*

3) Give loads of opinions and reasons for your opinions.

En mi opinión, debemos reciclar más porque... *In my opinion, we must recycle more because...*

You can use non-binary or gender-neutral pronouns in the exam — just make sure you use them consistently and that your adjectives agree.

If you're really struggling, ask for help in Spanish

1) If you get really stuck trying to think of a word or phrase, you can ask for help — as long as it's in Spanish.
2) For example, if you can't remember how to say 'homework' in Spanish, ask your teacher.
You won't get any marks for vocabulary your teacher's given you though.

¿Qué es 'homework' en español? *What is 'homework' in Spanish?*

3) If you don't hear something clearly, just ask:

¿Puedes repetir, por favor? *Can you repeat, please?*

You could also ask this if you're desperately in need of time to think of an answer.

Silence please! I'm taking my sneaking exam...

Don't panic if you slip up in the speaking exam — it's completely natural. Just correct yourself and move on.

The Listening Exam

Can you hear that? It sounds to me like a really useful page about the listening exam...

The listening exam has two sections

1) For the listening paper, you'll listen to various recordings of people speaking in Spanish.
2) The paper is 60 minutes long for Higher-tier students and 45 minutes long for Foundation-tier students. It's split into Section A and Section B:

Section A is the longer section — it's worth 40 marks. It contains comprehension questions in English, and you'll write your answers in English.

Section B is a shorter dictation section — it's worth 10 marks. You'll hear some short sentences and write them down in Spanish.

Doug had found the best listening practice for his GCSE exam — his Spanish neighbours.

Read through the paper carefully at the start of the test

1) Before the recording begins, you'll be given five minutes to read through the paper.
2) In particular, look at the questions in Section A. Use this time to read each question carefully. Some are multiple choice, and others require you to write some short answers — make sure you know what each one is asking you to do.
3) Reading the question titles, and the questions themselves, will give you a good idea of the topics you'll be asked about. This should help you predict what to listen out for.
4) You can write on the exam paper, so scribble down anything that might be useful.
5) You'll be given 2 minutes at the end of Section B to check your work.

Make notes while listening to the recordings

1) For Section A you'll hear each audio track three times, and then there'll be a pause for you to write down your answer.

- While you're listening, it's a good idea to jot down a few details — e.g. dates, times, names or key words. But make sure you keep listening while you're writing down any notes.
- Listen right to the end, even if you think you've got the answer — sometimes the person will change their mind or add an important detail at the end.
- Don't worry if you can't understand every word that's being said — just listen carefully each time and try to pick out the vocabulary you need to answer the question.

2) For Section B you will hear each sentence three times.

- For the first group of sentences, you have to fill in the missing words. For the second group, you need to write down the whole sentence.
- Keep in mind that you'll be marked for accurate spelling.

Don't worry — I'm all ears...

If you're still not sure of the answer after you've heard the track three times, scribble one down anyway — it's worth a shot and you might pick up some extra marks, especially if it's a multiple-choice question. Neat.

The Reading Exam

After all that speaking and listening, the reading exam offers some nice peace and quiet. Apart from the voice inside your head that screams "WHAT ON EARTH DOES THAT WORD MEAN?!" (Or maybe that's just me...)

In Section A, you'll answer questions about texts

1) The Higher-tier reading paper is 1 hour long, and the Foundation-tier paper is 45 minutes. Both are worth 50 marks and have two sections.
2) In Section A, you'll be given a variety of Spanish texts and then asked questions about them. The texts could include things like blog posts, emails, newspaper reports and adverts. The questions and answers will be in English.
3) Scan through each text first to get an idea of what it's about. Then read the questions that go with it carefully, making sure you understand what information you should be looking out for.
4) Next, go back through the text. You're not expected to understand every word, so don't get distracted by trying to work out what everything means — focus on finding the information you need. If you're having trouble with a particular question, you might want to move on and come back to it later.

Don't give up if you don't understand something

1) Use the context of the text to help you understand what it might be saying. You might be able to find some clues in the title of the text or the type of text.
2) Knowing how to spot different word types (e.g. nouns, verbs) can help you work out what's happening in a sentence. See the grammar sections (p.101-146) for more.
3) Make sure you put an answer down for every question — some of the questions are multiple choice, so even if you can't work out the answer, it's always worth putting down one of the options.
4) You can guess some Spanish words that look or sound the same as English words, e.g. el problema (*problem*), la música (*music*), el color (*colour*).
5) Be careful though — you might come across some 'false friends'. These are Spanish words that look like an English word, but have a completely different meaning:

el pie	*foot*	la ropa	*clothes*	el pan	*bread*	H actual	*current*
el éxito	*success*	largo/a	*long*	recordar	*to remember*	H grabar	*to record*

In Section B, you'll translate from Spanish to English

1) Section B asks you to translate short Spanish sentences (Foundation tier) or a short paragraph (Higher tier) into English. The sentences will be on topics you've studied, so the vocabulary should be familiar.
2) Here are some top tips for doing your translations:

- Translate a whole sentence at a time, rather than word by word — this will avoid any of the Spanish word order being carried into the English.
- Keep an eye out for different tenses — there will be a variety throughout the sentences.
- Read through your translations to make sure they sound natural. Some words and phrases don't translate literally, so you'll need to make sure that your sentences sound like normal English.

Don't be misled by false friends (in exams and life in general)...

As a reminder, you'll be reading Spanish texts in Section A and translating in Section B. You're welcome...

The Writing Exam

The writing exam is a great way of showing off what you can do — try to use varied vocabulary, include a range of tenses, and pack in any clever expressions that you've learnt over the years. You'll be *excelente*...

There are various types of questions in the writing exam

1) The Higher-tier writing paper is 1 hour and 20 minutes long and the Foundation-tier paper is 1 hour and 15 minutes long. Some tasks are only for one tier, but others appear in both — these are explained below.
2) Each task is worth a different number of marks, so you should spend more time on the higher-mark tasks.

F

Picture-based Task (8 marks)

You'll be asked to write four short sentences in Spanish to describe a photo.

Foundation

40 to 50-word Writing Task (14 marks)

You'll produce a short piece of writing in response to three bullet points. You'll need to choose between two questions and write about 40-50 words. Remember to write about each bullet point.

Both tiers

80 to 90-word Writing Task (18 marks)

You'll write about 80-90 words in response to four bullet points. You'll have a choice between two questions. It's really important that you write about each bullet point.

Higher

130 to 150-word Writing Task (22 marks)

You'll need to write about 130-150 words in Spanish, based on four bullet points. There will be two questions to choose from. For this task, make sure you give pros and cons and explain your answers in detail.

Both tiers

Translation Task (10 marks)

You'll translate five sentences (Foundation) or a short passage (Higher) into Spanish. It could be on any topic you've studied. See p.150 for some top tips for translation tasks.

Plan out your answers and carefully check them

1) In the writing paper, you'll have to translate English sentences into Spanish (Foundation) or a short English passage into Spanish (Higher). Read each sentence fully before you start. Don't worry — the translation will only include the vocab and grammar you've learnt.
2) For the longer writing tasks, spend a few minutes for each question planning out your answer. Decide how you're going to cover every bullet point and in what order you're going to write things.
3) Write the best answers you can, using the Spanish that you know — it doesn't matter if it's not true. It's your chance to show off your Spanish knowledge.
4) Once you've got something that you're happy with, go back through and check your answer. Here's a checklist of useful things to look out for:

Remember — you can use non-binary or gender-neutral pronouns in the exam (see p.148).

- Are all the verbs in the right tense and do they have the correct endings?
- Do your adjectives agree with their nouns and are they in the right place?
- Is your word order correct, including any negative structures?
- Have you spelt everything correctly, including using the right accents?

And lastly, don't forget your pen...

When you're nervous and stressed, it's easy to misread a question or skip question parts. For writing questions with bullet points, make sure you talk about each bullet in turn — tick them off as you go along.

Answers

The answers to the translation questions are sample answers only, just to give you an idea of one way to translate them. There may be different ways to translate these sentences that are also correct.

For dictation and translation questions, this symbol (|) shows where to divide the marks. There is 1 mark awarded for the first part of the text, and 1 mark awarded for the second.

Section One — General Stuff

Page 5: Numbers and Times

1) a) 17 b) 88 c) the second street on the right
2) a) A+B b) B c) B

Page 7: Times and Dates

2) a) yesterday b) Bath c) on Friday

Page 9: Questions

2) a) ¿Qué reloj | debería comprar?
b) ¿Con quién | bailabas?
c) ¿Cuántos platos | hay?
d) ¿De qué | hablas?

Page 13: Opinions

1) a) watching films at home
b) (They're) boring
c) (They can be) really funny
2) a) i) P ii) P+N
b) i) N ii) P

Section Two — Identity and Relationships

Page 21: My Family and Friends

2) a) the eldest
b) They enjoy the same activities. / They share several common interests.
c) her dad, his wife and her stepbrother
d) She and her stepbrother are the same age and have the same birthday.

Page 23: Describing People

1) a) B b) A c) C d) D

Page 25: Relationships and Partnerships

1) a) A b) B
2) a) C b) C

Section Three — Healthy Living

Page 33: Food

1) a) food with too much sugar
b) vegetables
c) finding options without meat at restaurants

Page 35: Physical and Mental Wellbeing

2) a) It's as dangerous as taking drugs.
b) not knowing where you are
not knowing how much you've drunk
c) They drank too much and had to go to hospital.

Page 37: Illnesses and Treatments

2) a) Water got into his tent on a camping trip.
b) If he feels worse than when he returned home.
c) He feels very cold.
d) Any two from:
Drink hot drinks.
Try to rest.
Wear more clothes if you're cold.
Have a bath before going to bed.

Section Four — Free-time Activities

Page 41: Music

1) a) easy to find new artists / easy to find shows
b) concert tickets
c) one hundred

Page 43: Cinema and TV

1) a) No le gusta nada | el cine.
b) Recomiendo películas | a mis amigos.
c) Los personajes hicieron | cosas divertidas.
d) Los efectos especiales | son extraordinarios.
e) En el futuro, me gustaría | actuar en una película de terror.
2) a) A b) B

Page 45: Sport

2) a) B b) B c) A d) C

Page 47: Going Out and Other Hobbies

1) a) The menu has | a lot of variety.
b) Starters are free | for children.
c) I want to try | a Chinese dish.
d) Soon I'm going | to ask for the bill.

Section Five — Places in Town

Page 51: Where You Live

1) a) Vivo en | un barrio agradable.
b) Me gusta vivir aquí | porque hay mucho que hacer.
c) Este fin de semana, | voy al centro del pueblo.
d) Mis amigos y yo vamos a tomar | el almuerzo en un restaurante español.
e) Fui allí el año pasado | y la comida fue increíble.

Page 53: At Home

2) a) B b) A c) B

Page 55: The Local Area

2) a) There isn't much to do in his region.
b) There aren't many cafés or restaurants. / They charge a lot for their food.
c) There are some marvellous buildings. / The art museum in his town is very interesting.

Page 57: Shopping

2) a) leather jackets
b) near the jumpers
c) go to the till to pay
d) The store is closing in thirty minutes.

Page 59: Directions and Weather

1) a) B b) C c) D d) A
2) El clima de mi región | suele ser húmedo en otoño. | Sin embargo, el año pasado | no llovió mucho. | Hizo mucho fresco y tuve que | llevar un jersey cada día. | Parece que nevará este invierno, | lo que es emocionante. | Para mí, las temperaturas frías | son las mejores.

Section Six — Environmental and Social Issues

Page 64: Effects on the Environment

1) a) Our actions | affect the environment.
   b) At the moment, we don't use | enough clean energy.
   c) This has negative effects | on nature.
   d) Fifty years ago, | there weren't as many clean options.
   e) In the future, one will need | to use fewer natural resources.

Page 65: Protecting the Environment

1) a) i) Clean the beach
      ii) It's important to protect the animals that live in the sea.
   b) i) Walking or cycling to school to use less energy.
      ii) Take public transport.

Page 67: Equality and Social Issues

2) a) unemployment
   b) associations
   c) discrimination
   d) opportunities

Section Seven — Social Media and Technology

Page 71: Technology

1) a) i) C ii) A b) i) B ii) C

Page 73: The Internet and Streaming

2) a) i) Spending time outside.
      ii) Someone could steal your data.
   b) i) Being able to get information quickly.
      ii) A virus could do serious damage to her device.

Page 75: Social Media

2) a) their parents
   b) to talk with their friends
   c) They're always waiting for new messages.

Section Eight — School

Page 81: School Life

1) a) C b) B c) C
2) a) 800
   b) You can find everything you need there.
   c) enormous
   d) It's very dirty.

Page 83: School Pressures and Difficulties

2) a) C & D b) B & C

Section Nine — Future Opportunities

Page 89: Career Choices and Ambitions

2) a) M b) H c) P

Section Ten — Travel and Tourism

Page 93: Where to Go

1) a) B b) B c) A

Page 95: Accommodation and Travel

1) a) by train
   b) It's cheaper than travelling by plane. /
      It's more comfortable than travelling by bus.
   c) a flat
   d) Any one from:
      It has a kitchen.
      It has a nice balcony.
      It's close to the station.

2) a) Nuestro hotel | no tiene ascensor.
   b) Los turistas tienen | dos maletas y una mochila.
   c) He ahorrado dinero | para reservar esta habitación.
   d) Habrá mucho tráfico | en la carretera.
   e) Espero que la vista | sea maravillosa.

Page 97: Tourist Attractions

2) a) in the north of Spain
   b) a beautiful cathedral
      various museums
   c) doing a tour through the streets

Section Eleven — Nouns, Articles and Linking Words

Page 101: Nouns

1) el zapato — los zapatos
2) la camisa — las camisas
3) la tradición — las tradiciones
4) el color — los colores
5) la vez — las veces
6) la mitad — las mitades
7) el valle — los valles
8) la amistad — las amistades
9) el ciudadano — los ciudadanos
10) la hoja — las hojas
11) la impresión — las impresiones
12) el siglo — los siglos

Page 102: Forming Nouns

1) Me gusta comer la comida mexicana.
2) El francés es una asignatura guay.
3) Fumar está prohibido.
4) Los españoles son simpáticos.
5) Ser famoso/a es complejo.
6) Volar puede ser muy caro.

Page 103: Articles

1) Comí un bocadillo de pollo.
2) El agua corre rápido.
3) Es profesora de inglés.
4) Quiere unas patatas fritas.
5) Juego al baloncesto los jueves.
6) No tengo regla.

Page 104: Subject Pronouns

1) ellos 3) ellos 5) él 7) ella
2) ustedes 4) vosotros 6) nosotras 8) él

Page 105: Object Pronouns

1) the window — la ventana **La** rompe.
2) the water — el agua (f) **La** bebo.
3) **Le** compró una falda.
4) **Les** enviaré un correo electrónico.
5) to you (inf., pl.) — os **Os** di el gato.
6) to us — nos **Nos** dijo el final.

Page 107: More Pronouns

1) What is your favourite colour?
2) the film that I saw yesterday
3) Have you eaten something?
4) That isn't true.
5) Yours is here.
6) I cooked for you.
7) They would go with you.
8) I will want that (thing).

Page 108: Prepositions

1) Hablamos sobre el tiempo.
2) El café está cerrado hasta el lunes.
3) Lo vi en la pared. / Lo vi sobre la pared.
4) Son de Valencia.
5) El perro corrió hacia mí.
6) Vivo dentro de la ciudad.

Page 109: Prepositions with Verbs and Nouns

1) He/She organised a party without telling me.
2) You managed to pass it.
3) He/She has stopped smoking.
4) I play in order to win.
5) I will close the door before going out.
6) I'm trying to drink more water.

Page 110: 'Por', 'Para' and the Personal 'a'

1) The train for Paris is arriving now.
2) I'll do it for tomorrow.
3) I watched TV for three hours.
4) I walk through the countryside.
5) They were keeping it for their children.
6) They rarely used to go out because of the heat.
7) No, the personal 'a' isn't needed.
8) Yes, the personal 'a' is needed because there's a word for a human being ('gente') after the verb.
9) No, the personal 'a' isn't needed.
10) Yes, the personal 'a' is needed because there's a word for a human being ('abuelo') after the verb.
11) Yes, the personal 'a' is needed because there's a word for a pet ('sus pájaros') after the verb.
12) No, the personal 'a' isn't needed.

Page 111: Conjunctions

1) La educación física es emocionante, pero es dura.
2) Me gusta la historia porque es fácil.
3) Como estoy enfermo/a, me quedaré en casa.
4) Si hace calor, voy a la playa.
5) Tengo clases de arte e inglés.
6) ¿Prefieres azul o verde?

Section Twelve — Adjectives and Adverbs

Page 115: Adjectives

1) el perro feliz
2) un postre vegano
3) los pantalones naranja
4) una botella reciclable
5) la hermana inglesa
6) un número comparable
7) lo peligroso
8) lo más divertido

Page 117: More Adjectives

1) el primer día
2) pocas tiendas
3) cada familia
4) ningún helado
5) sus libros
6) esas películas
7) el bolígrafo mío
8) aquel calcetín

Page 118: Comparative and Superlative Adjectives

1) Esta página es más fácil.
2) Soy tan alto/a como mi padre.
3) Faiza es mayor que Emilio.
4) Los libros son mejores que las películas.
5) Hoy es el peor día.
6) Ella es la menor.

Page 119: Adverbs

1) positivamente — positively
2) directamente — directly
3) socialmente — socially
4) diferentemente — differently
5) exactamente — exactly
6) perfectamente — perfectly
7) posiblemente — possibly
8) tradicionalmente — traditionally
9) evidentemente — evidently
10) suavemente — softly
11) auténticamente — authentically
12) anualmente — annually

Page 120: Adverbs and Adverbial Phrases

1) Mis zapatos están aquí.
2) Quiero salir ahora.
3) A veces viajo.
4) Vivimos lejos.
5) La tienda está allí.
6) Hay pájaros por todas partes.

Page 121: Comparative and Superlative Adverbs

1) Wafa come más rápidamente que yo.
2) Yo pinto mejor que ella.
3) Luis baila tan bien como tú.
4) Alba es la que habla más tranquilamente.
5) Ellos son los que mejor estudian.
6) Inoke es el que peor corre.

Page 122: Quantifiers and Intensifiers

1) Hay demasiados gatos aquí.
2) Es bastante interesante.
3) Tengo muchos amigos.
4) Cantan un poco.
5) Es un libro muy bueno.
6) Hay una playa buenísima.

Section Thirteen — Verbs and Tenses

Page 125: Verbs in the Present Tense

1) bailo
2) bebemos
3) discuten
4) rompen
5) aprende
6) mandáis
7) escribes
8) visitan

Page 127: Irregular Verbs in the Present Tense

1) **Comienza** a las tres.
2) **Queremos** leche.
3) Yo **doy** el libro a Lola.
4) **Puedes** entrar.
5) **Repiten** las direcciones.
6) **Pienso** que es importante.
7) Vengo a la fiesta también.
8) Vamos allí mañana.
9) Me visto rápidamente.
10) No tengo bolígrafo.
11) Los estudiantes tienen hambre.
12) La reconozco de la película.

Page 128: 'Ser' and 'Estar' in the Present Tense

1) **Está** muy enojado hoy.
2) Siempre **es** trabajador.
3) **Somos** de Hull.
4) **Estoy** en Bradford.
5) **Es** mi hermano.
6) Mi padre **es** doctor.

Page 129: The Preterite Tense

1) viniste 3) di 5) pidió
2) cagaron 4) fue 6) jugué

Page 130: The Imperfect Tense

1) cantabas 3) aprendía 5) estaba 7) volvían 9) éramos
2) decía 4) pagaba 6) tenías 8) seguíais 10) iban

Page 131: Using the Past Tenses

1) Ha viajado a España.
2) Ha corrido quinientos metros.
3) Han terminado el examen.
4) ¿Has comido ya?
5) Hemos escrito una carta.
6) Han vuelto a casa.

Page 132: The Future Tenses

1) vas a hacer, harás
2) va a tener, tendrá
3) va a bailar, bailará
4) voy a dar, daré
5) vas a poder, podrás
6) voy a jugar, jugaré
7) van a poner, pondrán
8) vamos a venir, vendremos
9) vamos a querer, querremos
10) vais a vivir, viviréis
11) va a decir, dirá
12) vais a saber, sabréis

Page 133: The Conditional

1) iría 4) hablaría 7) diríais 10) sabrían
2) cantaría 5) haría 8) vendríamos
3) pondrías 6) pediría 9) querría

Page 134: Modal Verbs

1) You have to study for the exam.
2) Juanjo doesn't know how to speak Spanish.
3) Can they / you come to the party?
4) We have to listen well.
5) I don't want to return home.
6) I would like to pay the bill.

Page 135: Reflexive Verbs and Pronouns

1) me llamo 3) se viste 5) me acuesto 7) nos sentimos
2) te llevas 4) se despierta 6) se levantan 8) os ponéis

Page 137: Verbs with '-ing' and 'Just Done'

1) estás trayendo
2) está abriendo
3) están diciendo
4) estáis corriendo
5) estamos bailando
6) estoy leyendo
7) están sirviendo
8) está siguiendo
9) Estaba pidiendo una carta.
10) Estaba estudiando en mi habitación.
11) El gato estaba durmiendo.
12) Estaba trabajando bien.
13) Acaban de ver la película.
14) Acabamos de comer el desayuno.

Page 138: Negative Forms

1) No fuimos a la biblioteca.
2) No tienen ningún pastel. / No tienen ningunos pasteles.
3) No hay nada aquí.
4) Nadie está en el coche. / No está nadie en el coche.
5) No es ni rojo ni verde.
6) Ya no vamos al gimnasio.

Page 139: Impersonal Verbs and the Passive

1) Se puede descansar ahora.
2) Hay que hacer ejercicio.
3) Se necesita ir a clase.
4) Hay muchos parques.
5) Vale la pena aprender este contenido.
6) Parece una idea maravillosa.

Page 140: The Subjunctive

1) You need the normal present tense 'viene'.
2) You need the present subjunctive 'sea' — it follows 'para que', which is used to express purpose.
3) You need the normal present tense 'tiene'.
4) You need the present subjunctive 'sea' — it follows a phrase that expresses an emotion.
5) You need the normal present tense 'va'.
6) You need the present subjunctive 'haga' — it follows a phrase that expresses necessity.

Page 141: The Imperative

1) ¡Canta esta canción!
2) ¡Ve a tu habitación!
3) ¡Escribe el mensaje!
4) ¡Tómalo!
5) ¡Di algo!
6) ¡Bebe el agua!
7) ¡Aprended estas palabras!
8) Ved este vídeo!
9) ¡Esperad aquí, por favor!
10) ¡Comprad eso ahora!
11) ¡Haced vuestros camas!
12) ¡Cruzad / Atravesad la calle!

Index

SPER42